The HEART *of* WHITENESS

The HEART of WHITENESS

Normal Sexuality and Race in America, 1880–1940

JULIAN B. CARTER

Duke University Press | Durham and London | 2007

Portions of chapter 3 originally appeared in "Birds, Bees, and
Venereal Disease: Toward an Intellectual History of Sex
Education," *Journal of the History of Sexuality* 10.2: 213–49.
Copyright © 2001 by the University of Texas Press. Reprinted
by permission.

CONTENTS

ACKNOWLEDGMENTS

For financial support I would like to thank the School of Humanities and Department of History at the University of California, Irvine. Additional support came from the James J. Harvey Memorial Dissertation Fellowship; Southern California Women for Understanding; The UnCommon Legacy Foundation; and Fellowships in the Humanities at both Stanford University and New York University.

At the University of California, Irvine, a truly outstanding ILL staff located many rare and ephemeral primary source materials on sex education, while the administrator of the History Department, Carol Roberts, winked at my extensive and unauthorized use of the Xerox machine. The archive staff at Harvard University's Countway Library of Medicine directed my attention to Robert Latou Dickinson's scrapbooks, where I first made Norma and Normman's acquaintance. Healthspace Cleveland has graciously granted permission to use their photographs of the statues.

The intellectual, personal, and collegial debts I've incurred during the process of this research have been enormous. Since 1992, Cornelia Hughes Dayton has paid kind and meticulous attention to my professional development and to the placement of commas, while Alice Fahs has urged me to keep my arguments firmly rooted in my sources. Yong Chen and the undergraduates in our 1994 and 1995 Asian American history seminars shared the intensity and joy of their work in a way that challenged me to pursue my desire to write and teach about race. R. Colin Fisher and Peter Catapano provided close to a decade of shared food, drink, and friendship; it is impossible to specify the influence their conversation has had on my work and on my ethical and political development. Edward Goehring and Carol Queen provided balance when my approach to sexuality got too abstract. Cathy Opie taught me how to talk about images and bought me glasses so I could see them clearly. Much of this book reflects Susan Harris's loving insistence that it is important to name things felt and intuited but not easily admitted into language.

Two more recent friends and colleagues, Marcia Klotz and Leerom Medovoi, encouraged me to stop fetishizing my primary sources and to focus instead on interpreting them. Their argumentative skills and personal affection were especially important in helping me write the article that eventually became chapter 3. Gail Bederman offered sharp criticism tempered with immense enthusiasm for the ideas buried in several chaotic early drafts of chapter 1. She had faith in this project when no one else, including me, could imagine where it was going. Heather Lee Miller commented on multiple versions of several chapters and also guided me through the early stages of the publication process. Lisa Duggan summarized the core argument of the dissertation in terms that forced me to confront the centrality of love to the meaning of modern whiteness. Her insight into the argument I had not at that time quite succeeded in making proved definitive for the direction this book eventually took. Richard White commented on chapter 1 and was instrumental in securing my academic employment at Stanford for a crucial postdoctoral year. An anonymous reader for Duke University Press prodded me to define my archive and to devote more room to discussing theory and methods. At an earlier stage, a reader for a different press wanted to know why the manuscript wasn't funnier, since so much of the material on which it rested was transparently absurd. Though I've pushed most of my jokes into the footnotes, I found this question immensely helpful in clarifying my own reactions to the primary sources.

Robin Nagle, director of the John W. Draper Interdisciplinary Master's Program in the Humanities and Social Thought at New York University, deserves special mention for her ongoing efforts to secure adequate pay and research funding, subsidized housing, office space, up-to-date computers, manageable teaching loads and departmental duties, and other essential supports for the postdoctoral teaching fellows she oversees. Without her commitment to the well-being of the temporary employees who so often fall by the academic wayside, this book would never have seen print.

The last few years of writing were sustained by Lisa Montanarelli and nico grey, queer scholars and creative writers whose shared commitment to strong prose has made this a much more focused book than it would otherwise have been. Their generosity is as outstanding as their literary skill. Lisa read the entire manuscript at least three times; nico edited out thousands of unnecessary words and spent hours talking with me about the political deployment and effects of normality. Each kept me company through more fits of overcaffeinated and loquacious authorial misery than I care to recall. Lynley Wheaton provided childcare and commented on the introduction. Finally, Allen Meyer picked up the slack when the process of rewriting kept me from carrying anything like my fair share of the labor of running our household. It is still more important that he counseled me to keep revising the manuscript long after I stopped imagining that this work could secure me a tenure-track academic job. My thanks are a small measure of my gratitude.

The Search for Norma

> She is modelled from recent measurements of
> 15,000 women from many parts of the United States
> and from various walks of life, including series of
> college students and other thousands of native
> white Americans. She is slightly heavier yet more
> "athletic" than her grandmother of 1890 and has
> lost the shrunken waist induced by tight corsets. As
> to the beauty of her figure, tastes will vary; fashions
> change ideals from one generation to the next.
> Norma is not meant to show what ought to be; she
> shows what is.
>
> "A Portrait of the American People,"
> *Natural History*, June 1945

With these words "NORMA—the average American girl" was introduced to
the public in the summer of 1945. Her body was straight and strong, her
arms were relaxed at her sides, and she looked directly ahead with the level,
proud gaze of heroic statuary. Her stance proclaimed her right to a prominent place in "A Portrait of the American People," cast in plaster and on
display in the Cleveland Health Museum. The portrait was a flattering one.
Norma was young, healthy, and unashamed, and she was as "normal" as the
combined forces of science and art could make her. That is, her curves and
planes were three-dimensional renderings of the statistical "norm or average
American woman of 18 to 20 years of age."[1] Norma was an emblem of the
national body, modern era, sexed female.

Norma was escorted by Normman, a strapping youth available with or
without a fig leaf. His figure incorporated the measurements of several
million twenty-year-old Doughboys, as well as those of young men in the

Ivy League.² Together, this upright pair embodied the triumphant progress of the years between 1890 and 1940. Norma and Normman were heirs to a modern world in which "improved nutrition, better care of our young, and advances in public health" promised increased stature and strength to the nation as a whole.³ They represent this book's major theme: the early-twentieth-century emergence of the ideal of the "normal" American, through which a particular kind of person came to be perceived as uniquely modern, uniquely qualified for citizenship, uniquely natural and healthy.

This modern, normal person was defined in large part through a powerfully racialized understanding of sexuality: Norma and Normman represented an ideal of specifically heterosexual whiteness, not simply a statistical composite of the American people. The statues dramatize the connection between "normal" modes of erotic intimacy and important cultural meanings of "whiteness" forged in the United States between the two world wars. This is so despite the fact that, at first glance, the statues appear reticent both about sexuality and about race. The article in which this introduction's epigraph appears mentions race only once, in its passing reference to "native white Americans"; popular newspaper coverage of Norma and Normman made no comment about race at all. Neither do such discussions make many overt references to sexuality. Yet the following chapters demonstrate that Norma and Normman should be understood as icons of a constitutively white kind of heterosexual eroticism in marriage. The normality they represented was inseparable from their race, at the same time that it was formed and expressed through rich cultural codes that gradually rendered overtly racial language redundant in many white-dominated contexts. These "race-evasive" codes took shape in the last decades of the nineteenth century and achieved tremendous power during the 1920s and 1930s.⁴ By 1945, when Norma and Normman made their debut, important elements of white racial identity were conventionally communicated through discreet depictions of normal sexuality. Indeed, one of the hallmarks of the "normal" whiteness these statues represented was the ability to construct and teach white racial meanings *without appearing to do so*.

The subsequent chapters analyze the discourses of modern sexuality through which whiteness became normalized and, thereby, hard to see. My argument is rooted in widely disseminated print sources which document the gradual discursive elision of white raciality in favor of discussions of marital love. These sources show that that elision took place through the rise

1. Normman and Norma, the "Average American Boy and Girl." Terra-cotta statues displayed at 1939 New York World's Fair. REPRODUCED BY PERMISSION OF HEALTHSPACE CLEVELAND.

of the concept of the normal in the early twentieth century. Normality discourse drew on and extended several earlier conceptual vocabularies, especially those of civilization and evolution, in a way which made it possible to talk about whiteness indirectly, in terms of the affectionate, reproductive heterosexuality of "normal" married couples. That is, "normality" made it possible to discuss race and sexuality without engaging the relations of power in which they were embedded and through which they acquired much of their relevance.

The "power-evasiveness" of normality originates in, though it is not restricted to, its mathematical meaning. In a statistical sense, "norms" are clusters of regularly recurring facts about a given phenomenon or population. The "normality" of those facts, within a statistical universe, exists only in their distribution and makes no reference to any quality of those facts beyond their occurrence. That is why *Natural History* could claim that Norma and Normman did not represent "what ought to be," only "what is." Yet Francis Galton, who is widely credited with having founded the modern study of statistics in 1864, did so in large part in order "to study social mass changes in man with a view to controlling the evolution of man, as man controls that of many living forms."[5] From its inception, then, modern "normality" involved both a positivistic claim about the pure neutrality of facts, and a distinctly eugenic element of judgment about which human bodies and behaviors were best. It also involved what would turn out to be a productive definitional confusion between what is common and what is ideal: for Galton and many of his colleagues, it was important to know what was ordinary, frequent, or common precisely so that one could shift the norm in the direction of the ideal. The power-evasive, the eugenically evaluative, and the definitionally confused elements of "normality" retained their importance well into the twentieth century. But Norma and Normman did not spring full-blown from Galton's forehead. As normality discourse entered U.S. popular culture in the early twentieth century, it drew on well-established conventions for representing conflict over issues of race, citizenship, and cultural reproduction through the language of "civilization."

Gail Bederman has demonstrated that between 1880 and 1917 civilization discourse provided a shared vocabulary in which Americans at every point of the political spectrum could argue for and against the legitimacy of the unequal distribution of power according to race, gender, and sexuality.[6] By 1940 "normality" described some of the same cultural terrain, and performed some of the same cultural work, that "civilization" performed in the first decades of the century. In fact, we will see that "normality" was deeply indebted to "civilization" for its conceptual content; normal Americans were necessarily civilized ones, and the two terms were sometimes used in the interwar years as though they were synonyms. But while their contents overlapped, their effects were significantly different. Where civilization discourse could facilitate political debate, the following chapters show that normality discourse generally worked to shut it down.

One of the most important effects of the concept of "normality," and the sign of its power in dominant American culture, was the increasing occlusion of racial and sexual politics in "polite" white speech.[7] Civilization discourse had often attempted to foster a similar illusion of peaceful, apolitical consensus about what it meant to be an American. It was quite common for late-nineteenth-century and early-twentieth-century, native-born, bourgeois Protestant whites to use "civilization" as a sort of shorthand for "the way well-bred people like us do things." When that shorthand was contested and its race-political agenda challenged, many whites responded by trying to remove their claim to ownership of the nation from political discourse.

They did this by appealing to the apparently neutral authority of evolutionary science. Evolution, as it was popularly understood in this era, explained the progressive development of peoples and nations from generation to generation. It was therefore an immensely attractive conceptual resource for racism. While evolutionism's interest in explaining change allowed for the argument that modern civilization was a natural improvement over "primitive" forms, its emphasis on continuity across time facilitated the position that American civilization was the hereditable property of the modern white persons whose ancestors had founded the original thirteen colonies. It is no accident that evolutionism had its widest and deepest reach in U.S. culture between the Civil War and the Civil Rights era.[8] Even though the language of civilization could be mobilized in overtly political contexts, evolutionist perspectives on civilization implied that social inequality—the dominance of native-born, financially secure, educated white men—was determined by heredity and so was beyond the bounds of meaningful dissent.

Representations of modern American civilization as an evolutionary achievement, in short, record the attempted depoliticization of white dominance in response to challenges to the entrenched racial order. This is where sex comes in. Because evolutionary thought emphasizes reproduction as the vector for inheritance and therefore as the primary mechanism for racial development or degeneration, an evolutionist perspective on civilization drew attention to the importance of a specifically sexual "fitness" among modern whites.[9] During the era between the two world wars, that evolved sexual fitness increasingly went by the name of "normality."

In the evolutionist context of its emergence, "normality" shared some important qualities with eugenics, the theory and practice of racial improvement through the reproduction of "desirable" elements of the population. Both normality discourse and eugenics drew on social-Darwinist vocabularies of development and degeneration to argue for the immense importance of correct sexual behavior, especially among the "better classes" of whites; both presented their vision of sexual control for the good of the race as though it was simple common sense based on objective scientific fact. But normality, unlike eugenicism or civilizationism, managed to acquire a mantle of political neutrality that remained powerful at least through the end of the twentieth century and that retains its dominance in many areas of U.S. culture to the present day. This book has two chief goals: first, to document the disavowed and mutually dependent racial and sexual hierarchies condensed in the notion of the normal; and second, to show that normality discourse appeared to be politically neutral in large part because it so often framed its racially loaded dreams for the reproduction of white civilization in the language of romantic and familial love.

In common speech during the interwar years, "normality" described a whole series of ideals regulating sexual desires and activities and, through them, modes of intimacy and familial structures. By 1940, this enframement had had the effect of helping to expand white racial definition to include most European Americans who adhered to these racialized sexual and relational norms. Erotically and affectively charged marriage became the privileged site for the literal and metaphorical reproduction of white civilization. At the same time and through the same gestures, that civilization's core racial value was redefined in terms of love. Though the statistical referent of the normal helped make its claim to neutrality plausible, it is as significant that the actual contents of the category were extremely difficult to contest: love was, by dominant cultural definition, an inherently benign force, politically relevant only in its ability to resolve conflict.[10] "Normality" thus provided a common, and deeply sexualized, vocabulary through which an increasingly diverse group of whites could articulate their common racial and political values to one another, while nonetheless avoiding direct acknowledgment of or confrontation with the many hierarchies that fractured the polity. The rise of the notion of the "normal" to discursive dominance was a crucial part of the process by which whiteness became not only reticent about its racial meanings but blind to its own struggles to retain racial power.

The Sexual Reproduction of Civilization
and the Political Innocence of Whiteness

The statues of the "normal" American boy and girl illustrate the way in which vague references to heredity and cultural development across generations could forge an ostensibly natural, objective, and politically innocent connection between whiteness, reproductive marital heterosexuality, and modern American civilization. Press discussions of Norma and Normman document the widespread belief that "normal" twentieth-century Americans were biologically and culturally superior to all other peoples. Harry Shapiro, curator of physical anthropology at the American Museum of Natural History, made this point explicit when he described the statues as manifestations of general "improvements" in the "physical development of the population" since the 1890s.[11] In Shapiro's account, as in many others, changes in the body were inseparable from changes in civilization. The slippage by which evaluations of physical development became evidence of cultural advance can be seen in Shapiro's comment that "both of these statues . . . leave little doubt that the figure is improving esthetically. . . . The average American figure approaches a kind of perfection of bodily form and proportion."[12] Modern, white Americans—"normal" people "like us"— were simply better than anyone else had ever been.

Shapiro's declaration of aesthetic progress merged with his celebration of the normal American body to suggest that the steady development of civilization to ever-higher levels could not be separated from the sexual health of native-born whites. Certainly it mattered to Shapiro and his readers that, by midcentury, "normal" Americans were comparatively safe from syphilis, polio, tuberculosis, and other diseases that had reached epidemic proportions in the late nineteenth century. But in terms of the future of the race, Norma and Normman's individual health was significant primarily as it influenced their reproductivity. Furthermore, because biological reproduction and cultural reproduction were equally necessary to the evolution of civilization, the health of what one might call their mode of reproduction was as important as their freedom from literal illness. The statues are material condensations of the widely held belief that the evolutionary triumph of modern civilization depended on and found expression in a particular normalized form of marital heterosexuality.

Just in case some readers needed a refresher course in the cultural logic

through which normal marriage both represented and enabled the reproduction of white civilization, Shapiro developed his claim about the natural superiority of modern Americans with the aid of several small photographs representing Norma and Normman's family tree. First came pictures of their plaster
"grandparents." These icons of bourgeois Victorian gentility were statistical
composites based on measurements from the 1890s. The lady exhibits "the
shrunken waist induced by tight corsets" and inclines slightly toward her male
companion as though they are conversing in modulated tones at some formal
social occasion. Their civilized whiteness is evident in their features, but above
all in their refined bearing.[13] The second pair of images depicts the mythical
progenitors of western civilization in the form of the Doryphorus of Polycletus
—better known as the Canon—and a voluptuous (though headless) Aphro-
dite.[14] Together, the photographs constitute a sort of family album document-
ing the increasing perfection of white civilization.

The six statues record the progressive development of whiteness by con-
trasting the aesthetic and physical ideals of past generations to those of the
present. The ancient statues share an impressive, if rather bulky, muscularity.
They look up to the task of laying the foundations of western civilization.
Harry Shapiro observed that ancient Greek statuary reflected the archaic
sensibilities of its creators, who valued "power rather than agility or speed."[15]
The Victorian pair, in contrast, are slender and graceful. They represent
elegance and polish rather than strength. Finally, Shapiro described Norma
and Normman as longer-legged, more dynamic forms than their racial predecessors.[16] As moderns, Norma and Normman inherited both strength and
elegance from earlier eras of white civilization: they are muscular *and* slender,
powerful *and* streamlined. Though they share racial / cultural traits with their
forbears, they have also surpassed them. The normal civilized whiteness they
represent is a uniquely modern one, and as such it is an evolutionary improvement over its own racial antecedents.

Viewed on their own, Norma and Normman can be taken for siblings.
When they are situated in a visual narrative of the evolution of racial ideals,
however, it seems clear that they represent mates, the ideal parents for the
new generation of civilized whites. The nakedness of all six statues is therefore not an empty nod to the artistic tradition of the classical nude. Rather,
that nakedness foregrounds sexual difference and the importance of the
sexual reproduction of the racial family. Across the millennia, Shapiro's
pictures suggest, white civilization has advanced through fruitful intercourse

between matched pairs of its best men and women. Because they were exemplary of a civilized sexual ideal, the presumption was that those reproductive couples were married; in any case, they had to be if their children were to be legitimate heirs of civilization. In short, the photographs illustrating Shapiro's essay in *Natural History* provided Norma and Normman with a high lineage of biological whiteness transmitted through marital heterosexuality. It is not incidental that the same representational gesture provided American civilization with a similarly lofty line of direct descent from the original democracy.[17]

Taken together, the three sets of statues constitute a visual argument that modern American civilization was the legitimately inherited, morally upright racial property of "normal" whites. Norma and Normman were embedded in a history of racially pure sexual reproduction that Shapiro collapsed into the developmental history of white civilization. These emblems of normality, that is, are also representations of the legitimacy and innocence of white dominance. Eons of material and cultural advances, transmitted via the marital sexuality of successive white generations, produced normal moderns organically rather than agonistically. Shapiro's use of the Athenian marbles to represent the origins of white civilization underscores whiteness's insistence on its commitment to and talent for democratic justice, while the collapse of cultural development into sexual reproduction constitutes an implicit argument that white civilization has progressed through the cultivation of marital love. In this narrative of civilization's evolutionary development, just self-government is a transhistorical matrix in which sex replaces struggle, marriage replaces race and class war, and the cultural and political life of the modern United States appear to be white property by nature and without conflict. This narrative suggests that the disavowal of political struggle over power was not epiphenomenal but central to normal whiteness.

The claim that political virtue was a continuous racial quality across the millennia helped to anchor white racial meaning in a politically innocent discursive space. It did not, however, mean that the race had not evolved since the fifth century BCE. The epigraph to this chapter emphasizes that the statues embodied "what is": Anglo America in the present tense. Norma and Normman were at the top of the evolutionary tree not only because they were white but because they were modern. As representatives of the mid-twentieth-century United States, an apartheid state which increasingly staked its identity and international status on its commitment to democracy, their whiteness was necessarily more inclusive of class and ethnic variation than that of earlier eras—that is, it was less restrictively defined by reference to high Anglo culture. When Norma and Normman moved from their creator's New York studio to their Ohio exhibition hall, a local daily paper ran a series of articles that underscore the statues' ability to represent the development of white civilization as though it were a steady procession toward enlightenment and freedom for all European Americans, not only native-born WASP elites. In one such article the Cleveland *Plain Dealer* contrasted the statues' athletic nudity to the overdressed and constrained Victorianism of the 1890s, when, it wrote, "Norma's Gym Suit . . . Covered All." The statues bore testimony to recent changes in "type of clothes, in attitudes toward women's freedom, in concepts of physical education, in public opinion."[18] Norma and Normman embodied civilization's progress toward freedom on a local, mundane level, easily accessible to those who were more excited by college basketball than by the remote glory that was Greece.

The belief that modern whiteness was uniquely egalitarian was nicely captured by the director of physical education at Western Reserve University, who summed up her response to Norma and Normman in these words: "As was said by the old mountaineer who lived in a town where a church and a school had been created for the first time, 'We ain't what we ought to be and we ain't what we're goin' to be, but thank God we ain't what we was.' "[19] The PE teacher saw Norma and Normman's magnificently white bodies as analogous to church and school, the core public institutions through which American civilization's ideological structures were both perpetuated and improved. The claim that the "normal" American boy and girl represent the same kind of progress as the founding of churches and schools confirms the sociopolitical importance of the married heterosexual pair. It also suggests "universal" access to normality: if being married was the prime qualification for transmitting civilization, literally millions of healthy, nominally Christian or at least morally conventional, reasonably well-informed modern heterosexual whites fit the bill. Further, the "old mountaineer' "s pious celebration of civilized institutions implies the inclusivity, the cross-class relevance, of the white ideals that the statues represent in a more rarified and abstract way. Shapiro's highbrow depiction of Norma and Normman's family tree collapsed political virtue into the legitimate reproduction of white civilization; the *Plain Dealer*'s more colloquial approach to racial history invited whites with less lofty genealogies to identify themselves with the march of national progress. Even if your grandfather said "ain't" you could still be normal.

At mass-cultural as on elite levels, then, normality discourse used the common cultural vocabulary of civilization's evolutionary progress in a way that tended to flatten out the distinction between political struggle and natural development. The folksy depiction of progress suggested that white domination over the American land was both natural and moral, while it concealed the genocidal violence of Native Americans' removal from the Old West by the simple device of ignoring it. The *Plain Dealer*'s stories about the development of civilization also depoliticized and naturalized half a century of intense struggle over (white) women's role in the polity: the long and bitter fight for women's education and suffrage is reduced to an unmotivated "shift in attitude," while modern women's "freedom" is illustrated by the rise in hemlines.

Yet while the real exercise of military and political agency as motors for historical change is disavowed, the *Plain Dealer* celebrates the bare physical existence of church and schoolhouse as a sign of modern civilization's achievement of liberty and justice for all. The net effect of such flattening, combined with the occlusion of racial violence and oppression, was to make the dominance of white civilization seem both natural and worth striving for—in short, to make whiteness normal. Whether it was represented in noble statuary or down-home colloquialisms, normal modern whiteness invoked the democratic dream of universal access to enlightened morality and free self-government, while it looked away from the struggles through which American government and white dominance were extended across the continent and, increasingly, across the globe.

Instead, normality discourse tended to focus on marriage, love, and babies. The importance of a carefully disciplined reproductivity to the continued progress of the race is captured in another headline from the *Cleveland Plain Dealer*: "Norma's Husband Better Be Good," it trumpeted. "Evolution Outlook Bright if Model Girl Weds Wisely."[20] Under this banner, the newspaper quoted a professor of biology's opinion that "rational . . . principles in mating" could eradicate "many of the ills that human flesh is heir to." With "proper selection in matrimony," the professor added, there was every reason to believe that future generations would "just keep on improving physically and mentally."[21] In such representations, modern civilization developed through the cultivation of marriage. Normal Americans, by definition, were whites who used their respectably reproductive sexuality for the betterment of race and nation.

From Civilized Nervousness to Modern Marriage

The subsequent chapters address distinct, though related, dimensions of the concept of the normal, first as its basic contours began to emerge among educated Anglo whites in the 1880s, and then as it expanded into mass culture during the first four decades of the twentieth century. Chapter 1 engages the late-nineteenth-century medical formulation of a particular kind of white body as the somaticization of modern civilization. I read theoretical, clinical, and popular narrative representations of nervous illness as constituting an attempt to define and describe the core essence of whiteness in the post-slavery United States. The literature on neurasthenia shows that the disease, and the sexual failures associated with it, indirectly expressed widespread white beliefs that the "cultured classes" were in danger of losing their inherited dominance over American life. Nervousness discourse therefore provides a window into "old stock" white fears that the best, most socially valuable part of the race was rendered physically and morally sterile by its extreme sensitivity, such that bourgeois whiteness might fail to reproduce itself and its civilization.

Norma and Normman's plaster "grandparents" of the 1890s provide a useful visual index of this construction of civilized whiteness as weakness: in contrast to the ancient Athenians and the modern Americans, the Victorian statues look enfeebled by their gentility. In neurasthenia discourse, the fear of white sterility found expression in exhortations to men and women of the "better sort" to preserve white dominance over civilization by cultivating sexual self-control. Sexual restraint enabled them to harness their sensitivity to the future of the race, directing their nervous resources toward the production of the next white generation. At the same time, the construction of whiteness as weakness helped to gloss over the social, political, and economic benefits whites gained from the real racial maldistribution of national resources.

The literature that describes neurasthenia does not use the language of normality, but in its representations of civilized whiteness we can see the convergence of many of the images and themes that would come to have definitional power in early-twentieth-century representations of whiteness as normal. Two of these were especially important. The first was an intensification of interest in marital sexuality as the central point or node for the legitimate reproduction of white civilization. Second was the discursive depoliticization of white dominance through the conflation of whiteness with the evolutionary development of ever-greater capacities for sexual sensitivity, responsiveness, egalitarianism, and love, a conflation which made it very difficult for whites to perceive their racial position in terms of oppression, exploitation, and injustice. But while these two themes would prove powerful in normality's self-representation, late-nineteenth-century discussions of civilized nervousness also differed from early-twentieth-century discussions of normality along several axes. Neurasthenia discourse's representations of whiteness foregrounded its physical weakness, while normality discourse emphatically rejected all suggestions of pathology; and neurasthenic whiteness was relatively explicit about its class and ethnic specificity and superiority, whereas normal whiteness defined itself in much more inclusive, and ever more power-evasive, terms.

In chapter 2 I argue that modern heterosexuality, which emerged in the 1920s and 1930s as an ideal of erotic discipline in marriage, was a central discursive site for the solidification of white power-evasiveness under the sign of the normal. In the marital advice literature that forms the core archive for this discussion, the sensitivity that late-nineteenth-century elites had argued was the hallmark of civilized whiteness was uncoupled from nervous illness. Instead, white sensitivity was newly framed as the capacity for shared erotic pleasure in egalitarian, loving marriages.

Concerns about white reproductive weakness did not simply disappear over the turn of the century. Rather, they were reframed by the consolidation of a relatively clear homosexual identity category. A rich body of historical scholarship has established that, both at the level of discourse and at the level of cultural experience, early-twentieth-century sexuality was increasingly organized in relation to the great homo / hetero divide.[22] In this era "homosexuality," and its more colloquial counterpart "queer," often connoted erotic weakness, degeneracy, and primitivism.[23] By the 1920s, fears about white reproductive weakness had realigned around the nightmare figure of the primitive pervert. Queer forms of sexual desire and gender expression acquired the capacity to represent sexual disability, which in the context of evolutionary discourses of civilization meant that failures of development and self-control were increasingly associated with same-sex object choice and opposite-gender presentation. White self-control, in contrast, found mass expression in the optimistic discourses of modern normality. A new generation came of age between the wars. Its plaster avatars, Norma and Normman, are not representations of white delicacy; they are whiteness regnant. The statues capture a widespread early-twentieth-century claim that modern normality was the triumphant answer to fears about the reproductive weakness of white civilization.

In chapter 2 I examine the way in which popular marital advice literature from the 1920s and 1930s reconfigured the Gilded Age's fear that white civilization was threatened by its own evolved superiority. Marriage manuals responded to the perception that modernity was undermining family and nation by constructing a newly intense kind of conjugal lovemaking as the antidote to divisive forces inherent in the machine age. Such works argued that shared erotic pleasure was the foundation of white married life and, by extension, white civilization. By modifying their gestures and adjusting their timing to guarantee mutual satisfaction, "normal" couples cultivated and demonstrated their self-control and sensitivity to the common good. Thus a vast mass-marketed literature on modern marital sexuality represented intercourse as a miniature rehearsal of the social and political values at the core of democratic ideology. It was becoming possible to imagine erotically charged marriage as inseparable from American citizenship in a way that legitimized the exclusion of homosexuals and other sexual "deviants" from full membership in the polity.[24] At the same time, the manuals' representation of tender concern for others as "normal" helped to sustain the dream that racial conflict, male dominance, and economic inequity were incidental to, rather than systemic in, modern civilization in the United States.

Marital advice literature's construction of ideal sexuality echoes neurasthenia discourse's representation of civilized whiteness as involving a strict regime of self-discipline harnessing white sensitivity to the good of the society at large. The interwar ideal of modern sexuality, however, extended that self-disciplined sensitivity from well-bred, native-born Anglo-Americans to the larger group of white people in general. This was the reason that the manuals could afford to be so much more optimistic than their nineteenth-century predecessors: American civilization's legacy of "high" or "true" whiteness could be preserved by expanding access to its central values *via* mass education in erotic self-control.

While I interpret marriage manuals as evidence of the mass-cultural implantation of bourgeois sexual self-discipline, it is nonetheless true that adults bought, read, and used such advice literature entirely at their own discretion. In contrast, hundreds of thousands, maybe millions of modern children, adolescents, and young adults were required to learn about the importance of sexual self-control in elementary and secondary schools and in the armed services. This is the subject of chapter 3, where I examine the way in which mass sex instruction for young people served to reinforce the correlation of heterosexual whiteness to normality. Early-twentieth-century sex education existed to convince students of the natural, apolitical connection between sexual self-restraint, an erotic ethic of monogamy in marriage, and the strength of white civilization. This was so despite the fact that sex-instructional materials very rarely discuss race or sexuality per se. Sex-instructional literature for children and adolescents communicated in an elaborately metaphorical and euphemistic language which emphasized that modesty and discretion were inseparable from civilized sexuality. Thus sex education was also an education in indirect expression. Desire and power, sexuality and white racial dominance were not matters for overt discussion, despite their ubiquity in "hygiene" and "family life" classrooms across the nation. A generation learned that decent people talked about these things obliquely. Being normal required learning to substitute the vague language of normal development for political analysis or cultural critique of existing sexual and racial relations.

Whereas in the late nineteenth century bourgeois whiteness represented itself as precious and besieged, by the Second World War white relational ideals were reconfigured as simply "normal," the apparently universal values shared by all right-thinking (or white-thinking) Americans. Sex education was one of the mass-cultural means by which this new, apparently race-neutral form of whiteness was transmitted to the first generation of Americans born and raised to be modern. In fact, this literature underscores the point that Norma and Normman have already illustrated: normality gathered much of its meaning from its indirect reference to modern whiteness as a set of universal values.

Though "normality" attained its greatest cultural power in the second half of the twentieth century, I conclude this study in the early 1940s for several reasons. First, it is significant that evolutionary / biological explanations of racial and sexual identity found their cultural and scientific authority challenged at this time. The nineteenth- and early-twentieth-century phenomenon known as "scientific racism" described human groups as "discrete and biotic entities" with clearly demarcated physical traits that signaled heritable intellectual and moral qualities.[25] Much contemporary research on sexuality proceeded from exactly the same premises, with the sole exception that most scientific racists were certain that racial traits were ineradicable and many sexologists thought that sexuality might be more fungible than that. But throughout the period 1880 to 1940, a generally evolutionist, biologistic perspective dominated print discussions of both race and sexuality in the United States and helped to suture them together.

These biologistic, evolutionary interpretations of sexuality were in decline before American entry into World War II. Although "glandular" (hormonal) therapies for homosexuality continued in the 1950s, by the late 1930s the trend away from physical and toward psychogenic explanations for sexuality was clear.[26] When the Committee for the Study of Sex Variance (the first major research group on sexuality in the United States) convened in 1935, its goal was to test "all the major etiological theories of homosexuality," and a number of its members were selected precisely for their interest in child development and mental health. In the Committee's 1941 report, it announced its conclusion that "the more 'pronounced deficiencies' of the sex variant were psychological rather than physical."[27] The same year, Alfred Kinsey published a highly influential article criticizing endocrine research and stating unequivocally that all such biologistic sexual science was inherently flawed. In his stringent critique he singled out the belief "that homosexuality and heterosexuality are two mutually exclusive phenomena emanating from fundamentally and, in at least some cases, inherently different types of individuals."[28] These publications seem to mark the end of the era when most sex researchers thought in the language of scientific racism and so suggest 1941 as a neat ending date for a study that devotes considerable attention to popular scientific discourses.

Approaching periodization from the perspective of race gives almost the same end date for slightly different reasons. By the early 1940s, as the criminal racial policies of fascist Italy and National Socialist Germany became known in the United States, intellectuals across the disciplines began to scramble for a new and less biologistic conception of race. In addition, African American agitation against segregation in the military and discrimination in defense industries during World War II opened the Civil Rights era, a whole new phase of American racial politics that would shape racial discourse for the next generation. Though the connections between race and sexuality remained profoundly significant during and after World War II, both the content and the context of those connections were different enough to warrant a separate study.[29] In short, I contend that it is not possible to develop an adequate understanding of race between the Gilded Age and World War II without attending to sexuality, and vice versa, but my cutoff date is not meant to suggest that after the war the two axes of identity suddenly stopped speaking to one another.

Sources and Methods, Boundaries and Centers

The diverse sources that ground this argument have several common threads. They are all, in their different ways, informative about the consolidation of marital heterosexuality as a distinct and privileged mode of experiencing erotic desire and pleasure; and all were chosen for their capacity to illustrate the way in which the rise of normality discourse helped to de-authorize explicit engagement with white racial meaning, and especially with white racial dominance. This particular archive demonstrates that one of the ways that whiteness became "race-evasive" was through the normalizing of deeply racialized sexual and relational ideals under the sign of "modern marriage." It also suggests that the collapse of normal whiteness into a marital ideal of erotic affection helped to expand the social category of whiteness across classes and, to a lesser extent, across ethnicities. Other archives, if investigated with a similar eye to the elision of white racial specificity in the early twentieth century, no doubt would illuminate different discursive strategies and effects: precisely because normality acquired a tremendously broad cultural reach, it can be investigated in many forms and from many perspectives.

For instance, one could choose to delineate normality's boundaries through close study of representations of perversion and the consolidation of homosexual definition in the early twentieth century, or through sources which record the ongoing importance of conflict over white racial definition and dominance. There is no shortage of source material for these interesting and valuable projects. Further, the scholarly consensus seems to be that comparative, dialectical, or deconstructive studies are to be preferred to more univocal ones, because their emphasis on the relational character of identity classifications makes it harder to evade their political implications. Such approaches have the additional appeal of testifying to their authors' political consciousness, while less dialogical strategies risk appearing naïve at best, perniciously ideological at worst.

Nevertheless, I have chosen to concentrate not on boundaries and relationships across categories of sexuality and race but on the comparatively claustrophobic subject of normality's internal descriptions and definitions of itself. That is one reason that I have grounded my analysis in print sources from the poorly defined yet fairly consistent genre we might call "normal sexual science." Theoretical descriptions of modern nervousness, sex advice for married couples, and educational materials about reproductive physiology and venereal disease all speak about sex from and to the position of civilized modern whiteness that the later materials refer to as "normal."

These sources' semi-scientific status authorized their relatively explicit discussions of sexuality as the allegedly apolitical vector for the reproduction of white civilization. Nevertheless, their authority in a popular (rather than medical or sexological) context could never be taken for granted simply on the basis of their scientificity: the mass distribution of these sources, and their publishers' bottom line, depended on their ability to speak in terms that their broad readership could recognize as legitimate and objective. Popular scientific writing, like that in marital advice literature or the Cleveland *Plain Dealer*, had to meet both genre-specific and popular-cultural standards of "normality" before it could see print. Such texts therefore offer us rich evidence for the contents of that category not only on the explicitly topical level but also in their mode of presentation, their assumptions about readership, use of illustrations, strategies of argumentation, tone, and so forth. It is also relevant that popular-scientific sources on sex were widely available. In the early twentieth century, they were often distributed free of charge through institutions like schools, public health clinics, and the armed services. Such mass-cultural publications offer access to some of the most authoritative and least controversial forms of knowledge about sexuality and race available at the time of their writing and distribution. Whatever we know or don't know about the reach and influence of individual documents, we can be certain that the positions they advance were "normal" ones. These sources not only described normality, they performed it.

The textual performance of normality involved a strikingly narrow focus. These sources are utterly self-involved; their world is inhabited only by themselves and by people like them. Though there are differences of opinion or approach among my sources, and even the development of distinct schools of thought about such things as the best strategies for teaching modern American children about sex, these differences pale when situated in relation to the overwhelming consensus that normal texts, and normal people, do not discuss the unequal distribution of social power or the conflicts to which it gives rise. Only very rarely do these normal sources go so far as to acknowledge the existence of people of color or of "perverse" forms of sexuality, and when they do appear, such acknowledgments are cursory. The absence of dialogic engagement with positions excluded from the category of the normal was so widespread that it appears to have been a constitutive element of normality, not an accidental one, a fact which makes these texts' refusal to engage in overtly political debate worth sustained consideration. Thus I work with "normal" texts despite some reservations about the ease with which the strategic reasons for that decision—which I will detail in a moment—can disappear behind its consistency with normative academic practice; unless they announce themselves as explicitly authored by and addressed to people of color and / or gay or queer people, most books about U.S. history can safely be assumed to be by and about heterosexual whites at the level of evidence as well as at the level of argumentation. Yet while I recognize the risk of appearing to participate in the marginalization and epistemological disqualification of non-normative subjects, there are several reasons—political, historical, and conceptual—that I believe it is valuable to concentrate on "normal" articulations of normality's meaning.

The first reason is a straightforward political urge to make whiteness speak its own name. Because white muteness about its raciality seems clearly connected to white irresponsibility in regard to its power, it is appropriate to push at that muteness in the process of its implantation, to explore the evidence it offers about how whiteness's self-definition as "normal" facilitated white ignorance and innocence in relation to ongoing racial inequality. There is a similar political satisfaction in mining heterosexuality's self-congratulatory descriptions of its naturalness and innocence for evidence of its historical embeddedness in unequal relations of power.

The second reason is historical. Grace Elizabeth Hale has suggested that whites became less articulate about race between 1890 and 1940 because their racial position became more secure. Whereas Emancipation, immigration, and industrialization had shaken the late-nineteenth-century sociopolitical order to its foundations, and so stimulated whites to define and defend their privileged place in the nation, Hale argues that by 1930 the white-dominant culture of segregation was so deeply entrenched that whites no longer needed to fear losing control over "their" civilization. One result was the increasing "blankness" of whiteness as a racial position.[30] My sources suggest that the contemporary name for what Hale sees as blankness was "normality." Sources that document normality's self-understanding at the moment of its emergence make it plain that the category was anything but empty or neutral, and so ask us to engage the appearance of "blankness" in new terms. Working with sources that are themselves apparently blank on the subject of race, and yet that turn out to be full of representations of whiteness, shifts the terms of current scholarly discussion about the history of white raciality in what I hope will be a productive way.

I will return to the secondary literature on the history and meaning of whiteness and its apparent emptiness in the next section. Here I want to suggest that segregation did not actually render whiteness blank. Instead, it provided the larger context in which whites' racial place in the nation could be displaced into discussions of marital sexuality: the (re)institutionalization of white power in the early twentieth century allowed, maybe required, a discursive shift away from the question of whether whiteness would continue to dominate, to the question of how white-dominant civilization could best be perpetuated. The popular-scientific sources on which this book is based answered that question by developing a definition of "normal" heterosexuality that emphasized marital romance as the mode of white civilization's reproduction. The internal focus of such sources, the complete erasure of sexually or racially non-normative voices that might have challenged their collapse of white raciality into the eroticization of married love, is inseparable from their claim to normality.

Collapsing white civilization into marriage required the conceptual, as well as legal, refusal to allow the legitimacy of love across the color line, and also of same-sex relationships. Peggy Pascoe has argued that miscegenation law was much less about sex per se than about who could marry whom; in her persuasive account, legitimate reproduction of the nation was the core political issue in courts' attempts to determine the racial boundaries of wedlock.[31] It is therefore not surprising that my "normal" scientific sources, reflecting as they do a depoliticized version of the segregated sociosexual order, silently assume both that sex takes place between married people and that married people are always and necessarily of the same race. Here again it is clear that normal sources distort the world in both sexual and racial terms. Early-twentieth-century Americans took their pleasure, fell in love, and sometimes married within categories of sex as across categories of race. Court cases, white-supremacist polemics, eugenics displays at state fairs, novels, and many other sources testify to the breadth and depth of contemporary white anxieties about the "contamination" of whiteness through interracial liaisons, and so scholars working with such sources generally focus on the tremendous significance early-twentieth-century whites attached to the policing of racial / sexual boundaries.[32] Yet the territory of white-on-white marital heterosexuality that those boundaries defended is virtually never discussed in racial terms.

This neglect needs redress because sexual desire and activity between men and women constructed not only racial edges but racial centers; both biologically and culturally, potentially reproductive sex lent itself to the consolidation of racial identity as well as to its transgression. At the same time, normal sources' insistence that "sex" is potentially reproductive in its essence worked to define whiteness in terms that mandated and naturalized heterosexuality. Many such sources suggest that the reproduction of white civilization in the twentieth century required husbands' and wives' mutual investment of sexual difference with erotic desire. The problematization and eroticization of married love in normal sources from the early twentieth century may reflect the instability of gender relations relative to race relations in this segregationist era, so that male dominance seemed less secure than white dominance by the end of the 1930s. It is more certain that the collapse of whiteness into love could not have appeared plausible outside the narrow bounds of a securely all-white context in which explicit discussions of contested race relations were already otiose. In short, the linked discursive processes of white deracialization and the invention of heterosexuality are vividly on display in "normal" mass-cultural sources that are less explicitly interested in "the race problem" than they are in affirming the natural rightness and sexiness of monogamous marriage between civilized whites. Concentrating on these "normal" sources therefore can facilitate critical focus on the self-justificatory logic of normality's political evasiveness.

This leads to my conceptual reason for choosing to focus on normality in conversation with itself, which is that norms appear to be inherently solipsistic. Francois Ewald proposes that a norm is "a way for a group to provide itself with a common denominator in accordance with a rigorous principle of self-referentiality, with no recourse to any kind of external reference point, either in the form of an idea or an object. . . . [A] norm, by virtue of which everyone can measure, evaluate and identify himself or herself, will be derived from those for whom it will serve as a standard."[33] In the purely statistical sense normality is a distributive relation within a data-set, such that phenomena or people defined as outside that set cannot meaningfully be described in relation to its norm. In a social rather than mathematical sense, of course, the early-twentieth-century definition of the normal by reference to a bounded racial and sexual group was tremendously consequential for people who could not plausibly claim membership in that group. Being excluded from the universe of people who count meant (and means) occupying a position that was always-already constructed by reference to what it was not: not white, not a native speaker of English, not married, not male, not able-bodied, "not quite our class."

This position is often much more socially alert than is a "normal" one. As such, it may generate both social movements for inclusion and critical analyses of systemic injustice. Non-normativity can be a position of considerable critical insight, because people whose lives are shaped by their difference from the normal perforce must know a great deal about both their own positions and the ones that oppress them. In contrast, being one of the normal people means being defined by reference to what you already are and so slides easily into the (empirically inaccurate) conviction that one's own position is simply natural and devoid of political meaning. Normality therefore implies a limited and ideologically corrupt perspective.

The difference between these perspectives is reflected in the different valences of the terms currently available to talk about these matters: "normality" (or "normalcy") can be, and usually is, used unreflectively, while "normativity" and "heteronormativity" record a critical stance in relation to normality's regulatory force. At the risk of seeming to ventriloquize the short-sighted arrogance of the normal, in this book I generally use the language of the normal. "Normality" is the term used by people who aspire to it, then as now, and so it seems appropriate to a study that focuses so closely on the claustrophobic worldview of the normal.

The critical difference between normal (solipsistic) and non-heteronormative (at least potentially critical) perspectives has a great deal to do with current scholarly preferences for analyzing both race and sexuality in terms of borders, intersections, mutual constitution, and dialogues. Whether they employ dialectical or deconstructive strategies, such relational emphases offer a necessary corrective to the infuriating blandness with which normative positions assume not only their universality and innocence but their ontological purity and epistemological superiority as well: there is a certain sense of triumph in demonstrating that whiteness depends on establishing the inferiority of blackness, heterosexuality on the abjection of homosexuality, for their basic meaning as well as for their power. Nonetheless, to treat white racial or heterosexual positions as though they acquire meaning *only* through their representations of and relationships to the categories of people they exclude is to forget the separatism and self-involvement inherent in the concept of the normal. If segregation provided the social and political context in which normality discourse developed, the self-referentiality of the norm provided the conceptual context in which whiteness and heterosexuality could focus myopically on their own small worlds, ignoring the existence of other positions while perceiving themselves as politically innocent, natural qualities of individuals.

On "Normality Studies"

Normality discourse, then, can be characterized as closing down the conceptual space for overly political discussions of racial and erotic hierarchies in the early-twentieth-century United States. Yet for all their refusal to consider the validity of different interpretative positions on white racial meaning or the natural superiority of heterosexuality, many "normal" sources from this period are highly articulate about one axis of difference: that of historical change. We have already seen that Norma and Normman were instantiations of the developmental progress of American civilization from generation to generation. Though their normality was profoundly self-referential in the sense that it referred only to the characteristics of potentially reproductive "native white Americans" and the culture they claimed as their own, it also acquired significance through its claim to superiority over earlier generations of civilized whites. Moderns were fond of representing their own historical moment as distinctly better than the recent past, especially in terms of the organization and expression of sexuality.

Yet while the emergence of a uniquely modern sexuality at this time is widely recognized, remarkably few historians have investigated sexual modernism as such. Most of those who do so have tended to accept their subjects' sense of difference from and superiority over the recent past as a reflection of historical fact.[34] In an influential early study of the subject, Paul Robinson defined sexual modernism as "a reaction against Victorianism," explaining that the earliest articulators of modernist sexual theory—men like Havelock Ellis and Sigmund Freud—were "quite self-conscious about their departure from . . . nineteenth-century sexual orthodoxy."[35] Christina Simmons, in contrast, has made a powerful case against taking the modernist claim of sexual radicalism at face value. She, and a number of feminist scholars following her lead, have argued that this claim was a ruse of patriarchal power, a way of turning attention away from the continuing political, economic, and psychological subordination of women by emphasizing the "liberation" of heterosexual expression.[36]

Though I find many aspects of this revisionist argument persuasive, the present work offers a different, and more race-sensitive, interpretation of the early-twentieth-century transformation of sexual relationships between men and women into modern normative heterosexuality. Just as Norma and Normman appeared more strikingly modern when posed next to their "grandparents," Ellis and Freud and many others secured their status as "moderns" by drawing attention to their difference from the "Victorians." Yet by emphasizing their difference from the past as the ground of their identity, they also revealed their continuing conceptual dependence on the past as the benchmark against which they measured their own progress.

Like the classical Athenian marbles that emphasized both Norma and Normman's modern sleekness and their ancient lineage of whiteness, moderns most often pointed to the past both to separate themselves from it and to claim progressive descent from it. If we recall Alexander Saxton's dictum that race is a theory of history, this double relationship to the past suggests a racial dimension to sexual modernism that has not yet figured in scholarly discussion.[37] The white moderns whose writing informs the present work were in a unique *racial* position in relation to sexuality: because they believed themselves to be the legitimate heirs to western civilization in America, they felt entitled to modify their legacy as they saw fit. Their sense of racially based ownership of the civilization they inherited from the Victorians authorized their interventions in the construction of new standards of sexual sensitivity and restraint, health and happiness—that is, of sexual norms. When moderns indicted the Victorians for their sexual pathologies, they were making an argument as much as an observation: they wanted to claim "normality" for themselves and their own generation's orthodoxies.[38]

With Foucault, I believe that to claim the status of normality is also to lay "claim to power. The norm is not simply . . . a principle of intelligibility; it is an element on the basis of which a certain exercise of power is founded and legitimized."[39] It follows that any self-description as "normal" should be treated with a certain skepticism, not to say wariness, about the political relations condensed and concealed in that gesture. For this reason, my approach to the literature of modern sexual normality is influenced by bodies of scholarship that have used such skepticism as a foundational interpretive tool: gay and lesbian history; queer theory; and antiracist feminist criticism. Though all these fields, like other branches of academic inquiry, have tended to be dominated by white scholars, they owe significant (if not always recognized) analytic debts to African American political and cultural criticism. Anti-lynching, Civil Rights, and Black Power activists played extremely important roles in developing the diagnostics of systemic social injustice that were taken up in the whiter contexts of the New Left and of the women's and gay liberation movements of the 1960s and 1970s.[40] It is therefore not surprising that antiracist feminism and gay and lesbian historical studies have long shared a characteristic skepticism about the naturalness, innocence, and universality of the category of the "normal."

At least since the mid-1970s, feminist scholars have been writing about the inseparability of race from the lived experience and politics of gender.[41] This literature is so well developed that I have felt free to put gender on the back burner in the current work; it makes periodic appearances where it is important in each chapter but does not constitute the principle analytic focus of my argument. It is nonetheless worth noting that my arguments resonate with those generated by feminist scholars exploring the problematics of representing desire in the context of racism and sexism. Ann DuCille, for instance, describes "the coupling convention" in U.S. black women's fiction as a political metaphor, "the outward and visible sign of the inward and systemic ills that plague American society."[42] DuCille insists we recognize such representations of marriage and family relations as serious approaches to a politically fraught domain laden with racial claims and patriarchal expectations. Deborah McDowell, Darlene Clark Hine, and others have also underscored the inextricability of racial, gendered, and erotic representations and social positionings in the early-twentieth-century United States.[43]

I have refracted such race-sensitive feminist historical interests through a queer lens. Though large swaths of contemporary queer life elide the radical antiracist tradition that informed the liberation movements of the late 1960s, some significant conceptual similarities remain. In many gay, lesbian, fetish, S/M, and other non-normative sexual communities, the meaning of any given form of erotic expression has been so actively contested that even pro-homosexual claims (e.g., "I was born gay") have long been recognizable not as universal truths but as positions in an ongoing cultural argument about sexuality. Queer theory is a form of engagement with this larger argument. One of its core commitments is the critical exploration of "the limitations, exclusions, and biases inherent within the process of delimiting sexual normality."[44] Queer-theoretical interests and attitudes therefore share with feminist and antiracist projects—with which they sometimes overlap—the political mark of their common emergence from liberation movements: all are motivated by the desire to expose and protest the fact that inequality and injustice are "normal" in American social, cultural, and economic life.[45]

Over the last decade theoretically informed queer sensitivity to the constructed and political nature of normality has helped to (re)direct scholarly attention both to heterosexuality and to the strong discursive connections between race and sex.[46] Yet despite their common origin in a politically alert skepticism about "normality" and its skewed perspective on the world, most often these topics have diverged such that in sexuality studies "race and sexuality" usually means "people of color and homosexuals."[47] Similarly, most critical work on whiteness has overlooked the significance of sexuality in the construction of white racial meaning and subjectivity.[48] To date, heterosexuality and whiteness have not been brought together into something one might think of as "normality studies." The present work is an attempt to forge a connection between the critical study of sexuality and the critical study of race such that "normality" becomes a subject for critical analysis *simultaneously* along both racial and sexual axes of difference and power.

Why hasn't this been done? Perhaps the most basic reason is a general sense that, however one approaches it, the subject of "normality" is a slippery one. Normality seems both immense and blank, ubiquitous and insubstantial, so that it is difficult to get a critical purchase on it except by catching at its ragged edges. In the effort to focus on its center, I have found it helpful to think of normality's apparent blankness as deriving from the power-evasiveness of its component parts, heterosexuality and whiteness. There is abundant evidence that whiteness is difficult for many whites to identify as a racial position at all, much less as a position one might study or work to change.[49] Heterosexuality also has trouble recognizing its positional particularity, preferring to imagine, in Michael Warner's words, "that humanity and heterosexuality are synonymous."[50] If normality is a slippery subject, then, it is because whiteness and heterosexuality share a certain unwillingness to acknowledge their own power and the many forms of coercion and violence that uphold their unearned advantages; both prefer to perceive themselves as natural traits, simultaneously noble and innocent of political meanings. The ideological character of this perception does not make it any easier to explode. It does, however, highlight the relevance of a scholarly practice demonstrating that that shared inarticulate conviction of praiseworthy innocence is not random or coincidental but records the extent to which early-twentieth-century "power-evasive" justifications of both white and heterosexual dominance were constructed and conveyed through the discourses of the normal that linked them together.

The complexity of the relationship between power and cultural visibility is also relevant to the difficulty of conjoining whiteness and heterosexuality as the double subject of "normality studies." On the one hand, the ostentatious appearance of blankness is often a trace effect of covert power operations at work.[51] In our own day's political and representational orders, many forms of power protect, fortify, and perform themselves by reflecting a smooth and empty glossiness to the inquiring gaze. Vulnerability to others' power, in turn, is often experienced and represented in terms of the inability to refuse being investigated and evaluated. Hence, much work in critical whiteness studies seeks to render whiteness more visible in order to render it less dominating and more accountable.[52]

But on the other hand, there are social positions in which even a glimmer of cultural visibility is something to strive for, situations of erasure in which the simple fact of representation can suggest a shift or opening in relations of power, and the possibility of an increased access to agency. Most queer engagements with issues of visibility register heterosexual culture's history of erasing gay and lesbian people's social worlds and critical perspectives, often through the very acts of investigation that claim to bring them into view.[53] As a result, a primary goal of gay, lesbian, and queer scholarship has been to carve out a space in which queer representations and interpretations have epistemological and political value, with a focus on making oppositional discourses register as disruptions in the relentless display of normative heterosexuality that goes by the name "American culture." The kind of "invisibility" that most concerns queer scholarship, in short, is of a different order than that which is of central interest in critical whiteness studies: it is the abject invisibility of having been eradicated from the representational field, not the powerful invisibility of the wizard pulling levers behind the curtain. Heterosexuality, from a queer perspective, is tiresomely overvisible already. Whiteness studies and gay / lesbian / queer theory thus engage issues of visibility and invisibility from different directions and with different needs. These differences doubtless have helped to obscure a crucial commonality between their analyses: across the disciplines (as in popular culture) it is widely believed that the tensions, struggles, and humiliations associated with membership in the "marked" and allegedly inferior subsets of sexual orientation and race (as well as of class, nationality, ability, and gender) dissolve under "normality's" magic sign.

Those who are excluded from the charmed circle are of necessity powerfully aware of its existence and the hierarchy of value it instates and enforces, and one result is that the invisibility or "blankness" of normality is much less credible to those who, for whatever reason, don't qualify for inclusion in that category.[54] Heterosexuality appears, from an explicitly antihomophobic perspective, much less natural than it does from one that presumes or accepts its dominance. Hence gay and lesbian history has given rise to interest in the history of heterosexuality, and queer-theoretical interpretation to this work's exploration of the concept of the normal. A similar trajectory has shaped the emergence of critical whiteness studies out of racially alert scholarship that originally sprang from and focused on the experience of people of color. I have already observed that much current work in the burgeoning field of whiteness studies notes the political significance of the white ability to avoid perceiving whiteness as a racial position. It is much less common for scholars to ask *how* whiteness became "invisible," or to connect that transparency to whiteness's historically specific cultural contents and meanings.[55]

This oversight stems in part from an influential argument that the reason whiteness does not appear to be a racial position is that it is an empty category. David Roediger, in what has become one of the foundational works of "whiteness studies," argues that whiteness is hard to see because it "is nothing but oppressive and false. . . . It is the empty and terrifying attempt to build an identity based on what one isn't and on whom one can hold back."[56] More recently, Manning Marable has argued that though racial formations change in concert with changes in the mode of production, "from the beginning whiteness was vacuous and sterile as a cultural entity."[57] In such analyses, whiteness appears to be "normal" because it is powerful enough to "hold back," that is, silence or marginalize, the voices of those who might testify to its specificity and its violence. In and for itself, it has nothing to say.

This view holds that whiteness has no cultural contents or meaning besides domination. Yet while white people have dominated the United States since its colonial beginnings, neither "normality" nor "whiteness" has always appeared to be empty. An identificatory label that refuses identificatory specificity bears all the marks of ideology at work, and as such it ought to draw our most sensitive critical scrutiny. When antiracist scholars assert that whiteness has no contents, they duplicate its claim that it is simply normal; their intervention is only at the level of evaluating normal whiteness as dangerous and violent. The attribution of "normality" is, in general, equivalent to an assertion that "there is nothing here to see or name." It is therefore skating close to complicity in a system that sustains its inequities by denying their existence. Thus, though most whiteness studies are motivated by a desire to reveal the political contents and consequences of whiteness, I am concerned that assertions of its emptiness may actually work to renaturalize the category in ways that produce political stasis rather than transformation.[58]

After all, the fact that "whiteness" claims to be "normal," that is, neutral and natural and universal, does not make it so. Norma and Normman embody ample evidence that, if heterosexual whiteness is "unmarked" at the beginning of the twenty-first century, it has not always been that way. In the early twentieth century, the racial and sexual beliefs, desires, practices, fears, hopes, fantasies, dreams, anatomies, regrets, rituals, compromises, physiologies, and failures of "normal," middle-class, white Americans were matters of intense interest to scholars and reformers of every stripe, as well as to millions of modern laypeople who produced and consumed popular representations of sex and romance. The sources on which this study is based establish beyond a doubt that many late-nineteenth- and early-twentieth-century whites were strongly aware of the racial specificity of the values they associated with "their" civilization, just as they discussed what a "normal" sexual expression and reproduction of those values entailed. Historical study can help us reconstruct the central cultural contents of whiteness during the years—only eight or nine decades, one long life ago—when the ascent of "normality" rendered those contents difficult for many whites to see and name directly.

Where Whiteness and Sexuality Intersect: Discursive History and Racial Ideals

Some readers will not recognize this work as historical in approach: not only do I rely on close reading of published texts, rather than the presentation of archival evidence, as my basic argumentative strategy, I am more interested in discourses than data, representations than facts. My sources offer little direct evidence of the way any real flesh-and-blood human being occupied the entwined categories "normal," "heterosexual," and "white," nor do I engage in extended analysis of their material consequences.[59] This is a deliberate choice and reflects my sense that more conventional historical methods, though fruitful for investigations of other kinds of historical phenomena, often find themselves unable to say much more about discursive constructions than that they are ideological.[60] In contrast, an interdisciplinary interpretive approach to the discursively available categories of selfhood can tell us a great deal about the lived experience of the past that more social-scientific methods and "harder" kinds of evidence cannot.

Identity categories are representational modes, and as such they can have the same kind of large-scale evidentiary historical significance as an era's architecture, fiction, or advertising. At the same time they are intimate and personal: they describe the temporally specific boundaries on the vocabularies with which people can ask and answer the questions "who am I," "who are we," and "who are you?" Identity categories are the words with which post-Enlightenment Westerners try to explain our differences from one another and our moments of recognition, our identifications with ourselves, and the ways these fail us. And fail they do. As Eve Kosofsky Sedgwick has noted, "it is astonishing how few respectable conceptual tools we have for dealing with this self-evident fact [that humans differ from one another]. A tiny number of inconceivably coarse axes of categorization have been painstakingly inscribed in current critical and political thought: gender, race, class, nationality, sexual orientation are pretty much the available distinctions."[61] Historians might add "era" and "religion," and disability studies scholars and activists are working hard to get "ability" included, but more additions to the list would not add up to a good description of the experience of the sense of self-in-the-world. Yet the inadequacy and clumsiness of taxonomies does not render them optional or unimportant. Neither does their ideological character mean that discursive analysis of them inevitably evacuates the political, as social historians have often contended.[62] On the contrary, identity categories have immense political as well as personal significance; our situation in relation to discourses of the self is and has long been an important part of how Westerners recognize ourselves and one another as humans and as particular kinds of humans, available for some relationships, jobs, and dwellings and not for others.[63] Precisely to the extent that "normality" functioned in early-twentieth-century culture as a euphemistic substitute for more explicitly politicized identities referring to sexuality and race, it demands that we attend to the discursive moves through which it acquired the appearance of blank emptiness and innocence.

This study, then, rests on the premise that the identity categories of sexuality and race—like those of gender, class, nationality, religion, and some forms of "disability"—are condensations of historical processes saturated with relations of power. Through these processes, individuals are positioned and position themselves as white or colored, normal or perverse, men or women, modern or old-fashioned, healthy or ill, respectable or marginal, and so forth.[64] This means that I do not see identity categories like "normality," "heterosexuality," or "whiteness" as descriptions of people's essential natures, consistent across time, nor as collections of more or less concrete traits that all "normal," "straight," or "white" people can be presumed to share within a given time. Rather, they are and were ideals to which no real person can ever quite conform, though the members of some social categories gain real social privileges by their perceived proximity to those ideals.[65] The following chapters tell the story of how "normality" came to serve as a sort of discursive umbrella under which white, heterosexual Americans in a formally democratic society could claim both physical and cultural ownership of modern civilization. I argue that normality discourse helped root that claim in the sphere of sexual conduct and values, at a highly disciplined point of intersection between body and soul, self and civilization.

One of the chief consequences of the ascent of normality in the interwar years was that white Americans acquired a language of neutral self-description that identified them with all the best ideals and achievements of civilization. That identification was sometimes used to bolster explicitly racist arguments about the inferiority of nonwhite Americans, but the evolutionary superiority of modern whiteness was implicit in the construction of normality even in the absence of overt racial comparisons. Norma and Norm-man are good examples of normality discourse's ability to celebrate white-ness without mentioning the existence of the "inferior" races. Indeed, nor-mality helped to construct modern whiteness as inherently superior to other races, and simultaneously as innocent of involvement in other peoples' polit-ical, cultural, and economic disempowerment. The fact that this discourse developed during the same years that the second Ku Klux Klan formed and flourished underscores the fact that "normality" was a cultural ideal, rather than a description of social reality.[66]

For this reason, I tend to read my sources not so much for evidence of what really happened, in terms of who exercised what forms of power in relation to whom, but rather for evidence of how a dominant racial class represented the legitimacy of its power. Such a reading strategy seems especially appropriate because many of the sources I explore were attempting to guide their readers' behavior into the normative channels the texts constructed and reflected. Prescriptive sources are in many ways dubious historical documents, offering only very problematic information about what people actually did.[67] This is largely because they had ideological and commercial agendas to fulfill but also because readers then, as now, were active and selective in their approach to texts; for instance, while we can establish that a specific marriage manual sold briskly for several decades, we cannot then deduce that people bought it for the same reasons and read it with the same reactions across that span of time. The disjuncture between normative sexual and racial discourse and its reception, or enactment in actual experiences, should not be forgotten. Nevertheless, this project proceeds from the premise that what people said in public, in forms that reached hundreds of thousands of readers, has its own kind of truth: it tells us a great deal about the "official" (read: normal, and therefore white and heterosexual) wisdom of the day, and in turn about the cultural values and beliefs in relation to which individual identities and political positions were formed. Dominant discursive constructions may tell us very little about the practices of everyday life, but they tell us a great deal about the systems of belief and power with which people had to live and contend. Without a rich understanding of the way in which "normality" was articulated in the modern age, we lack the proper interpretative context for understanding how real people lived their lives, under what psychic and cultural constraints they labored, and why they made the choices they did.

Perhaps this is the place to discuss the important question of exactly *which* whiteness I mean. One of the most fruitful insights of whiteness studies has been its recognition that not all whites are white in the same way. In the late nineteenth and early twentieth centuries, whiteness was fractured into many races—for instance, Celtic, Teutonic, and Mediterranean people were all "white," but their positions in relation to that larger racial category were not identical.[68] The historian Matthew Frye Jacobson has made an especially persuasive case against the notion of a "monolithic" whiteness in precisely the period about which I write here.[69] From the 1840s to the 1920s, Jacobson shows, massive immigration raised questions about whether legal whiteness (which had rendered immigrants eligible for naturalization since 1790) was an adequate qualification for full citizenship. The combination of a "universal" white naturalization law with a steady influx of immigrants meant that Americans of this era developed an extraordinarily nuanced perception of the physical and moral traits of different whitenesses. For all the nuance of this perception, however, the social distribution of power and privilege was often pretty simple: only Anglo-Saxons shared the racial heritage of republican self-government, and so all others were "probationary whites." As Jacobson puts it, an Irish or Italian immigrant's "racial credentials" as white were simply not "equivalent to those of the Anglo-Saxon 'old stock' who laid proprietary claim to the nation's . . . stewardship."[70] Only in the decades after the 1924 Johnson Act sharply curtailed immigration, Jacobson argues, did the relatively inclusive panethnic category "Caucasian" succeed the multiple, hierarchically arranged whitenesses of the previous eighty years.

When I speak of the construction and consolidation of "normal" whiteness across the era between 1890 and 1940, I do not mean to invoke a racial monolith where none existed. I do, however, mean to point to the widespread belief throughout this period that there was a sort of core racial essence that defined authentic American whiteness. In the 1880s, when my study opens, the "Anglo-Saxon 'old stock' who laid proprietary claims to the nation's . . . stewardship" were anxious about the threat to their dominance posed by the influx of white immigrants as well as by the post-Emancipation political realignment of the nation, and they expressed that anxiety by describing their own class-specific cultural ideals as the character or essence of "civilized" whiteness. In the 1920s and 1930s, when "normality" was coming to define a mass-cultural sexual standard at least theoretically accessible to all whites, that ideal racial essence retained significant elements of its older composition. In other words, who counted as "white" changed more, and more quickly, than the contents of the ideal of "whiteness" itself. Though the people Jacobson calls "old stock," "Anglo-Saxon," and "patrician" whites certainly had and retained a privileged relationship to ideal whiteness, that whiteness was not only a genealogical property of persons. It was also a series of interconnected beliefs about the virtues of self-cultivation and self-control in relation to the family, the nation, and civilization. Together these beliefs constituted a racial and sexual ideal of the "normal American." This ideal, rather than the various specific whitenesses of European immigrants, is the subject of this study.

Once again, Norma and Normman can make the point clearer. The statues derived their representational authority from their claim to truthful, accurate, transparent duplication of the statistically average measurements of American citizens in general. At the same time, it was a matter of public record that the statues reflected the measurements of "the old American stock," and that there were a disproportionate number among them of elite students from the Ivy League and the Seven Sisters.[71] "Normality" was, even at midcentury, a description of the scions of old Yankee families. Therefore we can say that "normality" did not need to justify itself by reference to any statistically normal population but co-existed quite comfortably with the acknowledgment that the "normal" was socially superior.[72]

In any case, it was manifest that the statues were much better-looking than the "average." Harry Shapiro of the Museum of Natural History wrote, "One might well look at a multitude of young men and women before finding an approximation to these normal standards. We have to do here then with apparent paradoxes. Let us state it this way: . . . the average is excessively rare."[73] Public acknowledgment that "normality" was a racial and sexual ideal derived from a patrician population did not make "normality" seem less normal, or even less democratic. When the Cleveland *Plain Dealer* conducted a "Search for Norma," inviting the women of Ohio to submit their measurements in competition for a substantial prize, it did so as a test to find out "if such a figure exists in life as well as in statistics."[74] Almost four hundred entries a day came pouring in, but 3,864 entries later, the paper concluded that "Norma remained a hypothetical individual."[75] The young woman who won the prize was no patrician; Martha Skidmore worked as a ticket-seller in a local movie theater and had been a gauge grinder during the war. But she won because her measurements approximated Norma's better than any others, and that approximation was enough for the Cleveland *Plain Dealer*. The "normal," in short, was an ideal. Apparently, "what is" was not, and everybody knew it.

This paradoxical, contradictory quality of whiteness registers its slippage back and forth from a material description or ascription of real Americans to an ideal, almost Platonic form to which no real person could conform. It is in this latter sense that I suggest that normal "whiteness" had relatively consistent meanings even though, at the same time, the racial category was both deeply fractured by ethnicity and applied in wildly unpredictable ways by naturalization and other courts.[76] The central contents of the category were much less flexible than the legal and social groupings of the persons who found themselves measured against it.

What were these central contents? I concur with Jacobson's suggestion that self-governance was the core value at the heart of whiteness. However, his scholarly interest in public-sphere politics and society leads him to neglect two crucial and connected issues: the specifically erotic, affective, and familial dimensions of self-governance, and the remarkable durability, against all evidence to the contrary, of the belief that whiteness is fundamentally "disciplined, virtuous, self-sacrificing, productive, far-seeing, and wise."[77] Jacobson, indeed, emphasizes that these white virtues were the qualities of an ideal citizen in a democracy, and he even notes that republican government requires its citizens to learn to control their passions. But where Jacobson moves on to note simply that "probationary whites" like the Irish or the Italians were widely depicted as problematic citizens inherently unable to curb their political passions in the interest of the common good, I emphasize "self-governance" in its sexual and emotional sense. The passions that could destroy the republican experiment were the passions of the bedroom as well as of the marketplace and the ballot box.

If "the Anglo-Saxon branch of the Teutonic race of the Caucasian group" failed to reproduce itself, no purely formal training in civics could replace the white "racial genius" for freedom tempered with responsibility.[78] If white husbands and wives could not work out marital relationships that modeled in microcosm the tolerant but passionate give-and-take of democratic citizenship, the nation lost its chief referent and school for social order. If white children could not be taught to take up their privileged racial burden of self-control, the foundations of American civilization trembled. Thus I focus my analysis on the way in which controlled *erotic* passion helped to define a bourgeois ideal of "true" American whiteness as the essence of civic and personal virtue.[79] This book, then, seeks to restore sexual desire and the problem of its management to its legitimate place in the construction of whiteness as ownership of the modern nation during the crucial era when mass culture was taking shape.[80]

I have already suggested that Harry Shapiro's use of Athenian marbles to represent the racial origins of modern normality contained an important, if inarticulate, reference to democratic political forms as a core component of the white civilization transmitted from generation to generation through sexual reproduction in marriage. I would like to conclude this introductory discussion with a brief discussion of two final sources. One is a semi-psycho-analytic work of cultural criticism and the other is a romantic Hollywood film directed at a broad popular audience; the first is self-consciously avant-garde, which is to say that it is proud of not being normal, while the second suggests that normality is the only route to happiness. Yet despite the difference in their genres, agendas, and expected audiences, they both represent heterosexual normality in terms of an implicitly racialized capacity for self-government. They can therefore illustrate something of the breadth of the representational frame in which race-evasive depictions of marital love worked to construct and communicate the power-evasive meanings of normal, modern whiteness.

In 1930 the leftist novelist and critic Floyd Dell argued that the material constraints on earlier civilizations had hampered both their sexual and political development: only with the coming of the machine age, he held, were people free enough to achieve adult heterosexuality.[81] At this time the term "heterosexuality" was just entering common use, so Dell felt it necessary to define the term for his readers. His definition conflates heterosexuality with modern marriage, which he describes in terms of the achieved capacity for independence and self-determination. The word "heterosexuality," he explained, derives "from the Greek 'heteros,' other, or different, or opposite—but having the sense also of being a 'mate' in that difference, as the one sex is to the other."[82] Desire for a member of the opposite sex, in Dell's eyes, was not genuine "heterosexuality" but only a biological response to sexual difference. As such, it involved a physical element common to all mammals. To qualify as adult heterosexuality, desire had to develop "through courtship and love-choice" to "sexual mating, parenthood, and family life."[83] Earlier eras of white civilization had lacked the economic stability to permit people to pursue this modern marital ideal; Dell explained that relatively primitive forms of white civilization "required an infantilized form of heterosexual love—one sufficiently docile to parental authority" in order to survive. As a result, romantic love and desire had been excluded from marriage, and people had turned to the perverse eroticism of "homosexuality, prostitution-patronage, and polite adultery" in the effort to compensate for the limits "patriarchal tyranny" placed on sexual development. In contrast, Dell argued, *"modern machinery has laid the basis for a more biologically normal family life than has existed throughout the whole of the historical period, or indeed in the whole life of mankind."*[84]

For Dell, sexual development from "infantile" perversity (ancient Greek homosexuality, extramarital courtly love) to normal adult heterosexuality (modern marriage) was unmistakable evidence that modern industrial civilization was better than any other had ever been. Dell's argument turned on the conflation of the modern and the adult with the normal, a conflation that underscores the racial assumptions structuring his paean to heterosexuality. The claim that truly modern lovers were the first to achieve true adulthood resonates with the era's racist and imperialist constructions of nonwhite people as permanent children, incapable of self-rule and therefore requiring guidance from more advanced races. Dell's insistence that adult heterosexuality was a uniquely modern accomplishment worked to align perversion with primitivism even in the absence of references to the existence of people of color.

Further, it worked to align primitive perversion with political and personal constraint and modern heterosexuality with freedom. Dell's persistent figuration of the past as sexually and emotionally stifled by "patriarchal authority" implies that what he called "patriarchal countries" in the present had failed to evolve to the level of self-determination he saw as the great accomplishment of the modern United States. When people from those countries immigrated to the United States, they sometimes attempted to restrict heterosexual expression into forms native to their comparatively archaic cultures of origin; thus, Dell explained, white immigrant groups sometimes failed to foster sexual self-government in their children.[85] If they were to become "normal" Americans, immigrants had to adopt the modern American vision of marriage as a free partnership between consenting adults motivated by mutual love and desire. And to the extent that they "grew up" enough to pursue the uniquely free heterosexual partnership of modern marriage, immigrant Europeans could hope to shed their "probationary" status and gain access to normality. At the same time, Dell's definition of heterosexuality implied that even an impeccably WASP heritage was not quite enough to guarantee that one's whiteness was fully normal. Normality required a specifically modern, indicatively white combination of erotic and emotional sensitivity and self-government.

One final source confirms that Dell's understanding of normal sexuality as instantiating an ideal of uniquely modern whiteness had representational counterparts in mass culture. MGM's hit 1928 film *Our Dancing Daughters* follows three young white women in their attempts to find happiness in marriage.[86] The plot follows a young flapper (Joan Crawford, in the role that made her a star) as she falls in love for the first time. Her frankness and energy make her devastatingly attractive, but the man she hopes to marry is beguiled by another young woman (Anita Page) into believing that Crawford is too "wild" to make a virtuous wife.

Crawford's beau is set up as easily recruited to this kind of judgment through the simple device of making him a rich Southerner. Just over a decade after *The Birth of a Nation* celebrated the revived Klan as chivalrous defenders of pure white womanhood against racial inferiors, audiences would have known how to read this character's regional origin and class as implying his belief that white civilization stood or fell with the chastity of its women.[87] At the same time, his status as an upright Southern gentleman suggested that he might not understand that flappers like Crawford could drink, smoke, and dance without compromising the sexual virtue that had been Victorian women's core contribution to white civilization. This suggestion is confirmed in a scene in which Anita Page's mother, strategizing about how to get all that money in the family, warns her that men are "old-fashioned" about their wives. Southern wealth, in this context, represents an ideal of whiteness that is infinitely to be desired for its stability, but that is simultaneously at risk because it is not modern enough to allow for the coexistence of self-government and erotic expressiveness.

Page therefore feigns what she calls "purity" by pretending she doesn't drink or smoke, by enacting physical timidity, and finally by apologizing for not being "modern." She drives her point home with the murmured suggestion that Crawford lacks the sexual self-control required for a position as a

Southern lady. So the eligible Southern bachelor marries Crawford's simpering antagonist. Alas, after the honeymoon he discovers that his lily-white, beruffled wife is a tippling gold-digger who thinks of marriage as a meal ticket and a license to stop performing the artificial maidenly purity her mother imposed. The only respect in which her performance of "purity" approaches authenticity is her complete lack of sexual interest in her husband.[88] Anita Page's character is a liar, a thief, and a drunk. Her insensitivity is the more damaging because it is matched by her lack of self-restraint; she seems to have no authentic feelings of her own, and she is appallingly indifferent to other people's.

The film depicts the demure "Victorian" blonde as emotionally and ethically rotten, while the modern "jazz baby" is stout-hearted and true. Joan Crawford's character demonstrates her white self-control in scene after scene. She sips at cocktails—but never gulps. She makes herself a pleasure to be around—but never leads men on. She "pets"—but never lets things get out of hand. She even performs the Charleston as a solo dance, so that it demonstrates her passionate vitality without suggesting that she is available to be touched. When she offers the Southerner what she calls a "friendly kiss," she is clearly startled by the intensity with which he responds and lets him see that that was both intensely thrilling and not what she had in mind.

Crawford's beau misinterprets her willingness to register that thrill as indicating faulty self-control, when in actuality it records the modernity of her whiteness: she is free enough to experience and express the depth of her feelings for him precisely because she knows how to control her sensitivity. When her dream of romance is dashed, she quickly disciplines herself to put her broken heart behind her without complaint or self-pity. Her apparently natural joyfulness is then exposed as the outward sign of good training and a strong will. The fact that Crawford's character is represented as the "right" wife for the Southern gentleman suggests that her virtues are racial ones. She stands for the energetic, but controlled, modern sexuality through which ideal whiteness was reproduced; she is Norma with a more fashionable haircut and in constant motion.

In contrast, the superficial whiteness of Anita Page's character, and her willingness to mobilize it to get what she wants, conceal her failure to embody its core modern values. The problem is not that her ancestry is doubtful. Rather, it is that her character is too tangled up in parental control and material considerations to develop to the point that Dell would have called "adult heterosexuality." But normality triumphs in the end. Page's character gets killed off for her failures of self-government: she falls down the stairs during a drunken tirade, and her death sets Prince Charming free to marry Crawford after all. In Hollywood, the wages of normal whiteness include getting your man.

Crawford's character highlights the odd contradiction in the normative ideal of whiteness, which is both "natural" to our open-hearted heroine and the result of constant self-restraint. Modern love required erotic sensitivity, but also social respectability; white marriage and the future of the race required a carefully calibrated amalgam of passion and sober self-control. Despite its mobilization of the conventional contrast between modern and Victorian sexuality, the film does not simply assess erotic expressiveness as inherently good. Sensitivity is crucial, but that very sensitivity makes self-government equally necessary and complex. Crawford originally loses her true love because she is not circumspect enough, while a third "dancing daughter" spends the film suffering because she lost her virginity prior to her marriage. Her misery is depicted not as the payback for her fall from virtue but as the consequence of a rigid, overcontrolled upbringing, which left her without the independence and self-discipline she needed to recognize the difference between sexual desire and the love that leads to marriage.

Discipline and restraint had to be internalized if white moderns were to make the normal marriages on which the legitimate reproduction of whiteness depended. At the same time, because those white marriages had a responsibility to combine respectability with fruitfulness, discipline could not dominate sensitivity. Thus Crawford combined passion, prudence, and purity in her performance as the ideal modern maiden.[89] The tension inherent in this position is registered in Crawford's character's name: she dances on tabletops, but she is called Diana, an ancient name for the ancient white virtue of chaste self-restraint. *Our Dancing Daughters* thus distinguishes between externally imposed repressive "Victorian" decorum and the modern capacity for genuine erotic self-government. Both were expressions of civilized whiteness, but the latter represented a more advanced state of civilization's development; the contrast between them therefore makes the modern form seem like a better approximation to the core racial ideals of sensitivity and self-control. In that sense, the marital erotics of "adult heterosexuality" make moderns seem more white, better at whiteness, than Victorians. Crawford's reward for her sensitivity and self-control is the class and race status of Southern ladyhood, but the benefits flow both ways: pure Southern whiteness receives a shot of modern sexual energy from its recognition of her as a legitimate mother for the race.

Our Dancing Daughters reminds us that highly sexualized explorations of the meaning, limits, and relative worth of modern, normal forms of whiteness were part of everyday middle-American life in the decades before the Second World War. The film launched Crawford to stardom and spawned two sequels, which played in Peoria as well as in New York and Los Angeles. At about the same time marital advice literature, middlebrow magazines, health exhibits at museums and world's fairs, sociological monographs, medical and psychological sex research, and other cultural media explored very similar subject matter in strikingly similar terms. Though class, regional, religious, and political differences certainly influenced both the content and the tone of many such explorations, by the end of the 1930s emergent mass culture featured a relatively "monolithic" ideal of normal whiteness. That whiteness was inseparable from a carefully governed normative heterosexuality. Statues like Norma and Normman and films like *Our Dancing Daughters* make it clear that, when it was under construction, "normality" was far from invisible or opaque. The following chapters examine the process of normality's construction, from its relatively contested origins in Gilded Age bourgeois culture to the point where it became, well, normal—so ubiquitous, so taken for granted, that its power became hard to see.

I "BARBARIANS ARE NOT NERVOUS"

Whiteness as Weakness: Nervous Exhaustion as a Racial Asset

In 1880, 1881, and 1884, a New York nerve specialist named George Beard published three immensely influential volumes that sought to explain to medical and lay America how and why the progress of civilization was making well-bred white people sick.[1] In these works and his many articles on the subject, Beard brought together a wide range of ailments under the single term "neurasthenia," explaining that while the manifestations of this newly named disease were various, their causes were relatively limited. The varied pains and weaknesses of neurasthenia, he wrote, all had a physical origin in an extremely sensitive condition of one or more of the three "reflex centers" of nervous response (the brain, the stomach, and the reproductive system).[2] Neurasthenia, also called "nervous exhaustion" or simply "nervousness," derived from an inherited physical incapacity of these reflex centers to respond to all that they could perceive. In other words, Beard's new disease reflected refined white Americans' sensitivity to the complex stimulations of modern life.

This chapter focuses on neurasthenia because the disease provides a useful context for understanding the subsequent construction of "normality." As normality would do for a later generation, Gilded Age nervousness linked contemporary discourses of race, class, and civilization into a fairly coherent statement about the world-historical significance of healthy reproductive sexuality among what were often called "old-stock" American whites. The disease thus can serve as a lens through which to focus on the articulation of race with class and sexuality at the end of the nineteenth century and thence to illustrate the interwoven beliefs about physical and social realities that helped to naturalize and justify white supremacy after Emancipation destroyed one of its chief institutional supports. The logic of the neurasthenia diagnosis rested on and reinforced a culturally powerful conceptual connection between whiteness and modern civilization; as a result, I interpret the disease as one site for the cultural (re)construction of a postslavery America in which white rule appeared—to whites—as both necessary and benign.

Indeed, though this interpretation is new in its focus on whiteness, scholars have long noticed and reacted against the politically troubling dimensions of the diagnosis. In 1973 the historians of medicine John and Robin Haller described neurasthenia as "a reservoir of class prejudices, status desires, urban arrogance, repressed sexuality, and indulgent self-centeredness."[3] In the 1980s Ann Douglas Wood added misogyny to this list, while the cultural historian T. J. Jackson Lears suggested that the symptoms of neurasthenia expressed a bourgeois "paralysis of the will" in the face of the increasing unreality of modern life.[4] More recently, Kevin Mumford has discussed the specifically sexual elements of the diagnosis in men, linking Lears's observation to "anxiety about lost manhood" and noting the connection between such anxieties and colonial expansion.[5] Thus for thirty years historians have been alert to the troubled and troubling social relations embedded in neurasthenia.[6] This scholarship has enriched my own interpretation of the diagnosis' racial dimensions and their relationship to sexuality, which have not yet been the subject of sustained inquiry.

My chief interest in the disease is as a window into the Gilded Age construction of whiteness as weakness, a construction that, paradoxically, bolstered faith in innate white superiority and fitness to rule. I show that the theory and diagnosis of nervousness expressed a widespread and debilitating sense of social powerlessness among bourgeois whites. In general, nervous weakness was a physical, pathological performance of the experience or fear of loss of agency and security. One of its chief manifestations was sexual exhaustion, which threatened to undermine the literal reproduction of whiteness; nervous men and women, as we'll see, were often represented as incapable of conceiving a new generation of productive and powerful Anglo-American citizens. Yet neurasthenia theory also reflected an optimistic sense of identity between bourgeois whites and modern civilization. According to Beard, these people tended toward nervousness precisely because they embodied modern civilization. Neurasthenics therefore had the potential to express modernity's full re/productive capacity and its loftiest ideals. Fulfilling that potential required a careful and consistent sexual self-discipline that helped to define what it meant to be modern at the same time that it helped to define what it meant to be white.

A note on the racial politics of this discussion seems appropriate here. There are excellent reasons to be skeptical of and impatient with economically and/or culturally privileged whites who complain about their sense of powerlessness. Yet it seems to me that this complaint is worth investigating, despite its clearly ideological dimension and the reality of white racial dominance, precisely because it has had such remarkable staying power.[7] Indeed, this chapter suggests that the oscillation between a smug sense of entitlement and a panicky fear of failure, or the sensation of losing control, has been a constitutive element of whiteness at least since the 1880s. Neurasthenia is worth revisiting in part because it offers such a clear vision of that oscillation, the dynamic interdependence of those two apparently opposite convictions about the meaning of race. I will show that white claims of weakness were inseparable from white bourgeois claims to legitimate ownership and dominance of American culture. Neurasthenia helps us see that weakness seems to have worked as a white racial asset.

For some readers, my approach will seem to replicate one of the most irritatingly arrogant and painfully consequential qualities of whiteness, to wit, its tendency to look at itself in the mirror and imagine it is seeing the whole world. Why do we need another representation of whiteness in conversation with itself? Part of my answer to this question is that an exploration of white self-absorption is not the same thing as a performance of it. Looking at the ways in which neurasthenia discourse constructed whiteness as weakness can help us understand white insistence on its own innocence in relation to racism. Though nervousness was a way for whites to talk about whiteness as both precious and vulnerable—a construction with terrifying consequences for the exercise of white power against racial and ethnic "inferiors"—its emphasis on weakness among whites helped to disguise the power relationships embedded in its constructions of racial and national modernity. Thus part of my goal in this chapter is to delineate the way in which whiteness was constructed in the Gilded Age as a self-referential set of ideals in support of the development of civilization, ideals which believed themselves to be not only innocent of racial terrorism but actually benign to the limited extent that they were relevant to the "lower races" at all.

Medicine, of course, is not the world, and even within medical culture Beard's theories were not universally accepted. A handful of well-known physicians among his contemporaries rejected neurasthenia altogether, and while the diagnosis was popular among clinicians for several decades, before 1920 it had fallen from medical favor in the United States.[8] On the other end of the middle-class cultural spectrum, many late Victorians took a spiritual stand against the godless scientific materialism represented by Beard and his ilk. Despite such oppositional voices, which I engage briefly at the end of this chapter, the language of "nervousness" and "nervous breakdown" entered popular culture and became part of the everyday emotional vocabulary of the twentieth century. Its remarkable durability indicates that neurasthenia spoke to many people about the conditions of their lives, and the state of the nation, in terms that they found meaningful.

It seems highly likely that the long-term success of the idea of nervousness records George Beard's remarkable ability to reflect his culture's conventional wisdom about sexuality, race, and modernization in America. In the historian Charles Rosenberg's words, Beard was "neither a profound nor an original thinker. His medical writings are a mosaic of the intellectual commonplaces of his time."[9] I have supplemented Beard's theoretical expositions with a variety of individual case histories.[10] I use these to check his theories against broader clinical practice and also against some of the most successful popular representations of the disease. At the end of this chapter I introduce a nonmedical account of the social scandal that erupted when a prominent Brooklyn minister, Henry Ward Beecher, was accused of adultery. I show that some journalistic representations of Beecher's trial draw on the same conceptual structures as the medical discourse of modern nervousness. The similarity of the description of white civilization under attack in these otherwise quite different contexts confirms that nervousness reflected a widespread bourgeois understanding of civilization as white property, developed through moral and physical self-restraint and sustained by the intersection of sexual and cultural reproduction. The different sources also emphasize the way in which that smug sense of racial superiority was entwined with anxiety over the possible loss of white self-control and social dominance. Turn-of-the-century expressions of the allegedly inherent, but never secure, identity between whiteness and modern American civilization constituted an argument for the world-historical importance of sexual self-discipline, and for the legitimacy of reserving social power for the well-bred whites who valued that discipline.

Neurasthenia and the Racial Body

From its inception, neurasthenia involved three interwoven elements: the individual body of the suffering person, with its specific predispositions and tendencies; the social body, or existing class-striated national context, in which each sufferer was embedded as a portion of some organ or limb; and the racial body, which incorporated both individual and social bodies through several generations, as they stretched out across evolutionary time. When Beard (or other contributors to the discourse of modern nervousness) wrote about any one of these elements, the other two were there as well, sometimes inarticulate, but giving depth and shape to the one being elaborated.

This multidimensional interrelationship is clear in Beard's description of neurasthenia's origins. Nervousness, he explained, was the result of complex interactions between individual bodies and the culture of postbellum America, especially in the industrial cities of the Northeast. This part of the world, he asserted, was home to a uniquely modern kind of civilization, which was "distinguished from the ancient [civilizations] by . . . steam-power, the periodical press, the telegraph, the sciences, and the mental activity of women."[11] These five developments contributed to a social environment marked by rapid material change, an unmanageable proliferation of information, and a correspondingly distressing degree of haste and competition.[12] Beard went on to note that America's unique atmospheric and sociopolitical climate made modernization even more disconcerting than it would otherwise have been: many of his contemporaries agreed that the American air was painfully dry and the range of temperatures extreme, while the people were unusually independent in religion, civil activities, and social and business interactions.

This description of modernizing America's social body folded into a description of the nervous individual through an indirect, but crucial, reference to the racial body. According to Beard, modern life made people nervous exactly insofar as they were embedded in the evolutionary history of modern American civilization. Nervousness was not caused only by modernization and climate, but by these things *as they affected people who were born into a special and privileged relation to national progress*. Native-born, genteel whites were the members of the racial body who inherited civilization from their ancestors, transformed it into its uniquely modern form, and transmitted it to their descendents.

Since nervousness usually attacked this group, the disease carried connotations of high evolutionary status. Just as inbred European royalty inherited hemophilia with their blue blood, the bearers of American culture inherited "a constitutional tendency to diseases of the nervous system."[13] Beard called this tendency the "nervous diathesis." This hereditary, physical delicacy of the nerves did not *cause* neurasthenia in and of itself. Rather, the nervous diathesis made its possessors extremely, painfully perceptive of their surroundings. The more stimulating those surroundings were, the more likely it was that the person with the nervous diathesis would develop full-blown nervous exhaustion. Conversely, in the absence of the inherited tendency to nervousness, the stresses of modern American civilization could not cause full-blown neurasthenia any more than a commoner marrying up could become a "bleeder."[14]

The clearest sign that a person was a member of this natural American aristocracy of nerves was superficial appearance. The typical nervous person possessed "a fine organization," which was "distinguished from the coarse by fine, soft hair, delicate skin, nicely chiselled features, small bones, tapering extremities, and frequently by a muscular system comparatively small and feeble."[15] Without mentioning race or class in so many words, Beard made it plain that the nervous diathesis was not to be found among the brawny laboring classes, or the stout peasants emigrating from rural parts of Europe, any more than among ex-slaves or Indians. The fine organization belonged to well-bred Anglo-Saxons.

Nervousness was therefore a "racial" trait in the simple sense that it appeared most often among white people. But just as modern civilization involved more than material development, the racialized delicacy of the nervous body was always more than skin-deep. The nervous diathesis was "frequently associated with superior intellect, and with a strong and active emotional nature."[16] The fine organization was that of "the civilized, refined, and educated, rather than of the barbarous and low-born and untrained."[17] Thus the physical refinement of the nervous body represented the cultural refinements treasured by the genteel middle classes as evolutionary achievements. The conflation of class with race here recalls the ideal, rather than real, nature of the "whiteness" that was under construction in the discourse of modern nervousness. The "fine organization" involved both a particular perceptual sensitivity, and a culture of bodily discipline, that together constituted an imaginary population of native-born, Anglo-American, bourgeois whites as personifications of modern civilization. Among the most fundamental elements of this imagined whiteness were a strong work ethic combined with a discriminating, even wary attitude toward fleshly appetites and pleasures.[18]

The nervous diathesis, in sum, signified an advanced evolutionary stage in individual bodies, in their society, and in humanity. Only people with the nervous diathesis could develop nervous exhaustion; only an advanced civilization could produce the nervous diathesis; and only a highly evolved race could create a civilization sufficiently advanced to give rise to modern nervousness. Neurasthenia was the end product of a long chain of racial developments, involving body, mind, spirit, and social order, which evolved slowly and incrementally across the generations. Pale skin—literal whiteness—was not enough. The nervous diathesis arose only in those whites who had inherited a specific ideal relation to American culture. In 1888, the temperance advocate Edward P. Thwing summed up this chain of associations, linking class, race, nation, civilization, and modernity in the simple statement that "barbarians are not nervous."[19]

Barbarians, and other racialized lower-class types, were not nervous because they lacked the physical, intellectual, and moral sensitivity and self-discipline that moderns had evolved. Beard acknowledged that otherwise healthy peasants sometimes displayed odd behaviors that looked like nervousness, but he explained that these meant that most primitive types "were simply unbalanced"—that is, they combined "muscular vigor" with "but little intellectual strength and very much emotion."[20] This combination might be exhibited as sexual appetite, or as outbursts of religious enthusiasm such as those displayed by the Holy Rollers, whose religious ecstasy led them to undecorous writhings.[21] Such behavior bore scant resemblance to the refined bodies, trained intellects, and delicately nuanced emotions of the modern neurasthene. In fact, Beard described such "unbalanced" peasants as "precious curiosities, relics or antiques that the fourteenth century has dropped right into the middle of the nineteenth."[22] The tendency to true nervous illness, Beard explained, was "developed, fostered and perpetuated with the progress of civilization, with the advance of culture and refinement, and the corresponding preponderance of labor of the brain over that of the muscles. As would logically be expected, it is oftener met with in cities than in the country, is more marked and more frequent at the desk, the pulpit, and in the counting-room than in the shop or on the farm."[23]

Such "brain-workers"—middle-class Anglo males—were the prototypical neurasthenics. Nervous collapses were almost commonplace among the great thinkers of the day: the roster of famous intellectual neurasthenes includes Herbert Spencer, Charlotte Perkins Gilman, William and Henry James, and Henry Adams. Academic or literary ambition, however, was not required. Simply doing the daily business of modernization could wear on the nerves. Beard represented nervousness as a disease most frequently found among professionals and businessmen, especially those whose business involved distinctively modern technologies. In fact, the railroad barons Leland Stanford, Collis P. Huntington, and Henry Villard all succumbed to bouts of nervous illness, apparently brought on by the strain of constant politicking amid the wild fluctuations of the Gilded Age's boom-bust economy.[24] Despite neurasthenia's image as an elite illness, however, there is evidence that, in actual clinical practice over the years, the diagnosis was applied to skilled workingmen, small farmers, factory girls, and other hard workers outside the ranks of the genteel. F. R. Gosling's quantitative analysis of 330 case studies published between 1880 and 1910 indicates that professional and artisan-class men received the most sympathetic medical treatment for nervous ailments. Some doctors also recognized the strain of poverty on working women's nerves. In contrast, doctors usually responded to prostrate laboring men and middle-class women with harsher judgments of nervous profligacy, hysteria, or idleness.[25] Thus we can venture to say that although clinicians applied the neurasthenia diagnosis more broadly than Beard did, they shared his general assumptions about the typical nervous person and his or her relationship to civilization. The labor of middle-class women in the home was culturally constructed as a natural expression of feminine caring, while the lower ranks of white ethnic working men were widely represented as shiftless, drunken, or otherwise unreliable: neither group seemed to play an actively effortful role in the routine business of modern civilization, and so neither had much excuse for nervous collapse. In contrast, financiers, professionals, and skilled workingmen and, to a lesser degree, working-class white women carried the weight of modernity on their shoulders.

It seems safe to conclude, then, that the typical neurasthene was an urban worker, usually educated and sometimes wealthy, who was forced into fierce competition and unrelenting struggle for access to limited resources. He or she was probably doomed to a life of strictly scheduled, disciplined labor as someone else's employee. In the genteel mind circa 1890, this seemed like a hard lot for Anglo women, whose sex and race was supposed to guarantee them the right to privatized labor in dependence on husbands or fathers. Such a fate was also contrary to the American dream for skilled artisans, professionals, and gentlemen: democratic rhetoric had long promised that all white men who were willing to work could hope for proud independence. The neurasthenia diagnosis in common clinical practice may well reflect the conflict between ideals of white American self-sufficiency and independence and the widespread material reality of uncertainty and wage-dependence, as a newly competitive form of capitalism came to dominate the American economy and created a permanent proletariat.[26] That conflict was often expressed and, presumably, experienced as the result of the influx of foreigners whose labor was cheap, and of the migration of free African Americans to the cities of the Northeast and Midwest.[27] Thus we can see that the clinical diagnosis of nervousness indirectly records the fact that all Americans faced unprecedentedly intense economic competition in the Gilded Age. Rather than pointing to the reorganization and manipulation of the national economy as the source of social insecurity, however, neurasthenia discourse suggested that racial weakness among native-born whites was to blame.

A good number of clinicians, then, drew a connection between nervousness and the work their white patients performed as productive members of the social body.[28] We can catch a glimpse of the importance of productive labor, and the strain of constant self-discipline, in Beard's list of causes of American nervousness. This list featured the wearing of watches and the necessity for punctuality, especially when doing business that involved railroads; the invention of the telegraph and the consequent globalization and acceleration of commodity values and fluctuations; the "unrhythmical, harsh, jarring" noises of the city, with an indictment of the elevated train; and the "rapid development and acceptance of new ideas," especially the theory of evolution.[29]

The theory of evolution, in fact, involved brain-work crucial to the advances of modern civilization. Evolution was theorized not only as an explanation for the origin of distinct species but also as the mechanism through which races made the painful ascent from savagery to nineteenth-century civilization. That ascent was confirmed by one of modern Anglo civilization's great achievements: the discovery that evolution was driving development. Evolution, then, was analogous to other modern scientific achievements, such as those that filled the city with harsh metallic noises. Like the elevated railroad, evolution constituted a significant source of strain on delicate nerves. Beard urged readers to

> consider the dazzling swiftness with which the theory of evolution and the agnostic philosophy have extended and solidified their conquests until the whole world of thought seems hopelessly subjected to their autocracy. I once met in society a young man . . . whose hair was white enough for one of sixty, and he said that the color changed in a single day, as a sign and result of a mental conflict in giving up his religion for science. Many are they who have passed, or are yet to pass through such conflict, and at far greater damage to the nerve centres.[30]

However painful it might be, this transition seemed like a necessary part of the ongoing intellectual work of civilization, which required people to abandon traditional belief in favor of scientific knowledge. Evolutionary theory made terrific demands on the brains of precisely the educated white men who developed and disseminated that theory. These people had evolved sufficiently to think in terms of evolution, and they were disciplined enough to force themselves to face its more painful implications, but they had not yet reached a point where such thought was fully incorporated into their natures—they had not yet adapted to a world ruled by rationality. Therefore, the "reflex center" of the brain reacted to the theory of evolution with a painful, jarring oversensitivity.

The prematurely silver hair of the young man in the above passage was a material sign of a mental, and moral, conflict. Like the respectable white woman forced to work for wages, the craftsman reduced to factory labor, or the gentleman financier who found himself ruled by the fluctuations of the stock exchange, the scientific thinker was confronted with a painful discrepancy between what he had been trained to believe was right and just and what his reason told him was true and necessary. This gap between ideal constructions of race and gender, on the one hand, and the actual conditions of everyday life, on the other, may well have been a common element of the modern experience in the last third of the nineteenth century. To the well-bred white people who inherited the nervous diathesis, that gap between the ideal and the real was also the blank despairing space of nervous exhaustion.

Sexual Weakness as Civilization's Sign

Well-bred Anglos taught their children to believe that, as the shapers and bearers of American civilization, they were both morally and materially responsible for the well-being of the nation and its future generations. This was a heavy and daunting burden for people who, acutely aware of widespread and fundamental changes in American life and of their helplessness to direct those changes, were far from certain that they could negotiate modernity themselves. The very sensitivity of perception that they believed made them central to civilization's progress also threatened to unfit them for full and vigorously productive participation in that civilization.[31] Nervousness might carry a certain cachet, but it had disturbing implications as well.[32] When the culture-bearers could barely keep up with cultural change, the legitimacy of their racial leadership was called into question. In the modern, scientific context of the Gilded Age, such questions took on an evolutionary thrust: does the evidence suggest that these organisms, these classes, are unfitted to their environment? Can, and should, a weakened racial lineage retain political and cultural dominance? If it does, does it not threaten the vitality of the whole social body, and the inheritance of the next generation? When the "brain-workers" who believed they inherited and led American civilization sank back on the sofa in darkened rooms, exhausted by pondering such questions, they had what seemed to them good reasons to fear that American cultural development would slow, or run off the rails altogether. The myopia enabled by their racial and class privilege, their very embeddedness in the structures of white supremacy that made them feel responsible for the future of the nation, also made it impossible for many of them to imagine a separation between their biological and cultural inheritances. As such people saw it, evolution (not politics or poverty) dictated that no other group of people could embody their heritage and take up the burden to which they feared they were unequal.

Because "brain-workers" lived by their wits in an era of extreme economic instability and fierce competition, their exhaustion also gave them good reason to fear literal bankruptcy. This is one of the reasons that economic images were prominent in many accounts of nervousness. Late-nineteenth-century doctors were fond of figuring the body as a zero-sum economic system, and many of them adopted Beard's metaphorical explanation that full-scale neurasthenia was the result of an "overdraft" of nervous energy. Those who lived within their means rarely went broke, but the nervous diathesis meant that nervous resources were limited. Potential neurasthenes were

> poor in nerve-force; their inheritance is small, and they have been able to increase it but slightly, if at all; and if from overtoil, or sorrow, or injury, they overdraw their little surplus, they may find that it will require months or perhaps years to make up the deficiency. . . . The man with a small income is really rich, as long as there is no overdraft on the account; so the nervous man may be really well and in fair working order as long as he does not draw on his limited store of nerve-force.[33]

Careful spending, constant self-restraint, was absolutely necessary in such cases if "nervous bankruptcy" was to be avoided. In this way self-discipline was linked to the capacity for social and individual productivity. Whites who kept themselves in "fair working order" thereby qualified themselves to contribute to white civilization, even if their economic and nervous resources were limited and their political supremacy challenged. Beard's account offers a disciplinary imperative in disguise as comfort: a white man who was not rich or powerful could nevertheless be part of the social and racial development of civilization, if he was rigorous about curbing his desires.[34]

Economic metaphors for nervous exertion repeat contemporary metaphors for erotic activity and its consequences. In nineteenth-century common speech, "to spend" meant not only to give money in exchange for goods or services but also to ejaculate. In what the historian J. G. Barker-Benfield has felicitously named "the spermatic economy," frequent emission was believed to render men demoralized, tremulous, and weakened—that is, in a state of nervous bankruptcy.[35] "Spending" too freely, without proper regard for the limits of one's resources, placed a great strain on the genital "reflex center" and so had pernicious effects on the entire nervous system. These were magnified if the spending was frivolous, wasteful, and self-indulgent; while marital intercourse could be exhausting, at least the outlay of semen and energy in the marriage bed could be viewed as recapitalizing the family business by investing in one's offspring. In contrast, any form of "unnatural" gratification—that is, nonprocreative sex, including masturbation, coitus interruptus, or intercourse with contraception—amounted to frittering away one's nervous inheritance.

One of Beard's case studies provides a clear example of the relationship between economic and sexual wastefulness or "over-spending" and the on-set of nervous exhaustion in the individual body. This patient, he wrote,

> presented such a picture of physical debility as is often described in the advertisements of charlatans [who claim to cure "lost manhood"], but which are generally supposed to have been made up for the purpose of terrifying young men. His eyes were red, swollen, and watery; the face was haggard and melancholy, and there was the characteristic and almost diagnostic timidity. Memory and the power of mental concentration had been seriously impaired. . . . The habit of masturbation, which had been faithfully followed in early youth, had been discontinued . . . but the effects—true spermatorrhea and neurasthenia—remained.[36]

In the spermatic / nervous economy, masturbation was foolish prodigality, the equivalent of throwing one's money away. Those with a "narrow . . . margin of nerve-force" could not afford to behave with such profligate abandon, for they would soon find that belated efforts at self-control could not always reverse the effects of wastefulness. The sexually depleted neurasthenic body was constantly struggling to pay the interest on its energetic loans but unable to make a dent in the outstanding capital.

Beard's own livelihood depended on his ability to help such nervous bankrupts recover independent standing, but he was not always sanguine about the chances of full cure. He concluded his notes on this particular case with the gloomy comment that "no information" had been received about the results of the treatments he had advised.[37] Yet all this suffering, anxiety, and waste could have been prevented by the simple cautionary strategy of a firm manly chastity until marriage and continence afterward. In the larger context of the evolutionary theory of nervous exhaustion, the story of the haggard young man reminds us that the material and moral dimensions of modern white civilization were always intertwined; it seems that the purely physical therapies Beard advised were not adequate to treat symptoms that had their origin in sinful failures of self-restraint. Even those agnostics who gave up their religion for science found that nature, like the church, required civilized white men to discipline their appetites. Once again, Beard's theories square with their clinical application. Doctors who treated working-class men for neurasthenia often behaved as though their characteristically sexual symptoms were signs of a culpable moral coarseness, a willful failure to live what the contemporary moral reformer Frances Willard called "the white life" of sexual purity and self-control.[38] Individual loss of self-control had social and racial consequences. When the haggard young man lost the ability to think clearly and to look his peers in the eye, he lost the power to participate as an equal member of the democratic polity. When he rendered himself sterile through masturbation, he wasted the productive potential of his body as a vector for the transmission of whiteness to the next generation, and so undermined the future of American civilization.

According to the conventional morality expressed in modern nervousness, truly refined Anglo-American women in the Gilded Age were neither economically nor erotically active. Nevertheless, "nerves" were an extremely common element of genteel femininity.[39] While we shall see that neurasthenia in women did have distinctly sexual components, and while case studies in medical journals indicate that practitioners were sometimes suspicious of middle-class women's nervous disorders, the sexual aspects of their sickness were much less obvious than was true among men. For instance, the novelist and nerve-doctor S. Weir Mitchell's popular works never interpret nervous women's typical emaciation as evidence of shameful self-indulgence at the expense of the nation and the race. Instead, Mitchell and his peers often depicted genteel white women as suffering from an undercapitalization which made it impossible for them to meet their social duties and still spare nervous strength for sexual activity.

Take, for instance, the history of "Mrs. C., a New England woman," who weakened her constitution by intense study in her adolescence. Still, she remained healthy until an early marriage led to three pregnancies in quick succession, "the last two of which broke in upon the years of nursing," and she began to lose "flesh and color." Nevertheless,

> she met with energy the multiplied claims of a life full of sympathy for every form of trouble, and, neglecting none of the duties of society or kinship, yet found time for study and accomplishments. By and by she began to feel tired, and at last gave way quite abruptly, ceased to menstruate five years before I saw her, grew pale and feeble, and dropped in weight in six months from one hundred and twenty-five pounds to ninety-five.[40]

Mrs. C. was obviously overspending a limited nervous inheritance, but her failure to curb her expenditure was not described as pathological or profligate. Her bountiful generosity was in keeping with her good breeding as a dutiful WASP woman. The Harvard professor (and sexist curmudgeon) Edward Clarke might have told her that she brought her illness on herself by intensive studying, thus sending blood to her brain instead of to her reproductive organs; Mitchell's more gallant account emphasizes her three children as evidence that she had not privileged selfish "mental labor" over marital and maternal forms.[41] In fact, the logic of her case history suggests that her breakdown came because she strained her sexual capacity past her body's limits.

Mrs. C.'s illness was bracketed by reproduction, its beginning marked by the cessation of menstruation, and her recovery by the reappearance of her monthly flow. Her doctor further noted that her flow remained regular "until eighteen months later, when she became pregnant." In this case, the sexual and reproductive imperative of genteel white women's nervous health was fairly obvious: Mrs. C. was sick when she could not conceive children, well when she was fertile. Her desire to be a good wife and mother was consistent with virtuous self-restraint in a way that the haggard young man's desire for solitary ejaculation was not. In the contrast between the two cases we can see a reflection of the era's constructions of the difference between white men's and women's sexual natures. Masculine sexuality was appetitive, feminine sexuality maternal. Thus the difference between Mrs. C and the haggard young man reflects the contemporary belief that women's sexuality was inherently more moral, more familial, than men's. Nonetheless, both men and women might fail to exercise the appropriate self-control, and in both male and female cases neurasthenia was the result of more sexual stimulation than the refined body's "reflex centers" could tolerate.

Other accounts of nervousness, not all of them as straightforward as Mrs. C.'s, confirm the importance of sex in the onset of the disease. The case of the Englishwoman with blue hands is illustrative.[42] This patient, a "naturally fine and highly cultivated" woman, "enjoyed good health until her marriage." Soon after, however, "she had a miscarriage, and then two subsequent pregnancies [that ended with] the birth of dead children. . . . The next pregnancy terminated in the birth of a living daughter . . . during it she had curious nervous symptoms,—e.g., her bed flying away with her, temporary blindness, and vasomotor disturbances."[43] Still, she did not become fully neurasthenic until all this reproductive trauma was capped by a series of "severe shocks from the death of near relatives." At this time, her symptoms began with "frequently-recurring attacks of fainting," accompanied by deafness, blindness, flushed face, and hands "clay-cold, often blue, and difficult to warm with the most vigorous friction." These attacks increased in frequency and her spine became extremely tender, "especially over the sacrum. Then came frequent and persistent attacks of sciatica, and gradual loss of strength." Eventually

> she became unable to do anything almost for herself, for the nervous irritability had distressingly increased. To touch her bed, the ringing of a bell, sometimes the sound of a voice, sunlight, &c., affected her so as to make her almost cry out. . . . If she stood up, or even raised her hands to dress her hair, they immediately became blue and deadly cold, and she was done for.[44]

Her heart began to murmur. Her appetite disappeared altogether, her skin took on a "dusky" tone, and she was unable to "sit, because the tip of the spine is so sensitive; any pressure on it makes her feel faint. . . . She cannot lie on her back, because her whole spine is so tender."[45] This woman's perceptions were so painfully heightened that she had to be anaesthetized before she could tolerate being carried, on a stretcher, to the city for treatment. Her doctor noted that when he first saw her, "merely laying the hand on the bed caused her to shrink, and she could not bear the lightest touch of the fingers on her spine or any part near it."[46]

Obviously, not all these symptoms could be directly referred to irritations of the genital reflex center; and unlike the case of Mrs. C., this case was not bounded in time by childbearing. Yet it's suggestive that even in this superficially asexual case, many of the symptoms return to the impossibility of touching this woman—or even her bed—without causing her excruciating pain. Her ailments are a map of erotic refusal. Not only did spinal sensitivity make it impossible for her to lie on her back, but the focus of pain in her sacrum and sciatic nerve transformed her pelvis, like her bedroom, from a space of sexual possibility to a site of sensory restriction and disease. This case does suggest sex, but in the negative. Instead of babies, this woman produced miscarriages and stillbirths; instead of being brought on by giving life, her nervous breakdown was precipitated by death in the family. As she became weaker, she produced a "uterine lesion," an internal wound or hole that can be understood as the symbolic opposite of a pregnancy. At the same time her complexion darkened: her inability to make a properly feminine contribution to civilization seems to have compromised her whiteness in a quite literal sense.[47]

In their different ways, these three cases of nervous collapse point to the critical importance of white sexual weakness in the logic of modern nervousness. In modern Anglo-America, white men and women of the disciplined classes could barely "go through the process of reproducing the species" without risking complete nervous breakdown.[48] And if these people became so oversensitive that they could no longer perform their marital duties, what was to become of the civilization they believed they both inherited and embodied?

> All our civilization hangs by a thread; the activity and force of the very few make us what we are as a nation; and if, through degeneracy, the descendants of these few revert to the condition of their not very remote ancestors, all our haughty civilization would be wiped away.[49]

If America was to continue to lead the world into the modern era, it was critical that those few refined whites adapt, reproduce, teach their children to restrain their appetites, and so perpetuate their civilization. The evolutionary imperative of reproduction meant that civilization's thread was spun out of sexual desire and potency—a fragile fiber indeed among the nervously refined.

Differential Diagnosis: The Problem of Illegitimate Culture

Neurasthenia thus marked the limits of refined whites' ability to bear and transmit the uniquely modern culture that defined their place in the social order and in the evolutionary history of civilization. When nervousness made reproduction difficult for the culture-bearers, their dominance over that culture began to slip, and it began to seem possible that upstart competitors might usurp the power to direct the nation—if not in this generation, in the next. Many historians have documented the rigor with which Gilded Age whites policed the boundaries of their privileged realm; for instance, both anti-immigration activism and racial segregation are best understood as exclusionary techniques, dramatic national performances of the difference between "legitimate" (native-born white) Americans and the people they saw as inferior outsiders. Yet the discourse of modern nervousness reminds us that not all outsiders were clearly marked by externals like dark skin or accented English. To some refined Americans, the most immediate threat to civilization came from the perceived loss of a unified, cohesive system of values, which they believed had once been common to educated Anglos and fundamental to their civilization. Neurasthenia discourse expressed this fear, about intraracial conflict over basic values, in representations of deception or fraud among whites who tried to "pass" as legitimate members of a high civilization to which they had no birthright.

Such representations rarely reflect simple social prejudice against the upwardly mobile. Gilded Age genteel culture approved of class rise because it confirmed the grand democratic principles that helped define white civilization, as well as the social Darwinian belief that native excellence finds its own level. Most often, stories of social fraud among whites suggest the centrality of strict self-discipline to white civilization and warn against the impending degeneracy of a once-proud nation forgetful of its own stringent moral origins.[50] Such concerns are manifest in the attention that the literature of modern nervousness devoted to differential diagnosis. In addition to their practical therapeutic considerations, diagnostic discussions of neurasthenia suggest a striking degree of concern for accurate identification of patients as particular parts of the social and racial bodies. Much diagnostic discussion turned on issues of appetite and self-restraint. The strength of a person's mastery over desire helped to determine whether a patient was a genuinely refined modern neurasthenic—a potential culture-bearer, an exemplar of white civilization—or whether nervous symptoms masked a fundamentally coarse, and therefore archaic, nature.

In theory it should have been easy to tell the difference between nervousness and other, less refined diseases such as hysteria: all one had to do was establish the presence or absence of the physically "fine organization" and its accompanying morality of self-control. But in daily clinical practice, appearances could be deceiving. By the end of the century, self-starvation among white women had begun to attract medical attention.[51] Under the name "anorexia nervosa," or "nervous lack of appetite," such self-starvation could appear as a symptom of neurasthenia, an extreme but understandable manifestation of civilized white self-control; both Mrs. C. and the Englishwoman with blue hands were emaciated, and many of S. Weir Mitchell's case histories presented the inability to tolerate food as a prominent nervous symptom. But self-starvation could render even naturally stout, ruddy bodies pale and delicate, and so could serve as a technique through which inherently barbarous bodies could lay claim to hypercivilized refinement. In such cases, Beard and other doctors held, the appearance of self-discipline and sensitivity masked a devouring hysterical ambition for sexual power.

It was an article of medical faith that hysteria involved a fundamentally vulgar duplicity and self-indulgent sensuousness of character, which remained intact while the telltale sturdy flesh melted away.[52] We can see this belief at work in medical warnings that, uninhibited by genteel morality, hysterics might stage their attacks "in order to excite sympathy and gain some desired end."[53] The rhetoric of one such warning suggests that the goal was masculine sexual attention:

> Attacks of this [self-induced] kind may be distinguished . . . by the frequency with which they occur in the absence of any exciting cause; by their never being produced under circumstances which would expose the patient to serious discomfort or real danger, but at a time and place discreetly chosen for the purpose; and by observing many little arrangements contrived in order to add to their effect. Thus the hair will often be so fastened as to fall at the slightest touch, in most "admired disorder"; and many analogous devices will be had recourse to, their number and variety depending upon the ingenuity of the performer, and the extent of her resources.[54]

The carefully, "discreetly" chosen time and place, the appealing frailty of the young woman: it was hardly a man's fault if he, like the hair, fell "at the slightest touch." Certainly some middle-class women, socially barred from taking an active role in courtship, may have wooed men with displays of feminine weakness. Yet this misogynistic fantasy suggests a more adversarial scene, in which a bedridden woman wrests sexual control from her healthy male friends and medical attendants and uses it to demand that her appetites be gratified. In this view, one way to decide whether a woman was hysterical rather than neurasthenic was simply to watch her closely for signs of sexual desire, duplicity, or other forms of self-indulgence and moral weakness. If any appeared, the doctor could deduce that the apparently nervous symptoms were self-induced or altogether false.

The paradigmatic case of this kind of hysterical duplicity was that of a Brooklyn woman who claimed to live without eating for more than thirty years. The historian Joan Jacobs Brumberg tells us that Mollie Fancher first came to public notice in 1866, when she was eighteen.[55] Fancher was a poised young lady from a middle-class family, and her lack of appetite was originally ascribed both to over-study and to an accident with a streetcar. The combination of genteel heredity, excessive disciplined brain-work, and a life among machines made her symptoms seem like a textbook case of modern nervous collapse. If Beard or Mitchell had had the treatment of her at this point, she would have been fattened up and married off in no time, and her case would be no more than a medical footnote in a treatise on nervous lack of appetite. But instead, the virginal Fancher became an international celebrity.

Many people, it seems, were willing to accept Fancher as a clairvoyant and spiritual athlete, whose wasted form was evidence of her moral superiority to gross matter. Such an interpretation was particularly galling to somatic neurologists like Beard, who saw the public's faith in Fancher as backsliding toward an archaic and superstitious religiosity characteristic of an earlier stage in the development of civilization. Scientific rationality dictated that Fancher must eat, because she lived. Therefore, her claims to abstinence from food must be a self-indulgent bid for attention; in turn, her deceitfulness and lack of moral restraint indicated that her emaciation was not nervous but a hysterical symptom of racial degeneracy. When women like Fancher were widely celebrated, men like Beard feared that the native white American stock had lost its putatively unique combination of intellectual and moral self-discipline, which had enabled the development of modern technological civilization.

For Beard and his fellows, the core of white civilization in the United States was its practical, productive rationality and the material wealth and technological development that stemmed from it. For Fancher and her admirers, that attitude was holding the nation back from its true moral and spiritual potential. Brumberg tells a story that highlights the mutual hostility generated when these ideals of American civilization collided. William Hammond, founder of the New York Neurological Society and Surgeon General during the Civil War, once offered to give Fancher a thousand-dollar check if she could "thought-read" its details—its number, the bank on which it was drawn, and so forth—through a sealed envelope. The only condition he placed on the experiment was that he, and two other physicians, had to be present while she exercised her powers. Fancher turned him down, retorting that her spiritual sensitivities would not serve her in the presence of someone as "gross and materialistic" as Hammond.[56] What was at stake here was the reproduction of white civilization. Fancher suggested that

Hammond, focused as he was on money and matter, was too coarse to understand the higher discipline that structured and sustained her life without food. He and his peers returned the insult with interest. Hysteria, in most medical opinion, reflected a weakened mind, which very frequently mistook its own illness for evidence of an elevated spiritual state. When a woman like Fancher claimed mystical powers derived from her triumph over the flesh, the newspapers called her *"spirituelle"*; Beard retorted that her anorexia, visions, and trances were hysterical and self-indulgent, not spiritual or nervous in origin.[57] Beard emphasized the racial primitivism of what he saw as exaggerated spirituality by conflating it with hysteria among "stout Irish servant girls, among the Southern negroes, and among the undisciplined and weak-minded of all races and classes and ages."[58] He went on to add that, "unlike neurasthenia," such enthusiasm "was more prevalent in the middle ages than in the nineteenth century."[59]

From a self-consciously scientific medical man's point of view, adherence to Catholicism, speaking in tongues, shaking and quaking with the presence of the Holy Spirit, participation in revivals, attendance at séances, and other manifestations of religious enthusiasm all suggested atavism, the failure to evolve into the modern era. As we have seen, Beard went so far as to suggest that deep intellectual engagement with modern reality would push truly civilized people to "give up [their] religion for science."[60] A respectably church-bound and unemotional Protestantism, to be sure, was fully consistent with gentility. But when hundreds of thousands of middle-class white Americans joined "Irish servant girls" and "Southern negroes" in seeking direct, transformative experiences of divine love, or pursuing connections with the spirit world in darkened parlors, thousands more of their hardheaded rationalist peers saw them as backsliders from true whiteness. The sheer popularity of the movement collectively known as Spiritualism forced materialists like Beard to wonder whether their own kind, the respectably restrained native whites who formed the cultural core of American civilization, might be degenerating toward madness and promiscuity. Mollie Fancher was not, in and of herself, a serious threat to modern civilization nor even to male medical authority. She aroused such intense medical hostility because she embodied a widespread cultural movement that defined self-discipline in terms that privileged the ethereal over the practical and productive, visions over labor, and that therefore threatened the foundations of white middle-class political and economic supremacy over the rest of the social body.

In sum, though Beard was unusual in the care he devoted to trying to untangle hysteria and neurasthenia from one another, the larger issues at stake in that differentiation were crucially important to many of his contemporaries.[61] Questions of materiality and morality, sexuality and deceitfulness, appetite and self-restraint cropped up repeatedly in late-nineteenth century American debates about the direction in which civilization was headed. Nervousness, after all, was not only a disease; it was a way of experiencing, representing, and often resisting the changes and conflicts within middle-class whiteness in the decades after the Civil War.[62] The diagnosis thus opens a window onto pressing questions of the origins and reproduction of legitimate power and influence over the cultural life of the nation, and the appropriate uses of social and sexual energies, for the perpetuation of the best qualities of the race.

Love in the Age of Mechanical Reproduction

One final "case study" can illustrate the way in which concerns about middle-class morality and sexual restraint intersected with larger worries about the boundaries and reproduction of white civilization outside of an explicitly medical context. Victoria Woodhull, like Mollie Fancher, was a Spiritualist, but there the resemblance between them ended. Woodhull never repudiated any of her appetites, and she seems to have had nerves of steel. Born into a large family of the class once known as the "dangerous poor," she achieved wealth and fame through a combination of brains, beauty, and dogged determination; she became the first woman stockbroker, the first woman to address Congress, and the first woman to run for president. And in November 1872 she used her newspaper, *Woodhull and Claflin's Weekly*, to break what became one of the most notorious scandals of the nineteenth century: a triangular love affair between the prominent preacher Henry Ward Beecher and his parishioners Theodore and Elizabeth Tilton.

The Beecher-Tilton affair has been the subject of a civil trial, extensive journalistic analysis, and many books and articles since Woodhull exposed it to public view; it is a fascinating subject but far too complex to recount here.[63] Its chief relevance to this discussion lies in the fact that *The Nation*'s editorial response to that affair drew on the same repertoire of images and concerns that structured modern nervousness. We have seen that neurasthenia theory and clinical practice represented a specifically restrained, yet creative whiteness as integral to modern civilization, at the same time that it depicted whiteness as threatened by the very modernity of the civilization it made. Journalistic mobilization of these images in coverage of Henry Ward Beecher's trial for adultery confirms that these complexly intertwined representations of race, sexuality, and civilization resonated on a mass cultural level as well as in medical theory and clinical practice.

Newspapers of every sort followed Beecher's trial zealously and in great detail. They did so because, in addition to its titillating subject matter and celebrity participants, the trial touched on many of the most contentious issues of the age, among them the legitimacy of white, elite Northerners' claim to moral leadership of the nation; the nature and permanence of the bond between husbands and wives; and the appropriate limits of spiritual passion in a scientific, rational culture. All these issues involved questions of genteel self-control that were fundamental to the legitimacy of white racial superiority. In sum, the trial offered journalists a public forum in which to describe, and attempt to clarify, the modern muddle of social and moral hierarchies.

E. L. Godkin, Mugwump editor of the genteel newsmagazine *The Nation*, took it on himself to retrace the contours of legitimate leadership of civilization with indelible ink and a firm hand. Godkin interpreted the Beecher-Tilton affair as evidence of the weakness of contemporary whiteness. As he saw it, the tales surfacing in the courtroom day by day offered incontrovertible evidence that many socially prominent, apparently refined people were barbarians under the skin: "if these were really pictures of American society in general . . . we do not hesitate to say that the prospects of the Anglo-Saxon race on this continent would be somewhat gloomy." Rather than acknowledge that "the Anglo-Saxon race" might not actually embody civilization's highest ideals (in which case its gloomy prospects were just as well), Godkin went on to explain that the circle around Beecher and the Tiltons was not genuinely representative of the standards and behavior of American whiteness. Instead, such people were imitation-genteel. Despite their posturing as ladies and gentlemen, their lax sexual behavior inevitably revealed them as "half-civilized people who have got hold of a code which they do not understand, and the phrases of which they use without being able to adapt their conduct to it."[64] "Half-civilized" people could not "adapt their conduct" to truly white standards because they lacked the rare, rigorous, and racially specific capacity for the necessary self restraint.

Still, the Beecher-Tilton scandal was newsworthy because its participants *looked* so "civilized"—they were wealthy, politically influential, and socially prominent. Godkin thus faced a problem we might describe by analogy to differential diagnosis: he had to theorize the difference between visible signs of civilized white refinement and its true essence. How could such socially elevated people turn out to be so bad at living up to the whiteness they appeared to embody? How could a family as old and reputable as the Beechers have produced someone so morally coarse, sexually self-indulgent, and duplicitous as Henry? Such questions come dangerously close to acknowledgment that civilized whiteness was not actually lived as it was imagined. Asking these questions draws attention to the gap between civilized ideals and real conduct and thus could lead one to reject white claims to evolutionary superiority, to identify the political nature and the injustice of the existing racial power structure, and perhaps even to oppose the violence and economic oppression with which white "civilization" preserved its dominance.[65]

Godkin's editorial for September 24, 1874, suggests that he, like neurasthenia theorists, contained this radical threat by focusing on the problematic prominence of machines in modern civilization. In Godkin's analysis, false claims to what he called "culture" were made possible by the forgeries of "Chromo-Civilization." Real culture, he wrote, did not automatically follow from good parentage but required "the breaking in of the powers to the service of the will" by means of "labor and self-denial." In a pointed reference to Beecher's emotional brand of Christianity, with its emphasis on love rather than judgment, Godkin added that "a good deal of [real culture] was obtained from the old Calvinistic theology, against which, in the days of its predominance, the most bumptious youth hit his head at an early period of his career, and was reduced to thoughtfulness and self-examination."[66] Godkin described legitimate religious practice in terms of a discipline concrete enough to raise a bruise. In contrast to this kind of "real culture," with its inheritance of Yankee intellectual and religious rigor, the squishy, self-indulgent spirituality of the Beechers and Tiltons of the world marked them as the degenerate bearers of what Godkin called "pseudo-culture." Their refinement was a matter of external appearance, and, according to Godkin, was produced and sustained by means of a modern mechanical trick rather than a labor-intensive process of shaping the self. A "chromo" was a tinted lithograph, such as adorned the parlors of the aspiring middle classes and the front pages of sensational scandal rags.[67] The "Chromo-Civilization," then, was one that spread a thin coat of brightly colored ink on blank, coarse paper, multiplied the sheets by the thousands, and distributed them at large to people who lacked the refined perceptions that permitted the truly cultured to discriminate between precious things and trash.

"The newspapers and other cheap periodicals," Godkin complained, "have diffused through the community a kind of smattering of all sorts of knowledge, a taste for reading and for 'art'—that is, a desire to see and own pictures—which, taken together, pass with a large body of slenderly-equipped persons as 'culture.'" The danger of such mechanically reproduced, illegitimate "pseudo-culture" was:

> [Its consumers] firmly believe that they have reached, in the matter of social, mental, and moral culture, all that is attainable or desirable by anybody, and who therefore tackle all the problems of the day—men's, women's, and children's rights and duties, marriage, education, suffrage, life, death, and immortality—with supreme indifference to what anybody else thinks or has ever thought, and have their own trumpery prophets . . . and philosophers, whom they worship with a kind of barbaric fervor. The result is a kind of mental and moral chaos, in which many of the fundamental rules of living, which have been worked out painfully by thousands of years of bitter human experience, seem in imminent risk of disappearing totally.[68]

Mechanically reproduced information and images, in this assessment, posed a direct threat to the legitimate re-production of culture, in part by helping people at a comparatively low evolutionary level pass themselves off as "prophets and philosophers" among the genteel. Even old-stock elites like Beecher, who could not plausibly be represented as barbaric social upstarts, might find their standards confused by the forgeries of "chromo-civilization" and so fall victim to the "mental and moral chaos" of life in the age of mechanical reproduction.

Mechanical reproduction, in Godkin's representation, interfered with evolution, diverting the main stream of civilization away from the refined, disciplined, intellectual whites who believed they were its most legitimate legatees. Modern modes of communication made debased "culture" available to the masses as a commodity, rather than reserving its purer forms to the classes as a prized birthright. This was a concern shared by many of Godkin's contemporaries. Among them was Anthony Comstock, who began his long career as smut-hound and censor by having Victoria Woodhull arrested for obscenity. Apparently Comstock was less concerned about the concealed immorality of a reputable preacher than he was about the social impact of publicizing that information.

One recent analysis suggests that Comstock sought to defend the sacred boundary between public and private, which was unbearably confused by the arrival in respectable mail slots of Woodhull's mass-reproduced accounts of other peoples' adulterous intimacies.[69] Certainly, Comstock agreed with Godkin that most people simply lacked the discriminating, educated taste that enabled well-bred white Americans to comprehend high culture; he feared that the mass reproduction of words and pictures, and their mass distribution, would give the coarse-minded access to culture without giving them the moral means to interpret it correctly. For him, the material object in and of itself was less important than the cultural values the object conveyed. "Slenderly-equipped" people might view artistic nudes and see pictures of naked people. The problem lay in the impossibility of securing the dominant, socially approved reading of any cultural artifact or piece of information once it had become available outside the narrow, restrained borders of genteel white society. To Gilded Age white critics like Beard, Godkin, and Comstock, it sometimes seemed that mechanical reproduction was undermining the bases of the white civilization that had made it possible.

This problem was the more pressing because so many contemporaries feared that the truly refined white bodies of the legitimate culture-bearers had very limited amounts of energy available to compete for cultural dominance; they simply could not match the high reproductive rate of machines. They could, however, learn from them. After all, machines were not entirely alien to the refined classes of "brain-workers." Machines, like nervous whites, were uniquely modern phenomena, and they could offer the culture-bearers images of themselves. The analogies with which Beard sought to explain neurasthenia underscore the intimacy between machines and middle-class whites. In his account civilization was like a series of lamps on a single circuit, drawing power from the force generated by the mental activity of the educated classes. The force of the generator determined the number of lamps the circuit could support. Therefore,

> [if] an extra number of lamps should be interposed in the circuit, then the power of the engine must be increased; else the light of the lamps would be decreased, or would give out. . . . The nervous system of man is the centre of the nerve-force supplying all the organs of the body. Like the [generator], its force is limited . . . and when new

functions are interposed in the circuit, as modern civilization is constantly requiring us to do, there comes a period . . . when the amount of force is insufficient to keep all the lamps actively burning; those that are weakest go out entirely, or, as more frequently happens, burn faint and feebly—they do not expire, but give an insufficient and unstable light.[70]

The mechanical metaphor here offered was not only applicable to individual nervous people but also to the social body and to the race. When the overstimulated central nervous system / generator of the social body began to brown out, the light of modern culture and civilization dimmed and flickered. Thus the sexual and spiritual floundering of the Beecher-Tilton ménage registered not only individual moral confusion but also the strain of the machine age on the nation and the race.

I suggested above that Godkin's complaints about the cultural impact of machines mobilized white solipsism so as to maintain white innocence. That is, when the political nature of American race relations, and the poverty of an evolutionary argument for white middle-class ownership of civilization, threatened to break into plain view, discussions of mechanized modernity could contain that threat. Machines could and did serve as metonyms for the civilized whites who claimed to have developed them. Thus when Godkin fulminated over the debasement of civilization by the spread of mechanically reproduced culture, he was talking about the increasing cultural diversity of the United States *and* doing so as though that diversity were entirely within varieties of more or less genuine or legitimate whiteness. Even in the context of complaints about loss of truly white control over the nation, it was possible to mobilize the claim that civilization was coextensive with genuine whiteness and that that position was a reflection of natural reality rather than a bitterly contested political claim in support of racial domination. In this way, discussions of the cultural consequences of mechanical reproduction could register fears for the perpetuation of white dominance while nonetheless preserving the plausibility of white claims to innocence of involvement in racial politics.

Beard's image of the modern body as a generator confirms the suggestion that machines in this discourse were metaphors for whiteness. His usage suggests not that machines were antagonistic to white civilization but rather that both machines and civilized whites would benefit from further development.[71] Eventually, Beard believed, biological and technological progress would make modernity less traumatic for civilized white bodies and minds. He hypothesized that new knowledges (such as evolutionary theory, or the principles of mechanical engineering) were exhausting because new circuits allegedly conducted electricity, or thoughts, against a resistance comparatively greater than that generated by "well worn pathways, where the resistance is brought down to a minimum." Self-control was easy when it was habitual. In familiar nervous circuits, "a very slight evolution of force is sufficient to produce the [desired] result, just as a very slight amount of electricity will pass through a good conductor, like a large copper wire."[72] Given a little time, white people would evolve into better conductors of modernity, offering less resistance to the free flow of new knowledges and technologies. Presumably, they would find ways to channel and restrain the impulses that modernity aroused; and thus their continued racial dominance would be assured.

The cheery optimism of this prognosis relied on the rhetorical ease with which technological developments (read: restored white supremacy) could be confused with biological evolutions. An editorial in the London *Times* synopsized neurasthenia theory by explaining that "the human machine" was like any other complex mechanism whose various parts or "engines" were all run by the steam "generated in a single boiler."

> If one such engine is hard at work, and is therefore using a great deal of steam, so much the less will be available to support the activity of the rest. For all functions of primary importance to the existence of the human race there are engines coeval with the race itself in antiquity, which have been perfected by long exercise, and handed down from generation to generation in a state of gradually acquired stability and amplitude. Such, for example, are the nerve-centres which combine in harmonious action the very large number of muscles that are collectively subservient to the maintenance of the erect posture.[73]

In this passage, the "human machine" evolves in both terms; bodies run on steam power, and engines, as part of the human family, acquire not only erect posture but a kind of social standing and wealth ("stability and amplitude") by virtue of their development "through long exercise," that is, through the application of self-discipline and focused rationality. The paragraph goes on to explain that upstart machines, like scientific innovators, intellectual women, and other new species, have to work harder for less security: "When the progress of civilization calls for the performance of a new function, whether it be of body or of mind, a new engine must be gradually provided for the purpose; and this which becomes developed in individuals long before it can be considered the common property of the race, will for a long period be inferior to more established centres in its power of endurance."[74] Because modern civilization had greatly increased the quantity and competitiveness of intellectual work but had not yet developed an "engine" to power such labor, nervousness was a kind of mechanical failure. The practical solution was to increase middle-class nerve-force, or the "boiler-power itself." With an enlarged well of energy upon which to draw, and with their self-control restored by that reserve force, genuinely white people would find themselves able to take part in the common life of civilization. From this optimistic perspective, mechanical prowess at reproduction could be seen not so much as a terrifying challenge to genteel mastery over modern civilization as an ideal for middle-class whites to follow.

Conclusion: From Nervousness to Normality

Neurasthenia, then, was a way of discussing widespread social and racial concerns about the impact of modernization on the white middle classes. Beard's disease brought together and encapsulated ideas about race, class, gender, and sexuality under the rubric of an evolutionarily achieved modernity. Further, the discourse of modern nervousness constructed modern civilization as part of the inheritance of native-born, middle-class, Anglo-Americans. Modernity and progress thus appeared to be naturally, rather than politically, linked to the refined white body. The link that sutured them together was the powerful self-discipline, and especially the sexual / economic self-restraint and its corollary commitment to rational productivity, that seemed to many Gilded Age Anglos the essence of their racial heritage.

On one level, this was an unsubtle bid for ownership of culture, a racial claim to the right to possess in perpetuity both the materiality and the meaning of modern America. On another level, however, the embodiment of modernity in "fine" white bodies suggests a certain doubt about the direction of change, a need to establish a natural foundation for the continued cultural dominance of the genteel classes. A nice middle-class girl like Mollie Fancher could be so traumatized by mechanized urban life that she reverted to the religious beliefs of the fourteenth century; a reputable old-stock WASP preacher like Henry Ward Beecher could be a liar, or, which was worse, could be so confused by the mechanically facilitated proliferation of false moralities that he lost his ability to distinguish the sacred from the profane. In a world where ladies and gentlemen could barely get out of bed in the morning, and machines could easily produce "culture" for the masses without apparent effort, it was becoming more and more difficult to identify the true culture-bearers with absolute certainty. Modern nervousness records not only the whiteness of civilization but a good deal of uncertainty about what that whiteness could and could not guarantee.

Such uncertainty stemmed, in part, from the real and common experience of individual economic helplessness in the face of industrial modernity. Several of the most prominent scholars of whiteness studies point to the connection between white material and cultural insecurity and the elaboration of white racism. For instance, David Roediger argues that "whiteness was a way in which [late-nineteenth-century] white workers responded to a fear of dependency on wage labor and to the necessities of capitalist work discipline."[75] Such class-sensitive accounts of race have expanded our understanding of whiteness as a form of property to which poor whites can cling when most other assets are out of their reach; at the same time, for all but the most destitute whites, whiteness helps to secure access to other material and political assets.[76] These materialist analyses are powerful. Nonetheless, the discourse of nervous exhaustion suggests that a pervasive sense of helplessness was not only something *against which* whiteness could identify itself. In fact it seems that the conviction of white weakness could be one of the "assets" of whiteness.

Nervousness was, without question, a reaction to transformations in the relations of production; recall Beard's emphasis on watch-wearing, stock fluctuations, business involving railroads, and other details of employment within corporate capitalism. The evidence about clinical applications of neurasthenia theory supports the contention that nervous collapse was a response to the increasing elusiveness of middle-class dreams of independent self-sufficiency. At the same time, nervousness was also a reaction to the loss of exclusive control over cultural capital, and a technique for maintaining a plausible position of innocence in relation to racist exclusion and violence. The emphasis on individual sensitivity, personal weakness, and the importance of self-control in neurasthenia discourse reflects the consolidation of a racial position that could not imagine itself as violently inhumane to "inferior" others. If we recognize that the ability to maintain a clear conscience while working for the preservation of white racial dominance was a social asset, we can see that the construction of whiteness as weakness was cultural capital in the bank.

One of the ways in which the construction of whiteness as weakness served white supremacy was by its mobilization of white solipsism or self-involvement. When Beard and Mitchell elaborated diagnostic and therapeutic techniques to address the pains of nervous sensitivity, or when Godkin and others excoriated Beecher's lapse in sexual and spiritual self-control, they identified whiteness as its own worst enemy. The appropriate response to white weakness was to strengthen and fortify whiteness; in their minds, civilization depended on it. Thus the construction of whiteness as weakness allowed activism on behalf of white dominance while it avoided direct recognition of the existence of people of color. The overt racial politics of nervousness were primarily intrawhite politics, in which the legitimacy of claims to whiteness was weighed in relation to white ideals of civilized self-control, productivity, and public service. By combining claims to weakness with self-referentiality, neurasthenia's mobilization of the "mirror trick" supported faith in white racial innocence from the 1880s to 1920, precisely the era in which segregation solidified, the gains of radical Reconstruction were rolled back, and lynching and other forms of violence in support of white supremacy accelerated to horrifying new levels.[77]

Challenges to white dominance, and belief in the fundamental innocence of whiteness and its constitutive ideals, continued across the turn of the century. If anything, they became deeper and more pressing as immigration continued to transform the actual population of the nation, as machines continued to dominate more and more aspects of daily life, and as urbanization and suburbanization changed the physical and spiritual environment in which young white Americans were groomed to take up the "burden" of developing and extending white civilization. In the first years of the new century neurasthenia was increasing steadily. Yet by the First World War, middle-class white Americans had begun to adopt a different vocabulary for describing their experience of modernity and their conviction of legitimate dominance over the nation's present and future.

Between 1910 and 1920, the language of nervousness gave way to the language of normality. As the next chapters make clear, emerging discourses of normality addressed many of the same concerns that nervousness had expressed. White emotional sensitivity, sexual self-control, fears about mechanization, economic insecurity, and spiritual anomie all played prominent roles in the discourses of modern normality. So did the claim that the future of civilization was inextricably bound up with white reproductive sexuality. But the increasing consolidation of homosexual identity, which gained momentum around the turn of the century, changed the discursive context for these concerns. By the 1920s, sexualized fears about white weakness had realigned around the contemptible (if sometimes fascinating) cultural figures of the degenerate "fairy," the mannish or man-hating woman, and the primitive pervert.[78] Political and moral values of self-discipline and self-determination, in contrast, found mass expression in optimistic representations of modern normality.

In part because sexual weakness was now constructed in relation to perversion, the emergent discourses of normality took up the thematics of whiteness in distinctly different terms. While both nervousness and normality linked a series of fears, experiences, and beliefs into more or less coherent cultural statements about white middle-class people's naturally privileged relationship to civilization, normality was much less accommodating to white pain than nervousness had been. In the conceptual world of which nervousness was a part, suffering could be met with a certain complacency as evidence of deep and refined feeling. Moderate pain was a natural part of middle-class whiteness. To some commentators, it seemed a kind of badge of self-control, the footprint of an inadmissible desire laudably overcome, like the metaphorical goose egg left on the forehead of E. L. Godkin's "bumptious youth" by his contact with the spiritual discipline of Calvinism.

Normality, in contrast, took the position that suffering—though widespread—was really not necessary. Modern whiteness continued to represent itself as uniquely capable of refined feeling, but pain was increasingly interpreted as a failure to respond rationally to its causes. Early-twentieth-century American reform movements were expressions of the belief that human suffering could be approached and resolved with the same confident, goal-oriented, problem-solving rationality that enabled modern technological achievements like suspension bridges and skyscrapers. Such triumphs rested on familiarity with the laws of physics and so appeared to demonstrate that nature was in no way antagonistic to modern civilization. The social engineering of the Progressive Era and interwar years reflected the heritage of optimistic nineteenth-century analogies between the social body and machinery. We shall see that the heritage of mechanical metaphors would inform normality on the level of the individual as well.

As the twentieth century opened, more and more people pointed to the skyrocketing divorce rate as evidence that something had gone seriously amiss in the reproduction of white culture, with immediate and dire implications for the reproduction of the family and the uniquely democratic civilization which grew out of sound family life. As nervousness gave way to normality, the whole complex of middle-class concerns about white weakness, white self-control, and their consequences for cultural and sexual reproduction was more and more often discussed in terms of the challenge that modernity posed to successful marriages. In the early twentieth century, however, that challenge was increasingly represented as no more daunting than any other engineering problem. If the nation was confronted with an apparent epidemic of human misery in marriage, the modern thing to do was to locate the origin of that distress and repair it as efficiently as possible.

But the construction of whiteness as weakness did not simply disappear. On the contrary, it was a resource for the production of a new kind of disciplined modern self, one that expressed its whiteness not through nervous collapse but through the cultivation of sexual pleasure. The allegedly exquisite sensitivity of civilized whites was increasingly expressed in terms of a special racial capacity for romantic love and erotic satisfaction in reproductive wedlock. In this new context, white vulnerability found new expression in representations of well-bred wives enduring years of humiliating sexual frustration before turning to divorce as the only remedy for their suffering. The next chapter examines the literature that explained unhappiness to a new generation of white Americans, and that taught moderns how to discipline their bodies and hearts in a way that could minimize pain while it buttressed white civilization.

2 THE MARRIAGE CRISIS

"Is Marriage Breaking Down?": Modernity and the State of (the) Union

George Beard was not alone in noting that modern, civilized white people found themselves unequal to the demands of conjugal life. Henrik Ibsen's play *A Doll's House*, which depicted marriage as an unbearable psychic and spiritual constraint on its heroine, caused a sensation in the 1880s that was still reverberating fifty years later.[1] In 1903 Bernarr Macfadden, the eccentric but popular prophet of racial advance through Physical Culture, bemoaned the "strife, bickering, quarreling . . . [and] misery" of most marriages.[2] By the First World War, he had been joined by a chorus of critics who collectively developed the claim that marriage was disintegrating under the impact of the machine age.

That chorus continued to grow for the next twenty years.[3] Between 1920 and 1940, modernization's impact on marriage was a central issue in American popular culture. Scholarly researches on matrimony gained a wide readership; some were published in several forms, aimed at both professional and popular audiences.[4] At newsstands, doctors' offices, and at home, magazine readers were offered a steady diet of articles like "Is Marriage Breaking Down?" and "The Modernization of Marriage."[5] The 1920 census is remembered by historians for its documentation that, for the first time, fully half of all Americans lived in cities; moderns were equally interested in its revelation that there was one divorce for every seven marriages in the United States. A questionnaire sent out by the National Probation Association in 1926 revealed that the level of marital discord was even higher than the divorce rate. Chicago and Baltimore had one "domestic relations" case in a city court for every three marriages of that year; Richmond reported one out of two; Omaha, two out of three.[6]

The statistical representation of marital conflict as a problem confronting cities, regions, and the nation at large illustrates the way in which moderns used the breakdown of marriage as a synecdoche for social disorder and disagreement: domestic discord divided Omaha, not only Mr. and Mrs. Citizen who happened to live in Omaha. When marriage could not endure, the nation itself seemed in danger of coming apart. The use of marriage as an index to the state of the union is not, of course, a twentieth-century phenomenon. At least since the founding of the Republic, American political discourses have generated and drawn on images of the family as the cradle of democracy, the miniature commonwealth in which people learn to work together for the good of the whole.[7] What was new in the early twentieth century was the development of a commercially successful body of marital advice literature suggesting that the bonds of marriage, and by extension the ties that constituted the nation and civilization itself, could be revitalized by means of the deliberate cultivation of sexual pleasure in the marriage bed.

The belief that marriage provided an index to the state of the nation helped make the subject of marital intimacy both legitimate and interesting to many upstanding citizens, authorizing an immense outpouring of writing about the perceived crisis of modern marriage. Hundreds of early-twentieth-century Americans, motivated by forces ranging from sincere conviction to the hope of making a quick buck on a marketable topic, added their two cents to the paper fray of argument and opinion. In this chapter I interpret this literature as a race-evasive, power-evasive response to the fear that white civilization in the United States might be destroyed by its own evolved superiority. In the first section of the chapter, I sketch out the major themes of the literature of marital breakdown, showing that the marriage crisis was widely explained as an expression of two linked problems. First, this litera-ture argued that technological development drove men and women apart by separating home from work, productive from reproductive spheres, with the result that husbands and wives had few common interests to bind them together. Second, it argued that moderns of both sexes internalized and expressed their civilization's mechanical values so that they became cold rather than compassionate in reaction to the differences between them; disaffection and divorce were the predictable results. In the second section of the chapter I turn to marital advice manuals, a popular subgenre of the literature of marital breakdown that offered solutions to the problems posed by modernization. I show that such manuals urged modern husbands and wives to emphasize and eroticize their differences, thus transforming the problematic gap between them into a source of heightened sensitivity and connection.

In its descriptions of marital sexuality as the antidote to the divisive forces inherent in the machine age, the literature of marital breakdown elaborated and disseminated the modern idea of "heterosexuality," that is, the erotic fascination with sexual difference that constitutes an immensely charged point of connection between men and women who are otherwise constructed as opposites. Marriage manuals mobilized the entwined fears of marital and national breakdown to underscore the importance of what they often called "complete sexual union." They argued, almost to a volume, that mutual sexual pleasure was indispensable to successful marriage, and with the larger literature of marital breakdown, they assumed that strong marriages were essential to the strength of the nation. The sociopolitical emphasis of the literature of marital breakdown suggests that it is appropriate to read marriage manuals' insistence on the importance of sexual pleasure across the gulf of sexual difference as a call to engage in civic activity, a disciplined and intimate enactment of the ideal relationship between citizens of the Republic.

Marriage manuals' descriptions of heterosexual love in marriage resonated with neurasthenia discourse's defensive depictions of the values at the heart of civilized whiteness, but they reworked earlier fears of intrawhite cultural diversity into a superficially much more liberal and inclusive vision of the basically benign nature of difference in a democracy. As a genre, marital advice literature claims that properly mated, normal modern couples instantiated in their private lives the larger virtues of their country: ideal marriage, like the ideal nation, was fundamentally just, characterized by tender concern for all its members, and committed on principle to the legitimacy and value of difference. Feminist historians have correctly assessed this literature's ideological confusion of heterosexual pleasure with social and political justice as working to obscure women's ongoing inequality both in modern marital relationships and in the public sphere.[8] Less attention has been paid to the subtle racial valences of the discourses of modern marriage: the sensitivity, self-cultivation, and self-control expressed in ideal modern marriage were profoundly racialized virtues. As chapter 1 showed, these virtues had long been represented as the pride of white civilization, and they have often been used to justify white rule in the United States. Thus marriage manuals' representational collapse of heterosexual love into citizenship helped to legitimize a race- and power-evasive understanding of whiteness as synonymous with all the highest American ideals of just, consensual political and personal relationships.

I conclude this chapter by arguing that the discursive construction of heterosexuality as the expression of the ideal relationship among citizens was simultaneously a normalization of the sexual self-control that had once been a mark of racial and class distinction among refined Anglo-Americans. In the Gilded Age, erotic restraint and the cultivation of sensitivity were primary ways of laying claim to fully civilized modern whiteness. Here I show that in the early twentieth century the sensitivity, self-cultivation, and self-control that had once marked their possessors as superior were increasingly demanded of all moderns who would be "normal." To the extent that heterosexuality was discursively constructed as a new foundation for national stability, then, we can suggest that *all* modern men and women were solicited to shape their erotic and domestic lives according to these newly normative standards in order to gain access to social and political legitimacy as Americans. Heteronormativity emerged at the level of mass culture, rather than in solicitations to elites. Yet the normalization of erotic self-discipline in marriage did not mean that its racial referents disappeared. Instead, the kind of ideal whiteness that had once set refined Anglos apart from other Americans was itself normalized. As its racial meaning was redefined in terms of the sexual performance of good citizenship, its cultural content became mandatory for more people, so that self-alignment with white racial ideals was increasingly represented not as a mark of distinction but as the basic requirement for participation in American life.

Like other mass-cultural products, the literature of marital breakdown constructed the collectivity it purported to address, interpellating members of the former white races into a new group of heterosexually self-disciplining white citizens.[9] This new group was bounded less by ethnicity or native language or religion or educational level than by the shared commitment to bolstering marriage against the onslaught of modernity.[10] That is, the literature of marital breakdown created an imaginary national / racial community composed of "normal" people struggling to sustain marriage in the context of the machine age.[11] Fear lest divorce should shake the foundations of civilization was evidence of fitness for membership in the nation, because it suggested personal alignment with the familial and civic ideals at the heart of whiteness, and, in turn, a willingness to adopt the disciplines necessary to shape body and self into conformity with those ideals.

To sum up, then, beginning at the turn of the century and cresting in the interwar years, Americans generated thousands of representations of marriages in every imaginable state of disarray, executed in every medium, and directed at every kind of audience. In their ubiquity and variety, such representations of marriage did immensely important cultural work. Their most obvious task was to solicit married couples' participation in the project of sustaining white civilization in the machine age. One of the basic strategies through which early-twentieth-century representations of marriage did this work was to describe modernity both as undermining marital intimacy and as holding forth the promise that it could be restored in a new and stronger form if only husbands and wives would love one another in a properly modern manner.

Among their most significant effects was the consolidation and normalization of heterosexuality, that is, the investment of sexual difference with erotic desire. Another was the massification or mainstreaming of erotic self-cultivation and self-control as a complexly racialized ideal. Where nineteenth-century WASP elites were taught to cultivate sexual self-discipline in part as a sign of their superiority to less civilized people, early-twentieth-century whites of diverse class and ethnic backgrounds were solicited to adopt erotic discipline as a sign of their legitimate membership in the modern nation. Representations of the modernization of marriage, in short, record the discursive suturing of normal heterosexuality to whiteness in the early-twentieth-century United States. It was through just such connections that whiteness gradually became "invisible," its racial specificity obscured by its claim to normality.

American History as Marital History: The Frontier Narrative

The literature of marital breakdown, despite its immense size and variety, displayed a generic commitment to a handful of themes and images that were repeated in dozens of different texts. These central themes are vividly displayed in a single exemplary source. The first page of the December 1925 *Harper's Monthly Magazine* bore a headline announcing the chaos of modern marriage. The subsequent article, by the psychiatrist Beatrice M. Hinkle, began by describing the present state of crisis:

> Among the many subjects agitating the minds of the people of the United States to-day none compares in its insistence and acuteness with the question of the future of the institution of marriage in America. A complete change of attitude, often in the form of a violent revolt against the former ideals and customs affecting the marriage relation, is in full swing and the general uncertainty and instability in the relation is probably more marked than in any other country. People all over the land are aroused by the disturbed conditions and they are arguing, writing, and preaching about it from all angles, in an effort to stem the tide of disaffection and disruption which is making such inroads upon this ancient institution.[12]

Hinkle's depiction of "people all over the land . . . arguing, writing, and preaching" about marriage did more than legitimate her own interest in the subject. It also summoned modern Americans to recognize themselves as such through their concern about the marriage crisis. To be one of the "people of the United States," as Hinkle and many others imagined that collective identity, was to be agitated and aroused, personally and socially involved in the "disturbed conditions" afflicting marriage. Having conflated worried interest in marriage with (interest in) the nation, Hinkle offered a short historical narrative to explain how the "ancient institution" had been rendered so uncertain and unstable. In doing so, she retold the history of the United States as the story of white marriage.

Hinkle and many others agreed that marriage had once flourished on the American frontier. The harshness of life among snowy woods and rocky fields had made pioneer men and women partners in the mutual task of "carving out a home and fortune for themselves . . . in the virgin soil."[13] This image of husbands and wives sharing the labor of bringing the wilderness under cultivation was an old one, but in the literature of marital breakdown their work did not reach its traditional goal of the glorious flowering of a virtuous republican civilization. Instead, the modern narrative pathway led toward a sterile world of machines and money. As the conquest of nature proceeded, Hinkle wrote, "the factory took over the domestic occupations of women, while the men became more and more preoccupied with the pursuit of material values." Within a few generations, these newly middle-class men found themselves "caught in a mechanism of their own creating," too deeply embedded in a world of money and machines to feel "the lure [of] the family or the love life," or indeed of any relationship that was not based on "opportunities for exploitation."[14] Industrial civilization drove a wedge between men and women by separating their experiences of labor. It also brought with its comforts a distance from nature, a degree of artificiality and mechanization, which extended into modern hearts and blighted warm impulses before they could bloom.

Hinkle, like many of her contemporaries, described American history as marital history in a way that underscores the effectiveness of marriage as a metaphor for the political relations that constitute the nation. Further, in her effort to describe the immense differences that threatened both familial and national cohesion, she mobilized a very common rhetorical opposition between the agrarian, organic past, when shared work made people feel connected to one another and to the land, and the mechanized, impersonal, self-seeking world of the modern city.[15] The contrast between nature and the machine was a conventional way of representing the transition to modernity.[16] In the context of the marriage crisis, that contrast provided Hinkle and her contemporaries with a politely apolitical and unanatomical language for figuring sexual difference: in the literature of marital breakdown, the core difference between men and women had nothing to do with genitals, wages, or citizenship, but rather appeared to reside in their relation to modernity.

Though Hinkle said that women as well as men were affected by the mechanization of everyday life, men appeared in her description as more mechanized, more ineluctably "caught" in modernity, than women. Women lost their occupations to the factory, with which they are not closely identified in Hinkle's story; in contrast, men internalized the machine. Other authors (and many filmmakers) portrayed women as the more modern sex, but however the sexes were aligned with the difference between the past and the present, representations of marital breakdown almost always developed in relation to the claim that modernization had rendered men and women as different from one another as domestic handcraft production was from work on an assembly line. Their partnership was therefore understood and represented as the materially and culturally productive (re)union of opposites. Marriage, in such representations, was a laborious achievement across the great divide of sex. Because marriage was also a metaphor for the nation, the difference between the sexes represented the existence of profound and significant difference within the polity, and connection across that divide represented a triumph of democratic respect for diversity.

The rhetorical contrast between nature and the machine, which constituted the sexes as opposites and so inflated the difficulty and significance of their union, simultaneously constructed difference between white and nonwhite races in a way that contributed to the consolidation and despecification of whiteness. The literature of marital breakdown was reticent on the subject of race, and so it is easy to forget that the frontier narrative was full of racial referents, and the frontier couple at its center was always presumed to be white. The whiteness of that pioneering couple is suggested by the historian Reginald Horsman's demonstration that the doctrine of manifest destiny was simultaneously an argument for white supremacy. By 1850, racial theories of the history of civilization had developed to the point that white Americans "could and did conceive of themselves as the most vital and energetic of those Aryan peoples who had spilled westward, 'revitalized' the Roman Empire, spread throughout Europe to England, and crossed the Atlantic in their relentless westward drive."[17] Through the end of the nineteenth century, the conquest of the American west was widely celebrated as an expression of an innate racial capacity for bringing civilization to previously barbarous or savage regions; so too was the leap across the Pacific in the Spanish-American War that brought the Philippines under U.S. rule. The "manifest destiny" of the antebellum years became the "white man's burden" of the Gilded Age and Progressive Era. Thus the image of the frontier couple bringing the wilderness under cultivation should be understood as a representation of the extension of white racial dominance, in a double sense: the frontier represented the geographical limit of white rule, while Horsman shows that participating in the westward expansion of civilization sometimes admitted otherwise "probationary" whites to the racial status of "Anglo-Saxons."[18]

Further, the iconic frontier couple was necessarily white because marriage was, in the nineteenth-century United States, a civil privilege linked to race.[19] Just as the rights of suffrage and jury representation were premised on a possessive interest in the nation that made them deeply incompatible with legal status as a possession, the right to exclusive bodily self-bestowal inherent in marriage was both conceptually and legally inapplicable to enslaved people. Because they did not own their bodies, slaves lacked the legal power to choose when, whether, and with whom to have sex. Enslaved people did not simply or always knuckle under to this particularly galling element of racial domination. Nevertheless, slavery formally denied slaves erotic, reproductive, and familial agency. Law and custom prevented slaves from marrying, but when slaves developed alternative sexual and kinship structures, racist whites interpreted these as evidence of racially innate promiscuity. This interpretation, and the corollary claim that "Negroes" were incapable of exercising rational self-control, proved far more durable than the legal institution of slavery. Thus ideal marriage, like membership in the nation, was not racially neutral even half a century after Emancipation, when the Freedman's Bureau had tied ex-slaves' access to citizenship to their willingness to standardize and legalize their unions.[20]

The implicit whiteness of the frontier couple suggests that, though the literature of marital breakdown mobilized the nature-machine opposition in ways that addressed gender more overtly than they addressed race, race was neither discursively derivative or secondary in its significance. Rather, the nature-machine opposition was a primary trope through which such texts represented difference along the axes of both race and gender. For many moderns, race and gender were intuitively intertwined; polarized gender difference was very widely represented as one of the evolved achievements of civilized modern whiteness.[21] The modern couple in crisis was implicitly white, but not in quite the same way as the frontier couple. Precisely because frontier husbands and wives had more in common with one another, the frontier couple represented an earlier, less complexly developed form of whiteness than that exhibited by urban men and women teetering on the edge of divorce. Horsman argues that participating in the conquest of the frontier served to confirm one's racial status as "Anglo-Saxon." Participating in the marriage crisis made one an American, according to a construction that assumed real Americans were white, but that also defined membership in the nation primarily in terms of commitment to rescuing civilization from the onslaught of the modern by fostering connection across difference. When the literature of marital breakdown described modernity as damaging marriage by deepening the difference between the sexes to the point that men and women no longer shared organic ties, it was simultaneously depicting the nation as constituted by the relations between white people and depicting whiteness as threatened by the civilization it liked to claim credit for creating.

The literature of marital breakdown, then, described both marriage and divorce in racially resonant terms. When Hinkle attributed divorce to the rise of the factory, she drew on a widely shared image of technological transformation as both the sign of civilization's progressive development and the sign of its self-destruction; this ambivalent image, as the last chapter showed, had a history of being used as a way to represent white dominance over civilization as both precious and vulnerable. The literature of marital breakdown consistently suggested that mechanization rendered the frontier couple's marital partnership obsolete in terms not only of the experience of shared work but also of the racialized capacity for emotional sensitivity and responsiveness. Already in 1897 the *Atlantic's* redoubtable essayist Agnes Repellier charged: "The old springs of simple sentiment are dying fast within us. It is heartless to laugh, it is foolish to cry, it is indiscreet to love, it is morbid to hate, and it is intolerant to espouse any cause with enthusiasm."[22] Thirty years later a college sociology textbook on marriage and family life explained this dried-up, cold-blooded state as the direct result of the rise of the machine:

> The machine has not merely multiplied man's productivity, it also has influenced his thinking and to a large extent made him a portion of the machine system. A basic content of our culture which influences both the acting and thinking of people is the stress on the mechanical. . . . The dominance of the machine is such that we literally think and have our being in terms of mechanics.[23]

Through that "we," the textbook constructed the community of its readers as modern, urban whites so embedded in and identified with the development of civilization that it was hard to distinguish between them and machines. Among the manifestations of this mechanical quality of modern life, the textbook went on, was the "standardization and sophistication" which "antagonizes romance and undermines its strength." That is, the identity between modern whites and modern civilization challenged the evolved emotional sensitivity that had allowed earlier generations of whites to cooperate in building families, communities, and the nation. In theory, increasing cultural sophistication could strengthen marriage, but "as always in the rapid reconstruction of culture, elimination and destruction have gone ahead of the rebuilding process, and for many sophistication means, not a deepening of idealism, but a skepticism with reference to it and a disposition too quickly to balance the books of matrimonial adventure and confess bankruptcy."[24] This sociology text used metaphors of tearing down build-ings and closing businesses in a way that linked the failure of white marriage to the industrial city. Dozens of other sources agreed that urban life under-mined the old-fashioned sentimental ties that had once nourished the de-velopment of white social values and of the civic culture that expressed and transmitted those values. This agreement may document the discursive association of such social ties, and the democracy made out of them, with the kind of "Anglo-Saxon" whiteness displayed by the frontier couple in contrast to the manifold whiteness of modern cities. Certainly, the diverse excitements of urban life constituted a direct challenge to the tight familial bonding of the fictional frontier household. William Graham Sumner, America's leading social Darwinist, announced that cities made "domes-ticity less attractive for either sex. Every interest in life is widened, and all of them compete with the home."[25] In "Middletown," the mythic "typical" city of the American heartlands, the sociologists Robert and Helen Merrell Lynd found that the members of white families shared few interests and spent most of their leisure time in public, surrounded by and interacting with automobiles, film projectors, and other machines.[26] As moderns became more and more intimate with machines, they seemed to lose access to and interest in one another.

Representation of moderns as mechanical suggested that civilization's material development had outstripped its affective and ethical development. The fear that an essential part of the racial heritage was being left behind was a recurring refrain in commentary on modernity. For instance, in 1931 the historian James Truslow Adams mused, "Any astronomer can predict with absolute certainty just where every star in the heavens will be at half-past eleven to-night. He can make no such prediction about his young daughter. From this fact—that one group of sciences has got entirely out of step with another—our civilization is becoming warped out of shape."[27] Adams's wit-ticism draws a sharp contrast between the astronomer's epistemological certainty about astral bodies and his vaguely panicked ignorance about modern sexuality and gender relations in his own family. "Our civilization" had a much better grip on the "hard" sciences than on social, familial, and sexual structures, a firmer sense of control over the movement of the heav-ens than over modern nightlife. For all his humor, Adams did not see this discrepancy as a laughing matter. The passage goes on to say that "it is possible that the sinister phenomena we see at present [such as the questionable sexual morality of the astronomer's daughter] are merely the wreckage of a period of change. It is either that or, like a fly-wheel that turns faster and faster until it reaches the rate at which it breaks to pieces, human society and the human mind may also explode into bits."[28] The same technological successes that defined modernity—and, not incidentally, that both physically enabled and ideologically supported U.S. imperialism into less modern, less mechanized areas of the continent and then the globe—brought with them an emotional, relational dislocation and disjuncture that threatened white civilization's survival.[29]

Violent images, often of explosions, dismemberments, or disintegration caused by contact with machines, were prominent in commentary on the breakdown of modern marriage and family life. A 1924 contributor to the *Journal of Social Hygiene* thought that something must be done about the "fundamental shake-up of the family . . . or occidental civilization may be decapitated by its own machinery."[30] A few years later Judge Ben Lindsey, also writing about the upheavals in modern sexual and family life, recorded that he often felt "keenly alarmed for the welfare of individuals who get themselves so entangled in the machinery of Change that they are in danger of being crushed in the wheels."[31] Images of mechanical violence provided a way for moderns to represent the vulnerability people felt as technological development overtook more humane values. Charlie Chaplin gave this vulnerability vivid mass-cultural expression in the famous scene from *Modern Times* where he portrays a worker whose eyes and hands are taken over and transformed by the machine he tends.[32] It is not an accident that the Little Tramp's mechanization is signaled by sexual assault: possessed by the industrial discipline that requires him to repeat a single gesture all day, the worker takes his wrenches to a woman whose dress has large buttons over her nipples. He seems to think he is tightening the bolts that stream by him on the conveyor belt. Losing the ability to distinguish between his own body and the body of the factory, he hallucinates other people as also made of machine parts, substitutes erotic aggression for respect or tenderness, and eventually throws himself into the gears.

In such images, the "standardization and sophistication" characteristic of the machine age produced both material wealth and emotional disconnection. That emotional disconnection was most often figured by men's and women's mutual noncomprehension. The preexisting chain of associations connecting machinery, modernity, and whiteness thus suggested not only the vulnerability of human bodies to mechanical forces but also the vulnerability of domestic ties, and through them, the vulnerability of whiteness as a set of consistent relational ideals that defined the nation and located it in the history of western civilization.

Cultural multiplicity, then, was one of the aspects of modernity often represented through images of sexual and familial dislocation. To moderns, the image of the astronomer's daughter out late in the city, or Chaplin's depiction of the Little Tramp and his sweetheart of the slums, could carry ethnic connotations: when nice young ladies rolled their stockings and painted their mouths, they were adopting working-class fashions originated by and associated with tough immigrant girls conspicuously uninterested in WASP standards of sexual self-control, while the Little Tramp's visual darkness, his inability to fit the bowler hat and striped trousers of an English gentleman, and his chronic failure to conform to his dominant cultural context all suggest that his peculiarity and poverty were connected to immigrant status. The declension narrative in which frontier marriage gave way to divorce in the modern urban industrial context was a story about the loss of a simple, vital foundation both for marriage and for the organic coherence of an American culture defined by and collapsed into Anglo ideals. Its warning about the probable consequences of marital breakdown for nation, race, and civilization was therefore an invitation for moderns to respond by settling the new frontier of modern marriage, consciously engaging in what the sociology textbook called "the reconstruction of culture" toward the goal of developing and universalizing the kinds of marital relationships that could hold the nation and civilization together.

At the same time the frontier narrative worked to obscure the power relations inherent in this racially inflected, heteronormalizing project. In the literature of marital breakdown, the correspondence between technological progress and emotional coldness argued that civilization had developed unevenly, such that materialism had gained ascendance over intimacy, and also that the inhumanity of civilization's progress was an unfortunate side effect of that uneven development. This literature's disavowal of modernization's structural inhumanity had a distinctly race- and power-evasive element in that it figured the suffering attendant on modernization as a purely emotional problem confronting the white men and women whose WASP racial heritage of sensitivity and connection was threatened by the rise of the machine, rather than as material problems for all people or for those whose racial and class positions made them especially vulnerable to exploitation and literal injury.

Beatrice Hinkle provides a helpful example of the way the frontier narrative's focus on white vulnerability obscured power relations and especially the reality of white dominance. In her account, American civilization developed through the joined productive and reproductive toil of white husbands and wives as they brought the continent under marital cultivation. Slave and coolie labor and Indian removal vanished in this revision of frontier history. So did the cultural and economic contributions of prostitutes, adventurers, solitary homesteaders, and all-male communities of (im)migrant workers. In their absence, the nation and civilization simply appeared to be white by nature, and completely homogeneous at that: the frontier narrative depicted pioneers as coming in matched male-female pairs, all engaged in the same work and all sharing the same religion, values, and goals. In this way the conventional, racially evasive account of American history as the history of marriage on the frontier worked both to normalize white dominance and to bury or disavow the existence of racial and cultural difference and struggles over power and resources. The image of the frontier couple substituted a simplified, artificially coherent vision of whiteness for the real complexity of nineteenth-century white racial definition and the differential distribution of its rewards according to ethnic, linguistic, and class markers. Further, when Hinkle used a narrative of marital gender-cooperation in a way that displaced also available (and objectively more accurate) narratives of race conflict, of sexual diversity, or of gender and racial exploitation on the frontier, she was telling a story about the true meaning of the nation, one in which marital solidarity between whites represented the ties that constitute the community of Americans.[33] The substitution of a gender-cooperative narrative for a race-conflictual one required both the elision of racial difference and the representational suppression of sexual politics. Through this move a positively Edenic vision of spousal love as the foundation of nation and civilization was made central to American history, while suffering in response to the loss of Eden appeared as a kind of white racial qualification.

In sum, the literature of marital breakdown mobilized the frontier narrative to make the argument that marital love is the core value of whiteness, and of the democratic civilization that allegedly expressed white racial essence. Yet at the same time, that literature insisted that the emotional responsiveness that allegedly sprang from shared labor on the frontier was inaccessible to moderns. Mechanization and urbanization separated men and women from one another and both from the sensitivity to others that made the community of the nation possible. Therefore marriage and the nation were on the verge of collapse, and a new way to bind Americans together was an imperative need.

Despite its repetitive insistence on the modernity of this situation, the literature of marital breakdown clearly echoes Gilded Age constructions of white civilization, its mechanical discontents, and the frightening consequences for race and nation. But while neurasthenia discourse depicted refined, native-born white Americans as infinitely sensitive to the suffering inseparable from the birth of the modern, marriage literature tended to depict a much broader audience of implicitly, vaguely white moderns as emotionally anaesthetized by their civilization's own achievements. George Beard had hoped that modernity would be easier for civilized whites to master once they evolved the capacity to live comfortably among machines. By the 1920s, much conventional wisdom held that the fundamental problem confronting moderns was that they were too deeply influenced by mechanical values to merge their interests and resources with others in the service of a stable family and civic life. Yet while the opposition between nature and the machine emphasized the fear that moderns had become unnaturally cold and unemotional, the belief that they had internalized mechanical values also suggested that marriage, like a radio or a Model T, could be repaired, rebuilt, and made to run as well as ever.

This was the specific function of the marriage manual. Marriage manuals were instruction booklets much like those that came with new appliances: they explained how to run one's emotional and sexual life in the machine age. Such guides taught moderns how to transform selfish, isolated, unhappy individuals into satisfied husbands and wives. More specifically, manuals taught their readers a distinctively modern form of sexual self-discipline calculated to cultivate the racial heritage of sensitivity and connection that they believed was essential to the nation and to white civilization. Oddly enough, these lessons in how to be a normal American proceeded through discussions about managing time.

"The Ever-Quickening Tempo of Our Times"

Marriage manuals proceeded from the basic assumption that, although life among machines made moderns emotionally unresponsive, marital lovemaking could provide an important point of connection. To the extent that husbands and wives could be solicited to shape their lovemaking in pursuit of shared intimacy, they had an absorbing project in common, and one from which both partners benefited as individuals while they strengthened their marriage and the race and nation of which they were members. The marriage bed replaced the homestead as the imaginary center of family life, the place where a couple could work together for a common goal. Sexual intercourse replaced shared labor on the land as the symbolic activity through which whites rehearsed in microcosm the relational virtues without which democracy could not work.

Through the same symbolic organization, sex could represent the coldness, the lack of connection, and the vulnerability that this literature described as characteristic of the machine age. If marital intercourse crystallized the failures of white civilization rather than compensating for them, the future of marriage, nation, and race looked dim. Many marriage manuals, like the larger literature of marital breakdown, argued that the breakdown of marriage reflected the way that mechanization exaggerated a basically natural sexual difference until men and women were all but unable to communicate or connect. This was, for instance, the core theme of Marie C. Stopes's famous and influential *Married Love*, first published in 1918 and continuously reprinted for decades.[34] Stopes explained the need for marriage manuals like hers:

> Love loses, in the haste and bustle of the modern turmoil, not only its charm and graces, but some of its vital essence. The evil results of the haste which so infests and poisons us are often felt much more by the woman than by the man. The over-stimulation of city life tends to "speed up" the man's reactions, but to retard hers. To make matters worse, even for those who have leisure to spend on love-making, the opportunities for peaceful, romantic dalliance are less to-day in a city with its tubes and cinema-shows than in woods and gardens where the pulling of rosemary or lavender may be the sweet excuse for the slow and profound mutual rousing of passion.[35]

Stopes used the opposition between nature and the machine both to emphasize the speed characteristic of the machine age and to highlight the difference between the sexes. "Haste and bustle," crowds, noise, and commercial amusements all distracted people from "peaceful, romantic dalliance" in the gardens of bliss. But while the literature of marital breakdown represented all moderns as alienated and cold, marriage manuals often represented men and women as alienated differently: men responded to the machine age by becoming more mechanical and moving faster than women. The difference between the sexes was a specifically erotic difference, and its essence lay in sexual timing.

Marriage manuals represented sexual difference as temporal difference partly because they shared the widespread assumption that high levels of conflict between the sexes were side effects of modernization. The feeling that life was moving increasingly fast was an important part of the experience of industrialization and urbanization. Technologies of speed were prominent in Beard's descriptions of the unique modernity of late-nineteenth-century civilization: the steam engine moved goods and people with unprecedented rapidity, while the telegraph made communication almost instantaneous. Such innovations, as I showed in chapter 1, were often described as causing tremendous nervous strain and suffering among refined whites. Forty years later, Raymond Fosdick, at the time a trustee of the Rockefeller Foundation and a member of the American Eugenics Society's advisory board, used similar images of breakneck speed to represent the modern. Fosdick pointed out that "when Napoleon was retreating in headlong fashion from Moscow, it took him 312 hours to complete the last leg of his journey from Vilna to Paris. Any traveler can now do it in less than 48 hours by railroad or in 8 hours by airplane."[36] He went on to tell his youthful listeners that the result was a disoriented nation "wandering in heartbreaking complexity," trying "to find some sure way out of this jungle of machinery."[37] When manuals like *Married Love* depicted marriage as damaged by a profoundly painful temporal dislocation between husbands and wives, they were drawing on a conventional representation of modernization in terms of the damage done by the "ever-quickening tempo of our times."[38]

The sense of being rushed and out of control, in our own day, is often described in the language of stress; I do not mean to discount the real emotional consequences of immense and rapid cultural change or, for that matter, of sexual mismatching. When used in this context, however, the conflation of sexual difference with temporal difference, and the assumption that both were manifestations of modernization, had the effect of obscuring relations of power along axes of both race and gender. I have already shown that the diachronic difference between past and present, primitive and modern, was also a synchronic difference between more and less "evolved" forms of whiteness as well as between whiteness and the allegedly less developed races. References to the temporal dislocations characteristic of modernity therefore carried racial implications that marital advice literature engages only indirectly. Instead, that literature displaced all discussions of difference onto difference between husbands and wives, in a way that enabled acknowledgment of intergender conflict while nonetheless evading engagement with gender politics.[39]

In the early twentieth century, white women were claiming an unprecedented social and economic independence. Though limited, these women's claims to independence, and to enfranchised citizenship in 1920, seemed to many contemporary observers to blur the line of demarcation between men's and women's traits and social roles. When contemporaries wrote about the meaning of difference between the sexes, it inevitably resonated with women's suffrage and commercial employment, and the complex questions these raised about the nature and meaning of citizenship. If women were really significantly different from men, their elevation to full citizenship meant that the nation as a whole might move in completely unprecedented directions. If the sexes were more similar than different, however, the natural foundation of marriage, the sexual division of labor, and the gender hierarchy were called into question. As one marriage manual put it, the fully modern wife "realizes that as an intelligent grown-up person and a voting citizen, as well as a wife, she has duties and obligations wider than she ever had before. She feels that there are other things more important in the general scheme of life than meeting her husband at the gate and having his slippers warming before the fire."[40] This passage is unusually politically explicit in its recognition that citizenship informed marriage as well as vice versa, but even this manual did not go so far as to acknowledge that not all husbands, however modern in other respects, welcomed the domestic presence of fellow citizens instead of personal servants.

Marriage manuals' representation of difference between the sexes as a temporal issue caused by modernization therefore should be interpreted as a way of simultaneously recognizing real conflict between men and women and evading the political dimensions of such conflict. Discussions of a profound difference in men's and women's erotic pacing record the disavowal of ongoing sexual inequality; in such discussions, erotic pleasure, rather than social justice, appeared to be the basic issue at stake. One manual asserted,

"If, anywhere and in any circumstances, the demand for equal rights for both sexes is *incontestable*, it is so in regard to equal consent and equal pleasure in sexual union."[41] Several others went so far as to suggest that the high divorce rate and the social disorganization attendant on it reflected the "amazing frequency" with which men ejaculated before their wives reached orgasm.[42] Marriage manuals could plausibly substitute discussions of sexual dissatisfaction for engagement with sexual politics because such temporal mismating was apparently endemic, even among men who were otherwise cultivated and considerate husbands. As one sensitive and genteel "Mrs. Smith" explained her separation to a judge in 1927,

> My husband . . . is always in a hurry about everything he does. If he goes for a walk—just a pleasure walk, you know—his impulse is not to stroll and steep himself in beauty and enjoyment as he goes, but rather to hurry as if he were bent on getting somewhere. You'd think he was going to catch a train and was late for it.[43]

The result was completely predictable:

> Of course, if I happened to be with him, he would forget all about me, in his impatience and nervousness, and would leave me far behind . . . just as if it didn't matter whether I came along or not. And so I don't care about taking walks, with only myself and my own thoughts for company.[44]

Night after night of one-sided sex could easily disrupt any marriage, and there is evidence that something of this nature was a common experience for white couples in the interwar years. The average length of intromission among comfortably situated Anglo-American men, according to a widely quoted marriage study published in 1931, was less than three minutes. Some 12 percent allegedly ejaculated immediately upon entry.[45] Yet while manual after manual constructs this pattern of intercourse as a serious failing that could wreck a marriage, they also indicate that many modern white men would find nothing wrong with it unless experts alerted them to its dangers. In fact, in the early twentieth century such sex had the distinct advantage of efficiency as it was then being defined: it yielded the maximum possible results in the shortest possible time, with a minimum of wasted motion.

The virtues of a businesslike approach to sex may have been, in some men's minds, the same as the virtues of a businesslike approach to business.

Quickness, reliable regularity of habit, and punctuality were highly desirable traits in modern commercial employment. Some men, if the hints in the manuals are correct, appear to have internalized the business ethic in their sexual lives to the extent that they were proud of their "efficiency in the sexual act" and may even have boasted of their capacity for instant emission as a sign of their potency, their ability to get things done.[46] Some women, for a variety of reasons, may have shared their perspective, or been willing to tolerate it. For instance, prostitutes might have appreciated quick ejaculation as making their job easier, and, to the extent that they understood themselves as trading pleasure for pleasure, working girls engaged in the culture of "treating" might have been comfortable with quick, businesslike sex after or as part of an evening out with a man. In such relationships, it is possible that sexual efficiency posed no significant problems.[47] But ideal modern marriage among middle-class white people was, in part, defined as such by its uncommercial, even anticommercial, nature.

I have already shown that the literature of marital breakdown often represented the fact that the household was no longer the center of production as a significant part of the reason that modern, mutually gratifying sex was necessary to hold marriages together. Many manuals argued that the shift was for the better, because the mutual interest of lovers was a nobler bond than the mutual interest of partners in economic struggle.[48] The business ethic had no place in the modern marriage bed. Hence one manual scolded an excessively efficient husband that "you may be a pretty fair business man . . . but as a husband you [are] a candidate for the divorce court."[49] Another manual marveled at the consistency with which "trained, intelligent men" who had "mastered the art of making money, of administering a business, of meeting the complex problems of commerce," were "ignorant, untaught primitives in their sex life."[50] Well-to-do white men were supposed to guard, protect, and foster the triumphs of white civilization, including marital love. They had a racial responsibility not to indulge themselves in the abrupt, self-serving sex allegedly characteristic of "primitives." When the white middle classes divorced, the foundations of the civilized world trembled: those who would sustain and perpetuate civilization first had to discipline themselves to sustain their marriages.

In the example above, "Mr. Smith" was not represented as "primitive" in any obvious sense; on the contrary, the image of him running for the train locates him firmly in the modern moment. Yet at the same time, his sexual selfishness and haste marked him as out of step not only with his wife's erotic tempo and her emotional need for companionship but with the ideals at the heart of whiteness. Truly white sex required the evolutionary achievement of the tender concern for one's mate that led the truly civilized to cultivate their sexual skills.

> In most mammals . . . copulatory behavior is instinctive, being not at all dependent upon imitation, learning, or experience. . . . In contrast complete copulatory behavior among the primates (that is among monkeys, apes and men) is reached only after a long period of experimentation and experience. It is not an instinctive behavior pattern, but rather a complex adjustment between two individuals. . . . In other words, adequate copulatory behavior does not come instinctively to men and women. The technique of the sexual relation has to be understood and learned in order to develop a satisfactory sex life.[51]

Because good sexual technique required intelligence and application, not all primates were equally capable of achieving it: self-discipline and mutual consideration were essential to "adequate copulatory behavior." Predictably, manuals often noted that "savages" lacked technique. "Savage" sexuality conventionally was represented as being "cruel and ruthless, with absolutely no regard for the partner."[52] Here was no "complex adjustment between two individuals." So "civilized man" was warned that he "who seeks gratification for himself alone, caring little or not at all for mutual satisfaction, descends to the level of the barbarian."[53] Conversely, the man who assiduously cultivated his wife's sexual pleasure thereby proved his status as "an *erotically civilized* adult."[54]

Civilized whiteness and mutually gratifying marital intercourse were sutured together in many manuals through descriptions of white women's sexual suffering and humiliation:

> The man reaches his climax quickly and the act ceases. The woman has remained unresponsive or, what is worse, she has been partially aroused or even highly excited but "left in the air." . . . The natural reaction of the man is to become relaxed, drowsy, and go to sleep. . . . [In contrast,] the woman, if she has remained cold, will too, perhaps, go to sleep, cold also in heart and spirit and with a dividing wall between. Or, if she has become stimulated and left unsatisfied, she may lie awake for hours, occasionally all night, tense and excited, unless she turns to auto-erotic relief. It requires but a moment of

picturing the situation, in imagination—the man satisfied, breathing deeply in sound sleep, while the woman lies at his side tensely awake with unsatisfied longing, or resorts to self-relief—to realize how inevitable it is that sooner or later there should escape from her in the silence of the night such expressions as, "selfish," "brute," "animal," "stupid," and the like, and that this fundamental disappointment should bring disharmony into their whole relationship.[55]

In the early twentieth century, as in the Gilded Age, these four epithets— "selfish, brute, animal, stupid"—strongly suggested the racial backsliding of white middle-class men who gave way to their coarser bodily appetites. In the throes of desire men like "Mr. Smith" forfeited their evolutionary inheritance of exquisite sensitivity to both physical pleasure and emotional intimacy. There were two possible results: either their wives joined them in substituting mechanical coldness for sensitivity and isolation for connection, or their capacity for white sensitivity was forced back on itself and became suffering. Thus bracketed by neurasthenia on one side and anaesthesia on the other, normal eroticism appeared to be characterized by keen enjoyment. And because men's commitment to mutual sexual pleasure was represented as a racial achievement, the normalization of enjoyment carried with it the suggestion of the normalization of whiteness. "Barbarians" never became sensitive enough to grow nervous, but with marriage manuals' help, they could at least be trained to pay attention to their wives' sexual needs.

Marriage manuals suggested that the defining experience of civilized sensitivity was mutual, and preferably simultaneous, access to sexual pleasure; strengthening marriage required that moderns learn how to synchronize their orgasms. Such shared bliss could go a long way toward dissolving the differences between more and less "evolved" forms of whiteness while it bound men and women together in what one manual called "a lifelong honeymoon."[56] Achieving that union required moderns to bracket racial difference, while devoting informed, disciplined, and unwavering attention to the difference between the sexes.

Heterosexuality: Sexual Difference and Simultaneous Orgasm

Many manuals include passages—sometimes entire chapters—stressing the depth and significance of sexual difference. A fairly typical instance appears on the first page of Marie Stopes's *Married Love*. Stopes insisted that, for all the hurt they caused, polar differences between the sexes were necessary and beautiful; from them, she wrote, sprang "the old desire of our race" for "life-long union with a mate." She described this desire as a fundamental characteristic of human beings:

> For some reason beyond our comprehension, nature has so created us that we are incomplete in ourselves; neither man nor woman singly can know the joy of the performance of all the human functions; neither man nor woman singly can create another human being. This fact, which is expressed in our outward divergences of form, influences and colours the whole of our lives; and there is nothing for which the innermost spirit of one and all so yearns as for a sense of union with another soul, and the perfecting of oneself which such union brings.[57]

Such passages did several kinds of work. First, given the context of marital advice literature designed to rescue civilization, these descriptions of sexual difference had a certain prescriptive undertone. They solicited readers to conflate "outward divergences of form" with the longing for love and the perfecting of self, a solicitation that took place through their representation of that conflation as a simple fact of nature. Further, Stopes's globalization of heterosexuality—"one and all" yearn for union across difference—suggested that the erotic desire for sexual difference was inseparable from full humanity: the implication was that those who failed to invest difference with this kind of desire had failed to evolve into fully modern, fully civilized white manhood or womanhood. Most manuals concurred that the sexual love of husbands and wives was the apogee of individual and cultural development.[58] "Heterosexuality"—the eroticization of sexual difference—began to come into mass-cultural focus through exactly such normalizing conflations of difference and desire.

Several manuals were explicit about the evolutionary development of heterosexuality out of the basic fact of sexual difference. For instance, Max Exner's highly successful 1932 work *The Sexual Side of Marriage* defined biological maleness and femaleness as "differences, attraction, [and] mating," before going on to explain that the "primitive attraction between male and female" had gradually been "elaborated into and adorned by the higher psychic and social elements" that constituted civilization:

> The most sympathetic [i.e., sexually sensitive] types became the best parents, and therefore brought the larger proportion of young to ma-

turity and hence survived against the less sympathetic types. It is mainly so that love in the world has grown. . . . From that first appearance of sexual sympathy grew . . . conjugal sympathy and parental sympathy. These two strands united to form the basis of the family. The sympathetic and social qualities and relationships developed in the family gradually extended . . . in turn to the nearest of kin, the clan, the tribe, the state, the nation. They underlie our entire social structure.[59]

Another text said of ideal marriage simply that the "consolidation . . . of physical sex and affection . . . is the peak of social achievement."[60] Heterosexuality, then, combined the erotic desire for sexual difference with the evolutionary elaboration of that desire into love; this combination was absolutely essential both for status as a normal modern and for the existence of civilized social order. In this construction we can see the collapse of sexual and racial normality into one another such that following the guidelines for married love could testify to one's commitment to nation, race, and civilization. Pursuing normal heterosexuality confirmed one's own healthy recapitulation of the evolution of individual development and social order. At the same time, it confirmed the legitimacy of American ideals about virtuous domestic and civic relationships that had a long history of being used to legitimize white dominance. Therefore, aligning oneself with normal heterosexuality had the effect of performing one's alignment with ideal whiteness. And so the more "heterosexuality" talked about itself, the less whiteness needed to say.

The literature of marital breakdown documented an emerging understanding of true whiteness as the enactment of love, a definition that excluded the recognition of injustice from the realm of the normal. The elaborate sexual self-cultivation and self-control required for fully normal heterosexuality helped to make this modern, power-evasive formulation of white racial meaning plausible by keeping moderns' attention focused on the sheer difficulty of the marital task in front of them. In Exner's words, "Marriage is not only an achievement; it is a difficult achievement. . . . It requires intelligent study, devoted application, and rigid self-discipline."[61] Margaret Sanger urged her readers to view the discipline required for married love as itself a stimulant to that love, arguing that the careful study of sexual difference "makes married life more interesting, more stimulating, more poetic and infinitely more mysterious. It appeals to the intelligence as well as the emotions."[62] Conscious pursuit of unity across the gulf of sexual difference was a prerequisite for and means of what Stopes called "the perfecting of oneself."

Here as elsewhere, the literature of marital breakdown interpellated people into normality through a barely veiled threat. As abundant examples from the histories of "delinquency" and "perversion" make clear, moderns who did not "perfect" themselves by pursuing heterosexual normality very often found themselves vulnerable to disciplinary "adjustment" at the hands of experts.[63] In contrast, people who willingly assumed the project of cultivating the erotics of sexual difference in marriage represented the triumph of white civilization over its own threatened failure. Careful self-cultivation and self-control, those classic hallmarks of ideal whiteness, allowed modern men and women to transform the cause of disconnection and unhappiness into the stuff of romance. Sexual difference, when subjected to proper management and saturated with erotic and emotional sensitivity, brought men and women closer together. But where in the Gilded Age such self-discipline was an important element of genteel WASPs' claim to be more civilized than anyone else, hence the legitimate owners and leaders of white civilization, marriage manuals summoned "one and all" to the task of perfecting the self through the deliberate, rational, modern cultivation of married love. Marriage manuals, in short, normalized a particular white ideal of sexual self-discipline by describing it as a basic, essential element of modern marriage. To the extent that any married couple aspired to that ideal, they entered into the disciplinary apparatus at the heart of whiteness.

I elaborate this claim in the next section, but first I want to detail the disciplinary technology that marriage manuals offered as the power-evasive solution to modernization's problematic exaggeration of sexual difference and its negative effects on marital love. In the world the manuals made, when wives and husbands could not get along their quarrels had nothing to do with pervasive domestic, political, and economic inequalities between the sexes. Marriage manuals represent unhappiness in marriage, at bottom, as a reflection of the natural discrepancy between the swift pace of male desire and the slow, subtler stirrings of female longing. In such situations, the rational, civilized, white thing to do was to develop a technology that could draw on nature as a resource, harnessing it and multiplying its power so that it could be put to more efficient use in response to a social need. It was in this modern spirit that manual writers advised their readers to cultivate their awareness of time, and offered simple graphs and charts to follow as disciplinary templates for negotiating a revitalized sexual union.

Such illustrations of temporal difference could refer either to distribution of desire across the calendar or to the time it took for each partner to achieve

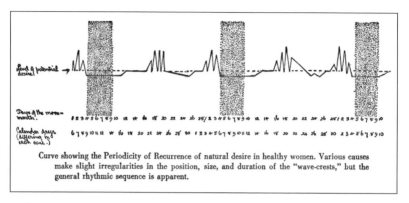

Curve showing the Periodicity of Recurrence of natural desire in healthy women. Various causes make slight irregularities in the position, size, and duration of the "wave-crests," but the general rhythmic sequence is apparent.

2. The Marriage Chart, from Marie C. Stopes, *Married Love* (NEW YORK: EUGENICS PUBLISHING CO., [1918] 1931).

climax in a typical sexual encounter. Marie Stopes was probably the first to develop a calendrical Marriage Chart: she used zigzag lines across monthly tables to demonstrate that women's sexual hunger rose and fell in predictable, more or less even cycles, apparently following the menstrual cycle. If men and women learned to take advantage of this cycle, she explained, they would find some of the discrepancy of pacing lessened, because women's responses were potentially faster and richer at some times of the month than others.[64] By the mid-1920s dozens of manuals included some version of the Marriage Chart. Almost all marital advice literature explained that civilized women were eager for sex at some points in their cycles and indifferent at others, though they disagreed about which points held the greatest erotic potential.[65] Yet despite variation in the details about periodicity offered from manual to manual, the point of discussing such cycles was consistent: marriage manuals urged moderns to plot women's desire on the calendar as part of a larger disciplinary apparatus that sought to delineate and resolve sexual difference through the pursuit of simultaneous orgasm.

Marriage Charts measured feminine cycles against an invisible record of masculine desire, which was presumed to be a more or less horizontal and constant line somewhere near the top of the chart ("physical sex desire in man is always near the surface and can be aroused at any time").[66] Making love at the peaks of women's cycles meant making love at the times of the month when white men and women most resembled one another in the pace and urgency of their desires and so were most likely to climax at the same moment; yet the analytic apparatus the manuals offered to help achieve this unification required that couples understand intercourse as a carefully engineered bridge across an immense sexual divide.

In this way men and women were urged to pay careful attention to sexual difference at all times. Marriage Charts held out the promise that disciplined attention to the difference between one's own and one's spouse's sexual needs would smooth out or prevent the hurt feelings and resentments that arose when both partners in a marriage could not find equal satisfaction and refreshment in their sexual practices. This promise resonates with the equally commonsensical promise that if moderns chose their mates wisely and made conscious decisions about when and with whom to reproduce, their children stood a better chance of being physically and mentally normal and healthy—that is, with the basic justification for eugenics. This parallel underscores the political disingenuousness of much common sense. Just as concern for future children's well-being trained people to accept constant evaluation of biological "fitness" of potential parents as reasonable and politically innocent, concern for the well-being of marriage itself trained people to accept constant monitoring of sexual manhood or womanhood as an ordinary and neutral activity.[67] The apparent scientific neutrality of the sexual and temporal discipline urged on married moderns was one of the major ways in which heterosexuality's embeddedness in relations of power was obscured.

But in the area of sexual timing, unlike the area of mate choice or any other, the manuals felt the need to warn their readers against being *too* disciplined in their pursuit of simultaneous orgasm. They seem to have thought it likely that modern couples would take the Marriage Chart as the basis for a sexual schedule which would then become a matter of inflexible routine.[68] Such scheduling may well have been common, since it was consonant with middle-class white ideals about sensible, methodical behavior:

> The more highly civilized and instructed the husband and wife have become, the more they attend to rules of conduct, whether in sports, or business, or marriage. Today the average married couple decide their marriage relations on some sort of plan. . . . How many children they should have, frequency of meetings in bodily union, and other intimate affairs are a matter of mutual understanding.[69]

This white kind of plan was a very civilized way to work out differences of opinion or taste without unseemly conflict or overt displays of power, but it was not a very helpful way to address eroticism. A timetable for intercourse, no matter how intelligently and consensually worked out, precluded the possibility of spontaneous, passionate connection and so could only intensify the troubling modern tendency to alienation in what experts agreed ought to be a moment of profound intimacy.

Manuals describe sex on schedule as defeating the purpose of the Marriage Chart, for it guaranteed a temporal disconnection and boredom that was the exact opposite of blissful union:

> The couple who want to travel onward from the first thrills of honeymoon days, so that custom will not stale the bliss of physical nearness, should never allow any form of love-making to become routine, or, worse still, a duty. The bride who reminds her husband to kiss her whenever he leaves or enters the house is killing the spontaneity of his caresses for her and forcing him to replace the irregularly recurring impulse to fondle her, with the prosaic habit of osculating punctiliously, in much the same way that he uses a doormat or toothbrush— because it is the scheduled time for this performance, not because he is irresistibly driven to the act.[70]

Sex between married lovers was supposed to provide a much-needed relief from the regimentation of white middle-class life, a corrective for the blank and hurried unfreedom of a nation of employees. Anything like a timetable for erotic activity was a reduction of love to a series of mechanical and repetitive gestures. Similarly, any tendency to try to standardize successful erotic procedure was unfortunate. One manual stated simply that, when couples made love, "no hard and fast rules can be laid down. The human is a machine not created in accordance with blueprints."[71] Even in the machine age, the manuals agreed, love could not be mass-produced. Accordingly, the modern husband was warned that he "must not think of [erotic technique] as something that can be made unchanging, once the best method is discovered, so that he merely needs to repeat over and over again the same thing in marital intimacy. The art of love . . . shrivels when it becomes stereotyped."[72] Another, similar passage was even more explicit in its warning that modern lovers should treat their dalliance as an art and not seek to discipline and rationalize their time together according to an industrial model:

> Individuals are not searching for a standard sex technique comparable to a procedure worked out by an efficiency expert in reorganizing a

business, or by a surgeon in performing a certain kind of operation. In this latter instances a scheme can be built up from experience that can be applied generally, since it represents the one good way of accomplishing the purpose in mind. Nothing could be further away from the art of love . . . [Couples] are not to struggle to conform, they are to work together to discover their own sex cravings and methods of satisfaction.[73]

Such passages have led at least one scholar to argue that marriage manuals were less conventionally prescriptive, less disciplinary, and more potentially culturally radical than most interpretations allow.[74] But despite their insistence that sex ought not to be mechanical, marriage manuals routinely describe the freedom to experiment as constrained by the fundamental temporal difference between the sexes, and by the mandate that true love found its truest expression in simultaneous orgasm. Love across and because of sexual difference was supposed to shape the larger trajectory of each erotic encounter between husbands and wives. The insistence on freedom and creativity in each couple's approach to a predetermined goal therefore recorded the internalization of discipline in the marriage bed, not its absence or subversion. If the "art of love" the manuals described was not entirely mechanically produced, it nonetheless used a standard technique and resulted in consistent end products: ideal marriages were those in which the partners cultivated erotic self-knowledge and self-control in the service of increased sensitivity and capacity for love.

In addition to Marriage Charts, some manuals offered graphs of sexual difference in erotic timing as tools for helping moderns track their proximity to the heterosexual ideal. Conventionally, the x (horizontal) axis of such graphs represented the timespan of a single erotic encounter, while the y (vertical) axis represented the intensity of excitement and pleasure. A successful encounter was one in which the line representing the husband and the line representing the wife converged at a high value on the y axis.[75] Simultaneous orgasm appeared, in geometrical terms, as a point of intersection. Here again, the graphic representation of sexual difference was also a representation of its resolution. Placing difference front and center, making it the core truth of erotic experience, allowed moderns to use it as a strategy for achieving unity in the moment of synchronized ecstasy.

But "allowed" is too relaxed a term. Many marriage manuals represented the deliberate cultivation of sexual difference for erotic satisfaction as mandatory. Note the imperative construction in the statement that the husband "must *consciously plan* to reach the climax at the same time as the wife. Therein the art of married love reaches perfection."[76] Marriage Charts and graphs solicited moderns to understand sexual difference in terms of an erotic discipline with a clearly defined aim: "mutual satisfaction with fully releasing, completely terminating orgasm in normal intercourse, all richly enhanced by a skillful art of love."[77] This was the central goal not only of modern marriage but of the entire genre of marital advice literature. Yet only a handful of books take on the task of erotic education in any detail. Most works repeat the formula for mutual satisfaction in its barest outline: couples should engage in some preliminaries before intercourse, and men should take care to restrain themselves so that they do not climax too quickly. The magic of simultaneous orgasm follows without detail as to how to get there, as though it sprang naturally and inevitably from prolonged intercourse.

The only advice about actual technique that appeared with some regularity was the observation that men would find it easier to defer orgasm if they alternated periods of motion with periods of relative inactivity. Few manuals offered more erotic instruction than this scanty outline, dressed up in an elevated language either of mysticism or of science. In either case, the emphasis was not on acts or techniques but on sexual difference and the properly orderly passage of linear time. For instance, *Happiness in Marriage* stressed "the necessity for a prolonged and definite period of preparation" and then went on to murmur:

> At the completion of the physical union of body and spirit, it is highly desirable that the participants strain [*sic*] the impulse to abandon control and to plunge forward into a precipitous movement toward the climax. . . . The crest of the first rhythmic wave has been reached. In order that the subsequent rhythm may reach an even higher crest, there must now follow a momentary ebb. . . . Therefore, follows a brief moment of rest, a period which permits the husband to regain the control, that might at this point escape even the strongest-willed of men. It is for the young wife a moment which definitely focusses her awakened passion and permits her to prepare herself for the culminating flight which follows.[78]

Such descriptions of intercourse are the verbal equivalent of the zigzag lines in graphic representations of arousal: peaks of intense feeling and quick response are separated by valleys of slow or no movement and little sensation. Like charts and graphs, these passages do not offer very much concrete information about how to please a sexual partner. Rather, they focus on the profundity and importance of synchrony, and therefore of self-control in the service of sexual difference. Page after page, manual after manual reminds the couple that it takes unwavering self-discipline, and conscious attention to the discrepancy between men's and women's sexual rhythms, for them to come together.[79]

There is something distinctly peculiar about a genre that justifies its existence by announcing an imperative need which it then refuses to address directly. The consistency with which marriage manuals evaded erotic instruction suggests that their central goal was not, in fact, the promotion of sexual pleasure.[80] Instead, manuals' obsessive focus on difference suggests that they used the promise of pleasure to promote a particular vision of marriage as the miniature domestic version of the relationships of mutual care that ideally constituted the democratic nation and white civilization. The precariousness of the claim that the modern nation and civilization were actually characterized by tender concern is one reason that manuals paid so much attention to erotic pacing. The focus on sexual difference as temporal difference worked to consolidate heterosexuality while occluding hierarchical relations of power between the sexes, between different groups of whites, and between whites and their racial others. Marriage manuals' suppression of these politically loaded differences allowed them to promote a vision of harmony and satisfaction as the defining experiences of marriage and, through it, of American life.

Manuals essentially promised that, if moderns responded to temporal differences in erotic pacing with proper self-discipline, other axes of difference would somehow be rendered neutral both in the domestic space and in the life of the nation as a whole. Simultaneous orgasm wiped out all obstacles to union: "If [the wife] derives the same full flavored, wholesome, and natural benefits from coitus as does the husband, if they merge into one ecstatic being during the glorious fervor of a simultaneous orgasm, then their marriage will find few obstacles to happiness and few will be the troubles and differences large enough to wreck so joyous a mating."[81] The social benefits were obvious. Orgasmic merger "into one ecstatic being" corrected and compensated for the absence of care for others, the injustice and exploitation distributed along axes of racial, sexual, ability, class, and ethnic difference that were characteristic of the social relations of the modern United States. In the language of the literature of marital breakdown, simultaneous orgasm overcame the isolation and social disconnection characteristic of the machine age. The centrality of that claim is one reason that many manuals described simultaneous orgasm with pastoral images. Exner's *The Sexual Side of Marriage*, which was a scientistic, rather "hard-boiled" work aimed at a college-educated and urbane readership, explained the relationship of prolonged erotic dalliance to mutual climax through the metaphor of a day in the country: "An exhilarating stroll in brisk air and sunshine of two lovers during which there is fascinating, stimulating interplay of the spiritual responses of their personalities will make infinitely more thrilling and satisfying the final mad dash down the hill together, to end in relaxation and sweet repose on the bank of a smoothly flowing river."[82] Exner's image suggests that the experience of sharing sexual pleasure bound men and women together in much the same way that working on the land had strengthened the ties of marriage on the frontier. Sex was stronger than the machine. In manuals adopting a more breathless tone in general, descriptions of simultaneous orgasm were hyperbolically elevated to the point of promising couples a glimpse of paradise:

> When two who are mated in every respect burn with the fire of the innumerable forces within them, which set their bodies longing towards each other with the desire to interpenetrate and to encompass one another, the fusion of joy and rapture is not purely physical. The half-swooning sense of flux which overtakes the spirit in that eternal moment at the apex of rapture sweeps into its flaming tides the whole essence of the man and woman, and, as it were, the heat of the contact vaporizes their consciousness so that it fills the whole of cosmic space. For the moment they are identified with the divine thoughts, the waves of eternal force, which to the Mystic often appear in terms of golden light.[83]

This imagery is so intense as to border on violence, resonating with the literature of marital breakdown's representation of divorce and social disintegration through images of decapitation and dismemberment caused by machines. Here, however, orgasm is figured as a sort of explosion, a rupture of boundaries leading not to disintegration but to the mystical experience of unity across difference. Other manuals described the unifying effects of simultaneous orgasm in terms that emphasized the extent to which marriage was a microcosm of the larger social order. The complete erotic fusion of husband and wife compensated for the cold and mechanical qualities of modern life, while the work it took to arrive at that intimacy taught valuable lessons in citizenship: "Consummated love has a softening, healing, inspiring influence. It often expands the sympathies, stimulates forbearance, and teaches self-denial, forgiveness, and consideration toward faults and foibles. . . . The harsh egoism is lessened, there is regard for the continual well-being of the other half of the unit and a reciprocal desire to give happiness."[84]

Representations of the discrepancy in erotic pacing that defined sexual difference provided manuals with an opportunity to promote sexual democracy: conscious adaptation of the partners' caresses made use of their contrary natures in the service of the common good. Such images of the social dimension of simultaneous orgasm return to the underlying claim that civilization depended on couples' ability to synchronize their desires: "Without . . . *mutual* satisfaction of the sex hunger, the home and civilization would soon be things of the past."[85] The thing the sexes had in common was the erotic pleasure they could take in their sexual difference. From this identity-in-difference sprang both the hope of blissful union and the need for constant negotiation and celebration of difference in order to achieve that union. *E pluribus unum*: marriage manuals thus constructed modern heterosexuality as an achievement analogous to the governmental structure and imagined community of the United States.

The Normalization of Whiteness

If the concept of democratic sexual self-government appears racially neutral, it is partly because its pursuit was so intimately connected to the power-evasive process by which whiteness became "normal." In the early twentieth century the American capacity for self-government was widely represented as a racial trait. For instance, one handbook for recent immigrants explained that the "Anglo-Saxon people is preeminent . . . in the art of self-governance. Of all the nations founded in the western hemisphere, only those established by settlers in which the British strain is predominant, have attained real stability or spread the blessings of democracy."[86] At the same time, polar difference between the sexes had long been a hallmark of civilized whiteness. The nature of that difference was called into question by the immense transformations in gender relations that influenced every aspect of modern life and that crystallized in women's admission to suffrage in 1920. The consolidation and normalization of heterosexuality—at once a relational ideal based on the eroticization of sexual difference and a civic ideal based on formal equality and mutual consideration—cannot be separated from contemporary changes in the content of gender, what it meant to be a man or a woman, that intersected in important ways with changes in white racial meaning.

In the last decades of the nineteenth century, the genteel consensus seems to have been that feminine sexuality was reproductive in its essence; refined white women allegedly experienced desire primarily as the craving for maternity.[87] White women's natural reproductivity served as a corrective to men's cravings for genital pleasure, which might exceed civilized moral control if not balanced by their wives' different priorities. In the 1920s and 1930s, however, though men were still assumed to be more conscious of their sexual needs, feminine white sexuality was sometimes represented as analogous to white men's, a shift that is registered in marriage manuals and other works on modern sexuality by the comparison of the clitoris to the penis as the erectile seat of erotic delight.[88] This new view of men and women as similar in the sexual pursuit of individual happiness had significant implications for racial meaning. If the difference between the white sexes turned out not to be so dramatic after all, how were whites to imagine and represent their evolutionary superiority to the "less evolved" races? If middle-class Anglo women's sexual desires could no longer be imagined as checking and balancing their husbands' lusts, what new standards of sexual morality and self-control could provide a solid foundation for the civilized social order central to the meaning—and high valuation—of American whiteness? When ideal married love no longer meant the willing submission of white wives in response to their husbands' sexual needs, and the principled self-restraint of white husbands in response to their wives' erotic indifference, how could husbands and wives perform the racially unique tenderness of their mutual regard?

Marital advice literature answered such questions by insisting on the importance of heterosexuality, the eroticization of sexual difference so that it could further sexual and social union.[89] The racial connotations of both sexual difference and the self-discipline necessary for mutually satisfying intercourse suggest that heterosexuality was one of the discursive sites where changes in the meaning of gender coincided with changes in the meaning of race. Matthew Frye Jacobson has argued that the varied white races of nineteenth-century immigrants were consolidated into a relatively monolithic "Caucasian" racial category by the middle of the twentieth century. His account suggests that the earlier stages of this unification coincided with the peak years of the "marriage crisis."⁹⁰ Like the reconfiguration of gender at this time, the reconfiguration of race had multiple origins in culture, economy, and law, including the "Great Migration" of African Americans out of the South (which peaked in the decade between 1910 and 1920) and restrictions on immigration after 1924. In response to such changes, by the early 1940s the multiplicitous racial environment of the turn of the century had given way to a "bifurcated racial climate" in which "the whiteness of the former white races became more salient than the differences between them."⁹¹

Another way to say this is that as the color line hardened in the early twentieth century, "probationary" whites were deemed better approximations of the WASP political and moral ideal of the self-governing republican subject than they once had been. This reassessment had a distinctly erotic element. Around the turn of the century, as respectable Anglo womanhood was reconfigured to include erotic appetite, one of the chief lines of demarcation that distinguished refined white women from what well-bred Victorians had called "females" disappeared. At the same time, nineteenth-century white ideals of refined manly self-restraint began to give way to a new valorization of primitive virility as the essence of natural maleness.⁹² The literature of marital breakdown suggests that the old genteel requirement of white self-discipline continued to inflect the new, and relatively ethnically inclusive, heterosexual ideal of forceful masculinity mated with erotic femininity but was modified and inflected by it as well.

Marriage manuals rarely used racially explicit language, but when they did their usage mobilized the conceptual connections that bound the modernization of marriage to transformations in racial definition. I have already noted that marriage manuals' descriptions of sexually inconsiderate husbands as "primitive" or "savage" worked to define men's erotic thoughtfulness and good technique as evolutionary achievements. Yet at the same time, such men were bad lovers precisely to the extent that they embodied and performed the efficiency characteristic of white civilization in the machine age. Husbands like "Mr. Smith" were represented as uncivilized by the very same token that they were represented as typically modern. This temporal paradox reflects the collapse of ideal whiteness, in both its erotic and its political modes, into the cultivation of sensitivity: the construction of machine-age whiteness as cold to the point of anaesthesia brought it into close discursive alignment with definitions of preindustrial whiteness as coarse, insensitive, and unfeeling. When measured against the new heterosexual mandate of shared erotic pleasure, all forms of white insensitivity appeared to have more in common than they had in the distinctly different sexual context of the Gilded Age.

Men's indifference to women's sexual rights and needs, in short, had much the same blighting effect whether it expressed barbaric tyranny or modern efficiency. Thus contradictory representations of men's sexual selfishness and haste as indicating both primitivism and modernity reflected the incorporation of the "probationary" races into a white racial definition that had previously taken its dominant referents from genteel Anglo culture. The new ideal of vigorous masculinity might have involved imperative, aggressive desires rooted in the evolutionary past, and this might have been a good thing for the strength of the race, but moderns were not supposed to let those desires gain mastery over them; they were supposed to harness natural energies for productive ends, like nurturing home and civilization. Men like "Mr. Smith" were potent, but that alone did not make them good sexual citizens. Similarly, when women like "Mrs. Smith" decided that they did not care for sex, they were mobilizing an ideal of white womanhood that had once signified their civilized superiority but that now indicated only that they were badly out of date. Simultaneously modern and "Victorian" in their coldness, such women found the sexually charged intimacy of modern marriage out of their reach.

The temporal problem confronting couples like the "Smiths," then, was not only about the difference in erotic pacing that distinguished women from men; it was also about the difference in erotic sensitivity and thoughtfulness that distinguished more and less "evolved" classes and races of whites from one another. Modern men and women, by definition, reconciled their temporal differences through the cultivation of heterosexuality, which allowed them to meet on the grounds of formal equality without addressing women's continuing subordination. Similarly, "old stock" and "probationary" whites could find a certain reconciliation through the careful combination of primitive sexual vigor and WASP self-discipline in ideal modern marriage.

This racial reconciliation, like the gender reconciliation of heterosexuality, worked by obscuring rather than resolving the hierarchical relations between the different kinds of whiteness. Marital imagery could make intraracial as well as intergender difference seem benign. One early-twentieth-century handbook for new immigrants explained that, while the putative English "racial genius" for constitutional law naturally guided the political life of the nation, the "imagination, adaptability, . . . art, music, decoration" characteristic of "the French man, the Italian, the Slav, the German, the Hibernian, the Scandinavian" were also valuable additions to the culture of the United States.[93] In this description Anglo-Saxons, the original citizens and "founders of the Republic," occupied a position of mastery and guidance in relation to the other white races, who contributed the feminine, aesthetic touches that make well-to-do white men more comfortable. The polyglot nation was represented as a bourgeois marriage in which some were more equal than others.

Cecil B. De Mille's film *Madame Satan* provides a more vividly sexual illustration of the way that the vigor associated with probationary whites could be incorporated into modern marriages without fundamentally challenging the ethnic hierarchy within whiteness. This 1930 drama tells the story of an excessively refined wife, Angela, whose frigidity drives her husband, Bob, into the arms of a chorus girl. On the level of the plot, the essential contrast between the two women is that Trixie likes sex and Angela does not. This erotic difference is visually represented through ethnic markers: Angela's tall, narrow figure, blonde hair, Roman nose, and round chin establish her as an "old stock" WASP, while Trixie's plump body, heart-shaped face, and bouncing black curls mark her as vaguely Irish.[94] The film represents the WASP woman as unable to let go of her self-control and the "probationary" white as lacking it altogether, stereotypes so predictable they would hardly be worth noting except that both ethnic / erotic positions are depicted as incommensurable with marriage. Bob and Angela are on the verge of divorce, while a series of situational jokes about how absurd it is to imagine Trixie as a wife make it clear that she is the kind of woman wealthy WASP men enjoy on a purely recreational basis. It is her sexual vigor, not her value as a prospective mate, that constitutes a threat to this marriage. Accordingly, Angela must let go of her respectability sufficiently to become sexy herself, while still retaining her race and class status as the kind of woman WASP men marry.

She does this by developing the persona of "Madame Satan" at a masquerade ball to which Bob has gone with Trixie. Madame Satan is everything Angela appears not to be—dark where Angela is light, scandalously erotic where Angela is repressed, amusing where Angela is reproachful—but she is also quite different from Trixie: mysterious where Trixie is obvious, elegant where Trixie is vulgar, and, most important, sensitive to sexual morality where Trixie is coarsely indifferent to it. Within minutes of her entry every man at the ball has flocked to Madame Satan's feet. When a furious Trixie challenges her to remove her mask, she refuses on the grounds that everyone has something to conceal and asks how many of the men clustered around her are pretending they are not married. Of course, they cluster all the closer, at which she laughs in triumph. The sequined flames that make up her extremely daring gown combine with her nom de guerre to underscore Madame Satan's mobilization of the moral wrong of adultery as the source of its excitement. Madame Satan thus combines a powerfully erotic presence with a marital ethic that makes her infinitely more fascinating than her cheap and easy rival.

It is no accident that this combination of sexual and moral sophistication is performed in a caressing French accent. More civilized than the shanty Irish, but unhampered by the Puritan strain in Anglo-Saxon Protestantism, the iconic French woman combines erotic, emotional, and moral sensitivity. The only problem is that Madame Satan's sensitivity does not prevent her from enjoying the company of married men like Bob. Sophisticated French ethics might turn out to include a certain tolerance for lapses in sexual fidelity; not so the Anglo-American marital ideal. So the plot twists until Madame Satan is forced to unmask. When Angela's blonde head emerges from Madame Satan's black sequined hood, Bob learns that his "frigid" wife is the exquisitely, passionately sensitive woman he hoped to make his mistress, while his "paramour" can be relied on to be completely faithful to him because she was really his wife all along. The film thus depicts the perfect white wife as a WASP woman who has assimilated a Continental erotic abandon into her existing capacity for moral and emotional self-control.

In this example as in many others, the reconciliation of the different white races depended on a distinct hierarchy within whiteness, crowned by continuing WASP dominance. Ideal modern marriage could incorporate a certain amount of "ethnic" difference, but only to the extent that the sexual charge associated with it remained subordinate to the "Anglo-Saxon . . . art of self-governance." When WASPs like Angela adopted the sexual intensity of "probationary" whiteness, their marriages would be strengthened and their reproduction assured. When Western European immigrants like Madame Satan practiced the self-government associated with Anglo-Saxons, they were that much closer to shedding their "probationary" status by performing adherence to normative white ideals. Such representations of successful assimilation helped to suggest that the lowliest "probationary" whites' continuing social and economic inequality expressed their failures to discipline themselves rather than the class and ethnic hierarchy with which they had to contend. For instance, the narrative logic of De Mille's film suggests that if Trixie had kept her maidenhood, refused to entertain married men, and put more effort into controlling her temper, she too could have wed a rich Anglo. Adherence to WASP disciplinary ideals did not become optional as whiteness expanded to include people from a greater variety of cultural backgrounds.

Rather, "probationary" whites were urged to adopt those disciplines, modernizing their sexual conduct and their understanding of marriage in a way that facilitated their assimilation into the imagined community of the twentieth-century United States. In his 1930 work *Love in the Machine Age* Floyd Dell argued that immigrants to the United States sometimes made the mistake of trying to preserve their cultural traditions of "patriarchal tyranny" over their children's sexual and relational choices.[95] Dell believed that the exercise of such parental authority over marriage prevented people from becoming self-governing adults. In earlier stages of civilization's development the resulting widespread "infantilism" had helped to ensure tight familial and social bonds, but it also produced erotic and gender systems marred by marital coercion, perversity, and infidelity; Dell specified "homosexuality, prostitution-patronage, and polite adultery" as symptoms of submission to archaic sexual authoritarianism.[96] In contrast, with the rise of the machine age truly "adult heterosexuality" and "normal family life" could combine in "the essentially democratic relation of modern marriage" for the first time in history.[97]

Dell's discussion turned on the conflation of the modern and the adult with the normal, a conflation that emphasizes the racial assumptions structuring his paean to heterosexuality: the claim that truly modern spouses were the first to achieve true adulthood resonates with the era's racist and imperialist constructions of nonwhite people as permanent children, incapable of self-rule and therefore requiring guidance from more advanced races. At the same time, Dell's discussion situated implicitly white immigrants as perverse not in themselves—Dell made a point of explaining that sexual compromise and "infantilism" were normal in preindustrial contexts—but in the context of the twentieth-century United States.[98] Modern heterosexuality required taking up the burden of free self-determination in personal as well as political relationships. The disciplined practice of sexual liberty produced loving, egalitarian, monogamous marriage as surely as the practice of political liberty produced just democratic government. As the principal of a Progressive Era night school for new immigrants expressed the political logic of this analogy, "liberty, in America, has always been indissolubly linked with union."[99] To the extent that immigrants pursued eroticized marriage based on the thrill of difference between formal equals, they proved themselves capable of adjusting to modernity, leaving the primitive past behind and becoming "normal," unhyphenated white Americans qualified to exercise their citizenship rights.

The realignment of racial politics around a consolidated, relatively inclusive whiteness such as Matthew Frye Jacobson describes is clearly visible in this new politico-moral definition of the normal citizen. The development of heterosexuality helped guarantee that modern whiteness was much more broadly accessible than the version articulated by late-nineteenth-century gentlefolk. In the Gilded Age, the "ethnic" whites, such as the Irish, Italians, and Jews, were likely to be classified as less perfectly white than WASPs on the basis of their presumed sexual license and its resemblance to the failures of self-control attributed to African Americans (with whom, indeed, they were sometimes alleged to fornicate).[100] During the years between the two world wars, the literature of marital breakdown worked to redefine sexual self-control in terms of the deliberate cultivation of eroticism between men and women. Emerging representations of erotic heterosexuality as the hope for the future of nation, race, and civilization cannot be separated from emerging conceptions of "probationary" whites as reasonably legitimate American citizens.

The marital metaphor for successful assimilation defined legitimate participation in the nation broadly enough to encompass literally millions of whites who adopted American marital norms. I do not mean to suggest that marital imagery had the force of law in relation to citizenship but rather to point to the way that power-evasive images of solidarity and complementarity between husbands and wives could make the hierarchical relationships between different kinds and classes of whites appear politically innocent, while ethnic and class differences appeared incidental in comparison to the basic familial values held by all "normal" Americans. The chain of associations that linked heterosexuality to marriage to the nation repositioned all but the most politically marginal and/or poorest whites (perverts, "hillbillies," whores and hustlers, the "feebleminded," and the young) as potentially docile, sexually self-governing, free citizens. Modern marriage, that is, represented a new racial and sexual credential for membership in the imagined community of the nation. At the same moment that the literature of marital breakdown expanded conceptual access to whiteness for previously probationary ethnic and religious groups, it specified the disciplinary requirements for "normal" marriage. To the extent that they met those requirements through the performance of modern marital heterosexuality, most whites, for the first time, could perceive themselves as "normal" in relation to the nation.

In fact, though adhering to dominant sexual and familial norms could certainly help probationary whites Americanize, such adherence was never sufficient to make people normal: poverty, accented English, and dark skin all continued to be marks of inferiority or marginality that could trump even the most rigorous conformity to modern marital ideals. Representations of whiteness as love, heterosexuality as liberty, and marriage as citizenship were profoundly power-evasive; whatever credibility they had stemmed from willful ignorance of the real differences in the ways that different kinds of whites were positioned in relation to the allegedly universal relational values of white civilization, and to the rewards of full citizenship, personal liberty, and cultural belonging that were supposed to accrue to "normal" whites. That power-evasion helped to produce race-evasion. When normal whiteness was represented in terms of a spousal love inseparable from sexual citizenship, more different kinds of Americans found themselves solicited to become "white," and the cultural-hereditary specificity and privilege of waspness eroded. Through just such discursive constructions the cultural contents of whiteness, unmodified, began to seem vaporous.

Conclusion: The Future Made Flesh

No marriage manual suggested, of course, that nation and civilization prospered when the mass of white citizens devoted their energies chiefly to pursuing sexual pleasure. Rather, the experience of perfect union provided white couples with a template for, and reminder of, the ideal experience of normal modern life. That reminder was necessary, in the cultural logic of early-twentieth-century America, because modernity threatened to undermine the foundations of the civilization that made it possible. Mechanization struck at the root of love; of family and home and marriage; of duty and pleasure; of labor and creativity; of the important differences between men and women, human and machine, old-stock WASPs and new immigrants. Modern white civilization was unstable and destabilizing. It was also cold and heartless and caused considerable suffering. At all these different levels, the machine age called into question the legitimacy of white dominance and the desirability of white civilization.

Marital advice literature invoked the fear of dissolution, the end of the WASP order of things, while it also answered that fear with the assertion that a new and improved modern order was already emerging. The brave new world the marriage manuals envisioned was one which preserved American civilization's legacy of whiteness by expanding access to its central disciplinary values via mass training in erotic self-control. The normalization of disciplined marital sex expanded the boundaries of whiteness to include a much broader range of citizens than earlier racial configurations had done. It also reproduced, in miniature, the mutual respect that made democracy possible, despite difference and inequality among citizens. The uniquely modern use of rational, scientific time management to enhance tenderness and intimacy appeared to offer further evidence that suffering was incidental, not essential to modernity; that progress was consistent with humanity; and that white civilization was essentially benign. By insisting that freedom and loyalty, consideration and care, were the core realities of truly modern marriages, the literature of the marriage crisis reassured whites that "their" civilization derived its power not only from technology but from the moral strength of respect for difference. That strength and respect were immanent in every disciplined act of marital lovemaking. Thus the sign of modern civilized whiteness, and of hope for the future of the nation, was simultaneous orgasm.

Simultaneous orgasm granted couples a glimpse of perfect union between men and women. But no matter how carefully synchronized the sex or how white the values it expressed, no marriage could be fully normal until it had borne fruit. Manuals were explicit about this point. When two separate lives were united, they created "a new entity, a new spiritual reality, which grows from that union as a child grows from the union of two cells."[101] Sooner or later, repetitions of this experience would lead "every normal couple" to want to make that fusion of selves as materially real as it could be.[102] Simultaneous orgasm was a sign of whiteness as an ideal relationship to the nation, but it was not its material substance. A new generation of pale bodies was required to carry on the legacy of the race. These white children were bred to inherit a country whose founding dreams of independent reason, egalitarianism, respect for difference, and personal happiness were performed in the act by which they were conceived. When their turn came, they would marry wisely and labor well. They would be the standard-bearers for civilization.

But how on earth could you communicate this vision to a four-year-old?

BIRDS, BEES, AND THE FUTURE OF THE RACE:
MAKING WHITENESS NORMAL

Sexual Knowledge and Normal Adjustment

Miss Isabel Davenport had agreed to meet with the interested girls after classes one Monday around 1920.[1] They reserved a corner of the auditorium for their talk, expecting perhaps seventy-five young women, but on Monday afternoon when Davenport arrived "there was already a large number seated and students pouring in mass down the stairways and into the two entrances of the room as for a general assembly. Thinking that the student body had been called together for some purpose and that our meeting would have to be postponed, I enquired of some of the young women what all the students were coming in for. They replied, for the talk on sex instruction."[2] Davenport convened this meeting because she wanted to conduct dissertation research into the sexual interests of "well-adjusted normal" adolescent girls.[3] But Davenport had no intention of conducting sex education for the entire student body of the New York Training School for Teachers, and so she had the doors of the auditorium locked against the crowds and began trying to winnow out the less serious students. She hoped that, if she managed "to discourage the weak and possibly morbidly inclined," only the healthy, responsible, and highly motivated students would make the effort to apply for inclusion.[4]

Out of the one hundred sixty-one students in the auditorium, only one dropped out. The rest generated over nine hundred questions.[5] Their interest certainly exceeded Davenport's stated expectation, but she registered no great surprise. With many of her contemporaries between 1913 and 1940, she took for granted that normal young moderns were eager to learn about sex.[6] She was nonetheless appalled that they asked such "childish and . . . trivial" questions about sex, questions which presented "a lamentable picture of ignorance and superstition" to her investigative gaze.[7]

In the early twentieth century as in the Gilded Age, allegations of immaturity and superstition carried connotations of a mental and emotional coarseness widely associated with the "primitive" races. Like hysterical women or sexually selfish husbands, Davenport's students remained at a low level of development regarding sex; they had failed to achieve the unique blend of thought and feeling that defined fully civilized white adults. Most of these students were within a year of earning the teachers' certificates that would authorize them to transmit white civilization to the next generation of Americans. Yet their training had omitted the information about the biological and social reproduction of the race that would enable them to fulfill their noble charge. Not only did they know next to nothing about anatomy or physiology; Davenport reported that the girls seemed completely oblivious to modern understandings of "love between the sexes as an element in normal adjustment."[8] The students showed no interest whatever in the "ideal aspects" of marriage "as an education and discipline and means of entrance into a larger and fuller life."[9] Equally ignorant of "scientific truth . . . and modern idealism regarding sex," these young people lacked both the informed rationality and the moral, spiritual, and aesthetic sensitivities that were the greatest achievements of white civilization.[10]

The "question at stake" as Davenport explained it, "is what the nation is going to do with the native racial tendencies of her girls." If the mating and mothering instincts of "well-adjusted normal" Americans were allowed to "go to waste" for lack of expert cultivation, the "inevitable result" was not only personal unhappiness but "social deterioration."[11] Conversely, careful guidance could foster the "development of the girl's native racial tendencies into conscious desire for wholesome love, marriage, and motherhood."[12] Boys, she added, were also susceptible to educational channeling of their sexual impulses and emotions toward the socially valuable end of fatherhood.[13] The end result of such training would be normal sexuality, the thoughtful, disciplined, marital lovemaking through which each white generation (ideally) passed its racial heritage of biology and culture on to the future. The construction of marital heterosexuality as a privileged site for the production and expression of white civilization's ideals contributed a certain urgency and cogency to the project of training children to be normal. Sex education—like marital advice for adults—was an educational technology for implanting the rational and relational values at the core of ideal whiteness in the population at large.

At least since the Enlightenment, sex education has been a part of the process by which privileged children are guided into adulthood; think, for instance, of the elaborate care with which Rousseau formed Emile's developing passions.[14] But sexual pedagogy has been pursued on a mass level only in the twentieth century. The movement for sex education in the public schools began in the years after 1910. During this decade, public concern about the loss of a unified, homogeneous (white) American culture reached a virulently nativist pitch, while an increasing number of people articulated their worries about the social consequences of widespread sexual misery and pathology. These fears intersected with an equally vocal optimism about the efficacy of education in curing most social ills. Isabel Davenport was only one of thousands who argued for an "adequate specific education" about sex as a form of national and racial hygiene.[15]

According to contemporaries, "a large number of the most enlightened people" were turning to education "in their search for progress toward the solution of the great sexual problems."[16] One important practical reason for this trend was steadily increasing enrollments in public schools during the first decades of the century. Schooling in office and technical skills, such as typing or draftsmanship, seemed to promise young white moderns stronger positions in the labor market of managerial capitalism than apprenticeships or other forms of on-the-job training. Especially as the Depression deepened, more and more young people deferred looking for a job and instead completed high school. Where a high school diploma was a mark of distinction in 1910, by 1940 it was common among whites. Thus, during the same years that marital sex advice was teaching adults that simultaneous orgasms could save white civilization, the youth of the race was a relatively captive audience in classrooms across America. Sex educators stepped in to teach them that the indicatively white management of sexuality in monogamous marriage was, in a word, normal.

Between 1910 and 1940, sex education was a major cultural site for articulating the bourgeois familial and social patterns that helped to define ideal whiteness, and for training young people of varied backgrounds to reproduce those normative patterns in their sexual behavior. Sex education held forth the hope that the first generation of Americans born and reared under fully modern conditions could achieve reproductive perfection in biologically and socially "normal" families. Toward this end, sex educators and reformers like Isabel Davenport tried to influence the terms in which ordinary boys and girls thought about sex. That is, they attempted to intervene in popular sexual discourses, implanting their vision of normal, modern family life in place of the vulgar sexualities that they perceived as detrimental to American civilization.

To date, the most comprehensive scholarly study of sex education in the United States is Jeffrey Moran's *Teaching Sex: The Shaping of Adolescence in the Twentieth Century*. Moran interprets sex education primarily as a social-control movement directed at preventing adolescents from having sex before marriage. Certainly, premarital chastity was a central behavioral goal of modern sex education. Yet this version of the social-control argument overlooks the significance of race. Sex education had an obviously eugenic dimension in many cases. Further, sex education was not only about behavior but about the shaping of the self in accord with "modern idealism regarding sex." The sexual self-control that was the chief goal of the movement for sex education in the public schools was a deeply racialized private virtue, a psychic stance in relation to ideal whiteness, as much as it was a behavioral mandate. The point was not simply to impose conservative morality on the young and vulnerable and to enforce it with whatever external means were necessary but rather to transmit the inner, disciplinary essence of white civilization to the next generation.

Further, it seems that sex education contributed to the homogenization of whiteness through its efforts to replace diverse sexual cultures with a consistent national approach to love, sex, and family life. Students in sex education classrooms not only learned that they should not have sex before marriage. They also learned that only one form of marriage, inspired by one kind of romantic love, erotically expressed in a uniform commitment to monogamy and instantiated in one sort of household structure, was "normal" for Americans. Sex education, in brief, offered diverse white Americans access to and training in the predictable, disciplined sexual and relational patterns that had once helped to ground WASP elites' sense of their racial superiority over the vulgar herd. The methodological and classroom materials generated in this culturally interventionist effort form the source base for this chapter. Though we will see that sex education strategies varied from author to author and over the thirty-year period under study, the pedagogical goal remained consistent. Young moderns were fairly systematically taught that only a domestic, marital, and reproductive mode of sexual expression was normal, that is, reasonably consistent with health and happiness. Deviation from that normal mode carried potentially serious consequences for the individual, the nation, and the race.

Frank Reticence

This was as true of communication about sex as it was true of sexual acts. As we will see, one of the characteristic traits of "approved" sexual expression was its distinctively modern style, which combined the ability to communicate about sex with a skilled, intentional evasion of the erotic. Training in this style was an important part of modern mass education in being a normal white American.[17] Because sex education in public schools was a major cultural site for developing and transmitting this modern mode of sexual communication, it helped to constitute the normal white American as such. Modern normality required the disciplined privatization of desire, its behavioral and linguistic containment within the (ideal white American) family and within a racially coded expressive etiquette.

I would like to clarify several points before I turn to close readings of sex education materials. First, the expressive etiquette in which I am interested here did not involve the strict exclusion of speech about sex, any more than the privatization of citizenship required the extirpation of passion from white marriage beds. On the contrary, a certain direct simplicity of speech was essential in the performance of normality. Moderns called this directness "frankness," and many valued it as a sign of a normal, wholesome sexuality. Shame about sex and discomfort at its entrance into language suggested something smutty and unwholesome in one's relation to it, a "Victorian" prurience that was inconsistent with modern ideals. But normal frankness and simplicity in sexual expression was not the same thing as the abandonment of self-control. Instead, frankness was a performance of a very carefully calibrated capacity for appropriate expression. Normal sexual communication required what I can only call "frank reticence."

This leads to my second point. While sex education was a technology for the homogenization of whiteness, its signature combination of frankness with reticence about eroticism was important in the modernization of blackness as well. A number of black feminist theorists and historians have pointed to the crucial importance of a carefully constructed and managed silence about desire in the construction of modern African American standards of respectability, especially as these referred to women's sexuality and subjectivity. Darlene Clark Hine, for example, has described the "culture of dissemblance" in which black women cultivated an appearance of openness and ease while concealing their inner selves and especially their eroticism.[18] Hine interprets black women's frank reticence as an armor assumed in response to the pervasive racist construction of blackness as hypersexuality. Importantly, the culture of dissemblance had both personal and racial dimensions: individual women hoped to find some shelter from sexual exploitation in their performance of sexual discretion and respectability, and many of them hoped that their "super-moral" stance would refute the myth of black bestiality and thus reflect positively on their race.[19] Evelyn Brooks Higginbotham adds that some relatively privileged black women used the association of sexual reticence with racial pride to justify their attempts to denigrate and control the sexual expression of less refined people.[20] At stake in such policing was the right to define which modes of sexual expression were acceptably black, and to whom. The implication is that a new racial ideal may have been formed for blackness as well as for whiteness. Was sex education a site for the homogenization and normalization of black racial meaning as well as for white? If so, what ought we to make of this parallel development during Jim Crow, when the difference and inequality of the races was firmly enforced? Before we can answer these questions we need more detailed information about sexual pedagogy in black schools—research into the limited archival record on the subject has just begun—but the indications are that for black children and youth as for white ones, the management of sexual expression and self-revelation was a major part of the pedagogical project.[21]

"Frank reticence," then, was not unique to whites but rather may have been significant in the early-twentieth-century reconfiguration of racial meanings more generally. Nonetheless, it was central to the discursive construction of the homogeneous, indicatively white sexuality called "normality." Hence my final preliminary point, which is that a uniform expressive etiquette of white sex was a discursive ideal that only gradually and partially came to resemble a social reality. The social historians Kathy Peiss and George Chauncey, among others, have documented publicly expressive sexual cultures (and conflicts over modes of expression) among urban whites from diverse ethnic backgrounds.[22] Such accounts suggest that, just as was true in the black communities Hines and Higginbotham discuss, class origins and aspirations exerted a powerful pull on the modes of sexual expression considered legitimate and appropriate within a given white community context. Not everybody wanted to be normal, and especially before the 1920s, there was no cross-group consensus about what normality involved in any case. As norms became more clearly defined, indeed, one might expect to find them more vividly contested in oppositional communities. Thus it would be a serious mistake to imagine that all white people were reticent or that the same rules of sexual expression applied in all the subcultures of whiteness in America. What I am trying to get at is the extent to which sex-education discourse worked to streamline and standardize the diversity of existing sexual cultures, in the hope that they could be rendered more like one another because they had all been rendered more like a preexisting white racial ideal.

That project would not have had any political or conceptual impetus if "normal" reticence had been integral to earlier, less monolithic versions of whiteness, or if those many racial positions had had more in common. Sex education was, in part, a technology for expanding a particular vision of whiteness, with its valorization of sexual self-control and privatized emotional intensity, and making these synonymous with modern white racial identity. This construction required the conceptual elision of sexually "sloppy" (that is, overly expressive) or otherwise deviant whites as well as the exclusion of more obviously racialized Others. Thus some working-class or queer or "ethnic" white positions retained racially probationary status on sexual grounds, while others gained relatively stable access to white racial privilege partly by virtue of their participation in the "normal" familial culture of sexual reticence and self-control.

Many historians of sexuality have documented the process by which diverse sexual cultures were pathologized in the early twentieth century, and several have used the records of normalizing agencies to recover descriptive data about those cultures.[23] Sex education has not figured prominently in such research in large part because sexual pedagogy in public schools never mobilized experientially explicit speech, detailed accounts of pleasure, vice, or perversion, or other expressions of familiarity with the multiple sexual worlds of the early-twentieth-century United States. These worlds were antithetical to the domestic, private space of the normal, and verbal acknowledgment of their existence could call one's own normality into question if it were not handled in an appropriately distant and judgmental way.[24] Therefore sexual pedagogues expended a great deal of effort and ink quarreling with one another about expressive etiquette in the professional practice of sex education. Their discussions on the subject constitute a rich metadiscursive archive of contestation over the rules for assessing and performing normal communication about sex. All, however, agreed that vulgarity was out of the question. In consequence, all young moderns who received formal schooling about sex were taught to employ an experientially indirect, usually either metaphorical or scientific, mode when talking about sexuality. Any other expressive mode was uncivilized, and as such marked its articulator as less than fully white.

In chapter 2 we saw an excellent example of this indirect mode of sexual expression in "Mrs. Smith's" description of her husband as "running for the train" while she preferred a "pleasure walk." There I argued that this metaphorical depiction of Mr. Smith resonated with contemporary constructions of savage sexuality in a way that made him, and other sexually inconsiderate husbands, seem like racial backsliders even in the absence of overt references to race. Here it is just as relevant that Mrs. Smith's demure image performed a double distancing from such savagery. Not only does she describe herself as a lady of leisure out for a breath of sweet summer air in the garden; she also avoids any hint of the sordid by the simple device of leaving bodies, emotions, and sensations entirely out of her account of her marital troubles. Her civilized whiteness is performed in her ability to communicate a wealth of information about her sexual experience without ever approaching the borders of the experientially explicit. In sex-education materials as in marriage manuals, the indirect discourse inseparable from normal sexuality contained important racial references. Being normal required verbal adherence to sexual and discursive ideals that were saturated with representations of and beliefs about race.

This was as true on the level of content as it was on the level of rhetorical explicitness. Much early-twentieth-century sex education discourse suggested that white superiority, which was manifested and reproduced through a specific form of marital heterosexuality, was biologically natural. Modern sex instruction for children and adolescents claimed that the combination of sexual self-discipline with tender, fruitful love between spouses was essential both for individual and familial health, and also for the future development of race and nation. Only this particularly civilized form of sexuality and family life reflected the natural order of things required for individual and social health and determined by evolution. Sexual self-restraint in modern marriage was simply right. There are clear resonances here with the use of nature images in marital advice literature—Mrs. Smith walked, like God, in the garden. Most modern sex education used references to evolutionary or medical science to make conventionally gendered, emotionally intimate, two-generational white family structures appear uniquely natural and healthy. In short, sex-education materials existed to expand, defend, and strengthen what a later generation would call the "nuclear" family. That term never appears in sex instructional materials from before the Second World War, however, and so it seems more appropriate to refer to that particular biological, social, emotional, and sexual configuration as the "evolutionary" family. This nomenclature is the more appropriate because it emphasizes the whiteness which sex-education narratives most frequently left implicit. Thus modern sex education was an indirect way of communicating not only the core disciplinary contents of ideal whiteness but also the "natural" supremacy of those ideals over all others.

In short, systematic training in heterosexism and in the civilized bourgeois etiquette of reticence was also training in racism. Mass sex education conflated the achievement of "normal" sexuality with physical health and the evolution of whiteness. And just as normal heterosexuality was, by definition, reticent about sexual desire and practice, normal whiteness was inarticulate about racial politics and power. Sex education literature's almost total silence about race should not be interpreted as indifference or inclusiveness. Reticence about race is not race-neutrality, and contempt for non-normative sexualities is not epiphenomenal in relation to the consolidation of the normative whiteness characterized by such reticence. On the contrary, whiteness was disseminated as normality in part through a pedagogy that depicted monogamous marriage as the natural foundation of modern civilization. This naturalizing pedagogy enabled sex educators to disseminate normative sexual ideals without mentioning the complex hierarchies of race that had originally given those ideals their specific contents; biological narratives helped them to universalize whiteness under the sign of the "normal." As it polished its strategies for communicating normality to the young people who represented the future of American civilization, sex education developed an approach to the reproduction of whiteness that worked by indirection, euphemism, and metaphor. Through just such techniques was ideal whiteness rendered normal, its erotic and racial specificity masked by a performance of racially coded sexual and expressive restraint and discretion.

Specific strategies for the normalization of sexual cultures took shape in relation to the widespread sexual beliefs and value systems sex educators wanted to supplant. Two such vulgar beliefs were repeatedly attacked as especially pernicious to individual and racial health. These were the "doctrine of necessity," or the belief that sex was necessary for men's health, and the belief that gonorrhea was "no worse than a bad cold."[25] The "doctrine of necessity" held that regular sexual intercourse was a biological requirement for men. This doctrine constituted a direct attack on the evolutionary family in that it justified white men's abandonment of sexual self-control and ignored the social and racial consequences. It therefore undermined the connection between sex and marital romance that was so important to modern whiteness, while it contributed to the spread of venereal disease. In turn, the belief that venereal disease was not particularly harmful discouraged infected people from seeking medical treatment or refraining from sex after the first, and most uncomfortable, symptoms passed.

In the effort to counter these beliefs, and the sexual values associated with them, sex educators developed two basic stories about what Davenport called the "scientific truth" of sex. One was a tragic narrative about the medical seriousness of venereal infection and the damage it wreaked in individual lives, in families, and in American society at large. The second story answered the doctrine of sexual necessity with a zoological narrative according to which eons of biological and social development culminated in the evolutionary family. The medical story of venereal threat was the focus of the earliest concerted efforts to introduce sex education to the nation at large, flourishing in the first two decades of the century, while the zoological story of the evolutionary family achieved its greatest popularity between 1925 and 1940.[26]

In the early 1920s, zoological / developmental education gained an edge over information about venereal contagion in cutting-edge pedagogical theory and in some schools and communities. Nonetheless, both strands of thought were reflected in educational materials widely available throughout the period under study here.[27] In my judgment, the relationship between them was not one of simple chronological succession but rather of ongoing contestation over what constituted a truly moral, fully civilized expression of the truth of sex. Although the contest between them was sometimes bitter, the two schools of sex education thought joined forces against a common enemy: the popular, commercial, pleasure-seeking sexuality that flourished in modern cities.[28] All sex educators shared the dream that the next white generation could be inspired by a vision of modern sexuality so compelling that they would gladly conform to the self-disciplinary norms it imposed. Free from venereal disease, repelled by the vulgarity of commercial and perverse sexuality, and secure in the knowledge that ages of evolutionary growth culminated in their marriage beds, they would engage in wholesome and fruitful sex in the service of white civilization.

The Tragic Tale of Venereal Contagion

In 1914 Charles W. Eliot, president emeritus of Harvard and president of the newly formed American Social Hygiene Association, described the venereal diseases as "most destructive of the white race," adding that they were "without doubt the very worst foes of sound family life, and thence of civilization."[29] The tale of venereal contagion was a story of the downfall of white civilization. What made it tragic was that the seeds of destruction were sown in the marriage bed by the very white men who were supposed to be the defenders of their families and the social order. As Allen Brandt has shown, social-hygiene activism gained momentum, and its first mass audience, in the context of the United States' extensive military activities of 1916 through 1918.[30] Mobilization on the Mexican border, especially, drew white reformers' attention to the moral and hygienic environment of army life. Predictably, they were horrified at what they found: camps encircled by saloons and houses of prostitution, official tolerance of the "cribs," and correspondingly high rates of venereal disease.

Partly in response to reformers' reports about the corrupt sexual culture of the armed services, the secretary of war formed the Commission on Training Camp Activities less than two weeks after the United States declared war on Germany in April 1917. The CTCA offered soldiers a variety of recreational and religious activities as well as mandatory sex education, all of which were designed to encourage sexual continence among the troops. Access to a "pure" camp culture, and lessons in continence, were intended both to reduce infection rates and to inculcate the sexual self-control and moral fiber that middle-class white morality demanded of good men, good soldiers, and good citizens.[31] The discursive connection between chastity, manliness, and American military strength is clear in the military policy of classifying venereal infections as injuries inflicted "not in the line of duty"— which is to say, as the moral and practical equivalent of shooting oneself in the foot to avoid active service, and therefore subject to court-martial.[32] This policy suggests that, in at least some powerful offices in Washington, men's selfish indulgence of sexual appetites outside of marriage was perceived as a direct challenge to the grand ideals of white civilization that justified the United States' entrance into the war.

While the law governing civilians did not have the power to punish those contracting venereal infections, extramilitary sex education for boys shared many of the assumptions and rhetorical strategies prominent in CTCA-sponsored instruction. From about 1910 on, most pamphlets and books for boys combined some explicit information about the medical consequences of contracting a venereal disease with emphatic messages about the social and racial ravages that syphilis and gonorrhea wrought. The chief difference between the two bodies of literature appears to have been that the literature for soldiers in the Great War typically emphasized the extent to which venereal infections made one's comrades bear the burden of one's moral weakness, while the literature for civilians tended instead to focus on the danger of infecting women and children. In either case, the thing that made venereal disease so utterly dishonorable was a combination of its origin in uncontrolled self-indulgence, with its tendency to attack "innocent" people who had not themselves engaged in acts of venery.

Brandt has shown that CTCA literature sometimes depicted prostitutes as an enemy analogous to German troops in terms of the threat they posed to the vigor of American manhood and the health of the nation's families and homes.[33] In civilian contexts, "civilized" standards of propriety dictated that whores must not be discussed in the graphic, matter-of-fact manner some-times used in talks to enlisted men. In civilian sex-hygiene literature, the rhetoric about prostitutes as sources of infection was transmuted into vague personifications of venereal disease as a traitor or spy which destroyed fam-ilies by insinuating itself into the intimacy between spouses. One pamphlet called venereal disease "a most sinister intruder" whose subtle influence could "absolutely wreck every hope of conjugal felicity."[34] Another writer warned that the convention of polite silence about the venereal threat made the "fatal treachery of gonorrhea" much easier.[35] Just as public exposure rendered political spies powerless, public education undermined vd's power to attack the home.

The metaphor of treachery in civilian sex education conflated the protection of the family (through continence) with the protection of the nation (at arms). This conflation underscores the fact that white ideals of manhood demanded moral and physical self-discipline in service to the weaker members of society.[36] It also highlights the importance of sex education: knowledge about the danger of infection was the weapon a virile man could use to protect "innocent wives," "newborn infants," the nation, the race, and civilization itself from the venereal threat. Thus we can see that narratives of venereal contagion drew on, and participated in normalizing, waspish middle-class ideals of gender in their attempt to enlist the entire nation in an educational war against venereal disease and, through it, the public sexual culture for which disease was a symbol.

Normalizing descriptions of white masculinity as a social ideal permitted reformers to warn boys of every background away from vice and venereal disease without requiring them to use the language of race, or to go into vulgar details about prostitutes or intercourse. Instead, the expressive etiquette governing this kind of sex education articulated the tenets of bourgeois white morality as though they were universal truths: in their world, true manliness lay in disciplining one's desires, and especially in resisting the treacherous lures of commercial vice. Most such works emphasized that only a moral weakling, a cad, or a fool would visit a prostitute and consequently become the means by which his home was conquered by sickness, his wife and children maimed or killed: "he is but a coward who does not shrink from buying voluptuous moments with the hazard of wife and child."[37] One popular 1914 sex instruction manual capped its description of the damages wrought by gonorrhea by inviting its readers to imagine a tiny grave with a tombstone reading:

Here lies a little blind baby,
so afflicted from birth,
offered up by its father as a
sacrifice to his pre-marriage sacrilege
of the sexual relation.

The young reader was offered a choice between being "the murderer of his own child" and being "a real man!"[38] A similar work from 1916 emphasized the martial prowess "real" manhood required. Resisting the urge to indulge in premarital intercourse was the only way a man could be sure he was free of all venereal infection at the time of his marriage. This resistance was "the biggest fight ever waged by man—a fight in secret—without applause."[39] In short, narratives of venereal contagion pulled out some very heavy emotional artillery in the battle to establish white middle-class morality's dominance over the next generation of American males. The normality of whiteness did not just happen; it was taught, in part by manipulating the visceral responses of a generation of adolescents through military metaphors of home protection.

Avoiding the erotically explicit, vulgar speech characteristic of corrupt sexual cultures in no way limited educators to vaporous, vague prose. It simply demanded that they speak clearly and simply, in a tone of upright frankness, about normal white manhood. Though it was generally less martial in its rhetoric, venereal education for girls also substituted very limited middle-class white standards of civilized gender for direct information about sexual acts or sexual cultures. As one pedagogue explained in 1911, "the appeal to normal healthy motherhood is all-sufficient with girls and . . . if only they are given the precautions and relations correctly they will strictly avoid anything which is likely to endanger this function."[40] "Anything," of course, meant premarital and extramarital sex. It also included marriage to men who were not white enough to stay chaste. The "correct" presentation of "precautions and relations" combined the performance of an almost aggressive frankness about reproductive anatomy with an equally marked obscurity about sexual experience. One of Margaret Sanger's pamphlets aimed at working-class women included a richly descriptive anecdote about a twenty-five-year-old whose husband had had gonorrhea before their marriage:

> The doctor found her flowing excessively, the cervix badly torn, the uterus sharply bent back and fixed, ovaries bound down and adherent, the tubes thickened; a leuchorreal discharge was present which contained gonococci, and other symptoms which made her sick and miserable. The doctor operated upon her, scraping the womb, sewing the torn cervix, opening the abdomen to remove the thickened appendix and inflamed ovaries and tubes. She convalesced beautifully, and had no bad or unusual symptoms for six months, at which time she returned with a renewed infection. Careful questioning extracted from the husband the confession that he had been "out with the boys," and had had a recurrence of gonorrhea.[41]

The scientific vocabulary of this passage helps to establish its message as objective truth, in part by performing the frankness that signaled an unconflicted, healthy attitude toward sexuality. Training in that modern expressive mode seems to have been at least as important to Sanger as the transfer of information about sex and disease: few tenement girls would have been able to picture the exact organs and conditions named in this passage, and the source of infection is never clearly specified on either the behavioral or the social level. Despite the obscurity of this passage, however, it makes two general educational points quite clear.

First, it teaches that anatomical objectivity is the approved, "clean" way to understand and represent sex. By putting scare quotes around the young husband's illicit activity—he went "out with the boys"—Sanger marks his colloquial form of sexual reticence as different from and inferior to her scientific one. His makes reference to the camaraderie of males and the "doctrine of necessity"; hers replies with the scientific evidence of the damaged woman's body. Second, the passage conflates that damaged body with a damaged family such that sex is anatomy is reproduction. Sanger's young woman was one of "the innocent" whose body was the prize in the war between pure white family life and corrupt, disease-ridden commercial culture. She suffered because, without access to the knowledge of contagion in her maidenhood, she had had no way to know what her choice of husband would mean for her health and happiness, or for the future of civilization and the race; similarly, she had no way to protect herself against reinfection.[42] Her ignorance was compounded by her husband's self-indulgent failure to protect her against disease, and as a result, invasive surgery rendered her sterile. Venereal disease had won this round of the war over "sound family life."

Here, as in comparable literature for boys, men's ability and willingness to discipline their sexual appetites to a white middle-class ideal appeared fundamental to the survival of civilization. But women shared the responsibility for protecting their capacity for "normal healthy motherhood." If they abdicated the white duty of guarding men's morals and their own purity, they betrayed their essential nature and paid for it with their health. Sanger managed to convey the message that strict adherence to middle-class white moral standards was indispensable to femininity, and to the reproduction of the race, without mentioning exactly what that roving husband did when he was "out with the boys." The extended list of infected body parts, and the tragedy of maternal capacities lost to white civilization, here stand in for information about prostitution, intercourse, and non-normative sexual cultures.

In short, venereal education used "frank reticence" to represent conventional ideals of white middle-class marriage as though they were synonymous with sexual health. That reticence was, in fact, inseparable from their concept of healthy sexuality. Though tragic narratives of venereal contagion are quite graphic in their representations of gender and disease, they are indirect to the point of coyness about sexual practice or sexual culture. Indirection was itself a performance of the normal, healthy morality it sought to implant. It was also a performance of mastery over one's speech as over one's desires. Such mastery was immensely consequential. Narratives of contagion presented strict self-discipline as the white weapon that would make the world safe not only for democracy but also for the normal marriages, homes, and families in which democratic civilization was born and nurtured. For instance, a pamphlet put out by the United States Public Health Service quoted the surgeon general to the effect that venereal disease was "the greatest cause of disability in military life"; the pamphlet enlisted civilians of both sexes in the fight against venereal disease by explaining that "the diseases, being highly contagious, have entered homes and marriage relations. . . . These diseases form a public health problem for civilians to solve in peace as well as in war." After appealing to the urge to protect "innocent young wives" and babies from a variety of medical horrors, the pamphlet expanded its rhetoric from home-protection to patriotic appeal: "No army and no nation can attain to its full vigor when its young men are weakened by venereal disease, when its women are barren, and when its children are defective."[43] The "test of war" proved that ignorance about sex rendered young American men and women vulnerable, and offered the enemy—whether germ or German—an advantage.[44] The tragic narrative of venereal contagion was a strong armor in purity's arsenal, and increasing numbers of public-school teachers stood ready to buckle it on.

"How Shall We Teach?": Strategies of Reticence

Yet for all its rhetorical potency, the "educational attack" in the war to protect the white American family against venereal disease faced a major difficulty in that a clear understanding of the danger to civilization required public reference to illicit sexual activities.[45] Delicate displacements of sexual matters onto lessons in WASP ideals of gender roles modeled a desirable skill at euphemism but did not conceal the fact that the knowledge of contagion necessarily included references to the possibility that one might pursue erotic experience outside of "normal" white marriage. In consequence, many people recoiled from the prospect of venereal education, believing it to be but one short step from actual viciousness. Even the president of the American Social Hygiene Association warned that the attack on venereal disease had to be "high-minded" lest it inadvertently incorporate "suggestions which might invite youth to experiment in sexual vice."[46] Among the basic tenets of sex education was the warning that it must be unlike all other kinds of education, "in that it must not seek to create interest and awaken curiosity in the subject in which it deals."[47] Some people, doubtful that sex educators could "avoid everything which tends to awaken or to intensify either . . . sex consciousness [or] sex emotions," elaborated the need for caution into an argument against teaching sex at all.[48] To them, the knowledge of contagion was itself a contaminant. In 1913 a Jersey City clergyman, John Sheppard, declared: "Just at present our ears are dinned with the fad of sex hygiene. Its introduction into the schools is discussed throughout the country. If ever there was a system diabolically devised to injure our youth, and to make them voluptuaries, this is by far the most effective."[49]

The rhetoric of war against infection that served sex educators also served their opponents. Sheppard's comment was probably a reference to a very public battle in Chicago in 1913. Jeffrey Moran has explained that during that year, Ella Flagg Young used her position as superintendent of schools to introduce a system-wide sex-education program in the Chicago secondary schools, arguing that "sex hygiene" lectures would help to protect the city's youth from the dangers of vice. Although Young had considerable support for her "Chicago Experiment," which was backed by such influential figures as Jane Addams, the lectures were canceled after one semester in response to intense disapproval from the (nonexpert but articulate) public and the city government.[50] In Chicago and around the country, people opposed to sex education in public schools expressed the fear that "sex lectures" would corrupt the youth of America. Unwilling to distinguish frankness from vulgarity, they argued that a consistent, disciplined, unwavering reticence about sexual matters was a more secure foundation of purity. They held that sexual expression had to be restrained at the level of official speech if it was to be restrained at the level of private action.

Another way to say this is that opponents of "sex lectures" sometimes registered their discomfort with the lecture format itself, which seemed to them to violate the most desirable expressive etiquette. If youths were to be discouraged from taking part in the public sexual culture of the city and encouraged to keep their sex private and familial, why should adults model a repellent publicity for them? Should sex instruction not be contained in the safely disciplined spaces where sex itself met physical and moral boundaries —that is, in the home and the church? In response, many educators argued that such strict expressive restraint was not actually good practical training for moral conduct, for the simple reason that modern American culture was already saturated with sex. One very influential sex-education handbook for parents started from the premise that only a child "completely isolated from contact with other persons, or . . . decidedly subnormal in . . . mental powers," could remain in total ignorance of sex.[51] Because truly modern parents were lovers, even the most civilized home was necessarily a sexual environment, and sexual knowledge was bound to emerge from it.[52] When young people went wrong, it was not because they had come into contact with public expressions of sexuality but because their relationships to modern society had been shaped by coarse, lewdly appetitive, commercialized sexual cultures rather than by calm, frank, morally sound scientific ones. As one esteemed educator explained the situation, "sex education from earliest childhood is inevitable. . . . We do not have the choice as to whether or not our children shall have sex education. We do have the choice as to what kind the dominating, character-forming sex impressions shall be."[53] From this point of view, purity was far better served when pure-minded people dominated the sexual conversation than it could possibly be if they tried to model a dignified distance from vice. Silence, sex educators believed, simply ceded the field to the vulgar.

The overt conflict between proponents and opponents of venereal education makes it easy to miss their common ground in the expressive etiquette of normal whiteness. The contest between them was not so much over values as over the best technique for transmitting them to the next generation. Civilized white reticence was equally valuable to both proponents and opponents of venereal hygiene education. Both sides hated and feared the overt sexual expression they associated with vice, and both reserved special scorn for the pleasure-centered sexual cultures that proliferated in modern cities.

Fear of the city as a source of moral contamination was not, of course, new or unique to the Progressive Era. The public, popular cultures of the urban working classes had long been understood as a threat to the purity of "our children," and as we have seen, the mass reproduction even of non-pornographic images had caused genuine alarm among some Gilded Age critics. But the scale of this threat appeared to be something new. Not only were more and more people living in cities in the early twentieth century but commercial amusements were being marketed further and further into the hinterlands. In 1913 William Foster, president of Reed College in Portland, Oregon, listed "the billboards and the picture postcards, the penny-in-the-slot machines and the motion pictures, some of the exhibits of quack doctors, most vaudeville performances, many so-called comic operas, [and] the dress of women approved by modern fashion" among the "schools of sexual immorality" which assailed youth in search of entertainment.[54] These early forms of mass culture were accessible to anyone who could spare a penny; neither an impeccable WASP heritage nor the inability to understand English necessarily disqualified or privileged one in relation to what were predominantly visual representations of the erotic body. Such mechanically reproduced amusements worked to standardize American culture, but not in the ideal white direction approved by sexual pedagogues. In Foster's argument, the ubiquitous sexual stimulation of modern life was dangerous because it prepared "young people to fall before the special temptations that beset all commercial recreation centers."[55] Commercial recreation seemed, in his description, to lead to commercial sex. Youth who patronized "saloons, dance halls, ice-cream parlors, road houses, and amusement parks" made themselves vulnerable to the "enemies of decency," who lurked there to seduce wholesome, farm-raised boys and girls into a mechanically mediated sexuality that killed the spirit and inevitably led to venereal disease.[56]

At first glance interpretations like Foster's seem to be no more than the usual fulminations of the upright bourgeoisie against urban wickedness, which it conventionally attributed to the innate profligacy of the "enemies of decency"—the poor, the "colored," the foreign, the perverse. But the expansion of whiteness in the early twentieth century to include previously "probationary" Americans under its disciplinary umbrella should lead us to look more closely. If a decorous ideal of self-restraint in sexual expression was really becoming central to a newly monolithic (or at least inclusive) white racial meaning, we should expect to see warnings about the dangers of modern, public sexual culture leveled across lines of class and ethnicity in sex education discourse, just as they were in marital advice literature. And in fact, the connection between the commercial motive and mechanical quality of much public entertainment, and the loss of sexual idealism and virtue, was not limited to depictions of the urban working classes at play. Middle-class forms of entertainment also drew criticism for their tendency to foster sexual curiosity and arousal. In 1924, the American Social Hygiene Association's director of education commented on the "oversexed environment" of American cities, in which "literature, art, the drama, amusements, social life, and even commercial advertising are pervaded with the sex appeal."[57] His list suggests that Americans of all classes were constantly solicited by a contaminated sexual culture. From this perspective, reticence was a distant dream. In 1933 an elementary biology teacher and progressive educational theorist from Bronxville, New York, argued that teachers and parents could not afford to "ignore the growing prominence of the sex motive in fiction magazines, books, newspapers, and motion pictures which exposes young people as never before to insidiously destructive influences which may logically be expected to undermine our traditional sex morals."[58] In this representation, mass-produced vulgar sexual expression posed a real threat to the survival of the sexual self-restraint at the heart of white civilization. Pedagogues, far from sponsoring sexual thoughts in innocents, sought to inculcate middle-class white ideals of purity, restraint, and familial containment—"our traditional sex morals"—in people who otherwise would almost certainly fall prey to the contagious bad influences of urban, commercial, public culture. Sex education, in short, could help to implant and normalize an appropriately civilized, family-focused self-restraint where all the alternative forms of sexual expression, collectively known as vulgarity and perversion, would otherwise flourish.

Sex educators' commitment to a "decency" they defined in terms of the white family helps to explain the startling frequency with which books and pamphlets for adolescents described the impact of venereal disease on infants.[59] Asking young men and women to imagine the brief and painful lives of children born with syphilis or gonorrhea allowed sex educators to dwell on the terrifying consequences of deviating from "normal" sexuality, while still foregrounding the hope for healthy parenthood.[60] Information about prenatal contagion was intended not only to frighten adolescents into chastity but also to call out and develop their nascent parental urges to cherish and care for children. This strategy also offered an opportunity to teach the ideal white virtues of civic responsibility and sensitivity to the feelings of others. Purity for the sake of the coming generation was morally and socially superior to purity that derived only from fear. As one writer put it, "the lad who is 'good' merely for the sake of his own skin is a poor creature; the finest lad—who might perhaps hazard his own individual fate—will refuse to gamble with the souls and bodies of those others who shall be his own flesh and blood."[61] Appeals to consider the health of future children had a selfless nobility or chivalry about them that was whiter than warnings limited to the dangers of premarital sex for its participants.[62] Such appeals tempered selfish fear with familial love and social consciousness, altruism and compassion. In this way they taught ideal white virtues while they dissuaded from vice.

This perspective seems to have guided the decision to include a photograph of a syphilitic baby in Irving Steinhardt's manuals *Ten Sex Talks to Girls* (1913) and *Ten Sex Talks to Boys* (1914). In the manual for girls, the photograph appeared in the middle of a long passage addressing and sympathizing with the infant depicted there: "Poor little syphilitic baby! No one loves you nor wants to hug and kiss you except, perhaps, the poor mother who had the misfortune to bring you into the world."[63] The photograph makes the reason plain. The infant's skin is badly discolored, cracked, and apparently sloughing off; its mouth gapes and is crusted with diseased tissue, and, just at the limit of the camera's focus, its eyes wear the fixed and unnerving stare of death. The image is the more disturbing in that at first glance the baby seems terribly distorted, its feet almost as large as its head and too close to it. A second look reveals that the picture is actually two photographs, one of the head and one of the feet, juxtaposed on the page in a way that heightens the horror of the composite image while it discreetly avoids showing the infant's genitals. The image of the syphilitic baby represents disease with great clarity, while it crops all other obvious information about sex out of the picture.

To Steinhardt, however, the syphilitic baby offered a model not only of sickness but of maternal selflessness and social service. After a long description of the baby's "repulsive" body, he comforted it, saying, "It is hard on you, poor little sufferer, but even you are serving a purpose . . . and helping to pave the way that other babies' lives may not be so blighted in the future. You are helping on the work of opening the eyes of a heretofore indifferent public to the ravages of these vile diseases of immorality, and making them think a little more about the lives they should lead for the benefit of themselves and their future offspring."[64] The image of the syphilitic baby was meant to make civilized young people recoil, not from the unfortunate infant so much as from the racial backsliding into self-indulgent insensitivity that could make them responsible for such suffering in their own children. Importantly, that image, and Steinhardt's discussion of it, avoids explicit references to sexual acts and organs beyond the single word "immorality." Thus, while Steinhardt used painfully vivid images to teach the importance of controlling one's acts for the common good, the example of the syphilitic baby suggested that a normal, healthy approach to sexuality required representational self-restraint as well.

Despite its reticence about sexual behavior and anatomy, the syphilitic baby example was a graphic rendition of the failure of civilized whiteness and a powerful incentive to conform to its ideal of sexual self-control. Indeed, sex hygiene's deliberate play on young readers' emotions seems to have reflected the survival of a venerable, and indicatively white, technique for drawing public attention to shameful social conditions. The cultural historian Karen Halttunen has argued that graphic depictions of suffering in mid-nineteenth-century abolitionist literature reflected a Romantic fascination with vicarious sensations. An important strand of Anglo-American humanitarian thought held that exposure to others' suffering inspired a feeling of sympathy for one's fellow creatures; this experience allegedly uplifted and enlightened the viewer. It also had an important social aspect: in Halttunen's example, sympathetic suffering with the image of a slave being whipped was supposed to strengthen the white viewer's commitment to fighting slavery.[65] In this view, confronting other people's pain head-on and imagining how one would feel in a similar situation was a necessary part of the process through which whites were trained to fight for an ever more civilized, more just, more democratic nation.[66]

But by the early twentieth century, the sympathetic suffering once inseparable from well-bred American whiteness had gone out of fashion. To many moderns, its sensationalism was vulgar and troublingly morbid, while its basic premise, that civilization advanced through sensitivity to pain, was cruel nonsense. However venerable the WASP tradition to which it referred, the example of the syphilitic baby could not teach white ideals about normal marriage and family life to a new generation of Americans, many of whom did not share that heritage of refined self-cultivation. A broader definition of whiteness required a less ethnically and class-specific educational strategy.

In addition, a more modern definition of femininity and of family life demanded a new representational strategy, one in which both mother and infant could play a positive role in further development of the nation and the race. By 1919 a general consensus began to emerge that an emphasis on disease was poor preparation for civilized adult sexuality, and more and more voices called for education about "the moral, the normal, the health-ful, the helpful, and the esthetic aspects" of sex.[67] Simply avoiding explicit representations of sexual acts and behaviors was not enough; many moderns in the interwar years argued that representations of any form of sickness or perversity might taint young imaginations. The narrative of contagion was perfectly consistent with sex educators' short-term goal of premarital self-restraint, and it did model useful lessons in indirection, but it was not likely to encourage "truly clean and wholesome companionship between boys and girls," the foundation for "the union of body and spirit" in modern marriage.[68] Venereal disease simply had no place in normal modern sex-uality. By 1925 tragic tales of venereal infection were no longer at the vital center of sex education. Stories about normal families took their place.

The Birds and the Bees: Indirect Education

In contrast to the tragedy of venereal contagion, the story of the evolution-ary family was optimistic and uplifting. Its basic outline was simple: sex was, to those who understood its true nature, synonymous with modern mar-riage. Marriage and family life had developed over ages of evolutionary refinement until they achieved the ideal form of tenderly expressive, sexually exclusive, intelligently fruitful monogamy. This message made evolutionary sex education much less controversial than narratives of venereal contagion had been. After all, what could be more "normal, helpful, healthful, and esthetic" than a pedagogy that naturalized and universalized the ideals of reproductive wedlock at the heart of modern whiteness?

Answer: a pedagogy that avoided mentioning the human experience of sexual arousal and satisfaction. The story of the evolutionary family offered young moderns an elaborate education in the expressive etiquette of normal white sexuality, which meant using and understanding euphemisms and metaphors while appearing completely unembarrassed about their underly-ing referent. Whether offered in the form of pamphlets, lectures, or hands-on classwork, sex education in elementary and junior high schools of the late 1920s and 1930s tended to focus on what was called "nature study." As the years passed, students were made acquainted with the process of reproduction in a variety of animals and plants. In these lessons, young Americans were taught that modern marriage was mandated by evolution. Reproductive marital heterosexuality was represented not only as biologically normal for moderns but also as naturally superior to all other forms of sexual expression, emotional connection, or family structure. Yet human bodies and relationships were very rarely mentioned in these lessons. Instead, schoolchildren under the age of ten or twelve were taught, quite literally, about the birds and the bees.

This indirect mode of instruction took its theoretical justification, and its basic narrative outline, from popularizations of Ernst Haeckel's famous theorem that ontogeny recapitulates phylogeny.[69] Haeckel posited that each individual person's life repeated the processes of evolutionary development.[70] The recapitulation of sex, therefore, began with "the primal segmentation of the cell." In the unimaginably distant evolutionary past, as at the moment of conception in modern human beings, each organism was complete and sexless and reproduced by the simple method of dividing itself in two.[71] Only with the development of the vertebrates did distinctly different sexes evolve. At that world-historical moment, reproduction became sexual. According to this widespread account of the evolution of sex, heterosexual attraction appeared to be an evolutionary achievement of the race. It was also the natural endpoint of the developmental narrative for moderns. Though sex-education materials were generally very cagey about acknowledging the existence of people whose desires were not directed toward possibly reproductive heterosexuality, contemporary sexological writing on perversion extended the recapitulationist argument to its logical conclusion: "perverts" manifested both racial primitivism and personal childishness. In civilized white adults, "arrested development" was both a personal failure to grow and a mark of a potentially racial failure to evolve.[72]

Recapitulatory understandings of sexual development constituted a powerful argument for delaying young people's access to information about the human experience of sexuality. Some critics of venereal education expressed their objections to teaching about disease by suggesting that the nervous impact of such lessons could cause "morbid tendencies" and "arrests in normal development."[73] A similar caution influenced the stance which held that, because elementary schoolchildren's development was still not far advanced, it was most appropriate to offer them lessons about organisms representing early stages in the evolution of life. Pamphlets and books for children, and teachers' reports from schools, suggest that many young-sters began their sex education with flowers.[74] Children with imaginative parents, or in especially advanced schools, were allowed to plant large seeds, such as beans, and pull some of them up at different times, to observe the stages of germination.[75] Others watched a teacher dissect a large flower such as a lily, or were shown illustrations of its different parts, or simply heard them described. However the class was conducted, the children were ex-pected to learn two things: that all life comes from eggs, and that before an egg can hatch, a fertilizing agent is necessary.[76] Stress was always placed on the process of pollination, to emphasize the point that all beings have two parents: "By itself the pollen could not grow to be a seed. The egg needs the pollen and the pollen needs the egg."[77]

In fact, of course, not all life comes from eggs, and it is not remotely true that all beings have two parents. It is a charming irony that the lilies so often used as examples in sex-education literature are cultivated from bulbs, which reproduce asexually. But the point of such nature study was not a good grounding in botany. It was indoctrination with the idea that, even among relatively primitive life forms, "sex" was synonymous with reproductive activity and emotional interdependence between women (egg-producers) and men (fertilizers). The lessons about reproduction offered in this indirect way were inseparable from lessons about normative gendering. Conve-niently ignoring the astonishing range of sexual techniques among flowering plants, sex educators used them as metaphors for human parents. The blos-som, with its ovary, sweet fragrance, and showy petals, stood for feminine white womanhood, alluring and passively receptive to the advances of its apian visitors. The bees (or wasps or moths) bumbled and pushed their pollen-laden way into the heart of the flower. One popular manual for children went so far as to call the relationship between insects and flowers "making love."[78]

As nature study went on, pupils examined or read about fishes, frogs, and birds. With each kind of creature, the elementary points about dual parent-hood and fertilized eggs were repeated, but a few new points were added as the lessons progressed up the evolutionary scale. These points emphasized that loving marriage and careful parenthood were natural for modern hu-man beings. Evolutionary development from simple animals to complex ones was depicted as the progressive development of parental devotion. Fishes, because they are ancient and cold-blooded animals, were used to represent the primitive era before the development of family love. Under the subheading "The Mother Fish Neglects Her Babies" one popular pamphlet for ten-year-olds explained:

> The baby fish are produced in great numbers because so many of them get lost or are eaten by other fish or by birds or other animals. The father and mother fish cannot take care of their young ones. . . . Fish, you understand, are rather low in the animal kingdom, and they have not yet learned how to take care of their young. You will be surprised to know that a mother sunfish would not know her own babies from any others that might be swimming about in the water. I am sure you are glad that you are one of the human race, which knows so much more and takes so much better care of its boys and girls than any fish would know how to do.[79]

Having disposed of fish as unsuitably "low" models for human families, sex-education materials turned youngsters to the study of amphibians. As parents, frogs had made clear advances over fishes in that frog eggs are protected by a jelly, which makes it difficult for predators to get a grip on them and also serves as a lens to intensify the sun's heat and help them incubate quickly. But frogs had to be left behind, for the advances of amphibian civilization did not extend to any form of parenting. Birds introduced the elements of family life into nature study:

> Perhaps you have seen the birds chasing each other in the spring and have supposed that they were fighting. Not at all! The male birds frequently fight each other when they are courting the female, but the two mates do not fight. They build the nest together; they help one another; the male carries food to the female when she is on the nest; he protects her from harm; and if we may judge by his actions he loves her in very much the same way that your own father loves your mother. Of course then he would not wish to fight her! He is merely giving her the substance from his own body which she can then put into the eggs so that the baby birds will be part his and part her children.[80]

Such passages serve as reminders that the goal of all this nature study was not accurate knowledge about animal sexuality, social behavior, or reproduction. Rather, it was designed to indoctrinate youngsters with a specific vision of sex as synonymous with bourgeois WASP constructions of gender, ideals for modern marriage, and normal family life. Floral metaphors for marital intercourse and fables about robins disseminated the same vision of normative heterosexuality as the tales about healthy manhood and womanhood in social hygiene literature. The chief difference between the two major schools of modern sex education was that the haze of suggestion and allusion was even thicker in nature study than in lessons about the dangers of venereal contagion. Indirect speech on sexual matters had a great deal to do with the success of evolutionary sex education: stamens and pistils, eggs and nests were far easier and safer to discuss with children than human genitalia, prostitution, and venereal disease.

Birds were especially useful in sex education attempts to naturalize monogamous, gender-polarized, intimate white heterosexuality. Many birds pair-bond, at least for a given mating season; some common species divide the work of reproduction and chick-raising along lines that lend themselves to anthropomorphic gendering; and they often appear to be devoted parents.[81] Exceptions to these generalizations were usually suppressed but sometimes came in handy as indirect warnings against deviant sexual behavior. One educator reported an incident in her classroom that underscores both the characteristically metaphorical quality of modern sex education and the extent to which it could be effective in transmitting normal whiteness to the masses as though it were simply natural. The teacher had used cowbirds as an example of bad parenting: the male bird, she said, "mates with the mother bird and then flies away, giving no thought for the mother or the young ones." The female cowbird does what an unwed and abandoned mother should: she leaves her eggs in another bird's nest, to be incubated by a "foster mother."

> A big, square-backed boy from the rear of a tenement-house district, hearing the story of the cowbird, kicked a stone and announced, "Say, I call that cow-bird father a mean skunk." Perhaps, if we teach our boys before adolescence, we may safeguard them from becoming irresponsible fathers and from bringing children into the world until they are ready to protect them.[82]

The student's recorded judgment is that the cowbird was "mean"—a term that communicates both economic and emotional selfishness, and that therefore suggests he had understood the importance of tender familial affection and mutual support to legitimate modern sexuality. Even "square-backed," primitive louts from the tenements could grasp nature-study's fables about the importance of love and sexual self-restraint. They could also express their disapproval of sexual misconduct forcefully and clearly, yet without resorting to vulgar explicitness. If discreet avian metaphors could teach slum dwellers—among the "lowest" whites of their day—both the relational norms and the linguistic discretion required for normal whiteness, surely there was hope for race and civilization.

Many, perhaps most, sex education programs stopped their evolutionary storytelling with birds.[83] In 1915, for example, approximately 1,500 freshmen were required to take biology at a large high school in New York City. Their curriculum included instruction in nutrition, "hygienic habits of living," and the "fundamental principles of the reproductive function" in flowering plants, fishes, insects, and birds. Explaining this program, the head of the biology department said simply, "We do not think it wise to discuss mammalian reproduction in mixed classes in the first year."[84] This reticence was deliberate and widespread and was intended at least in part to protect young people from the sexual shocks and possible morbid consequences of too much knowledge too soon. High school students were still too young to mate, and so they were too young to be taught about mating. That could wait until they had finished recapitulating the youth of the race and were ready to settle down to breed the next white generation.

Consistency with the recapitulatory schedule of sexual development was only part of the reason for such reticence, of course. Sex education distinguished itself from lessons in vice in large part by the care it took to avoid topics that could arouse students' interest in sex and possibly inspire them to seek extracurricular instruction. This concern for the instructional performance of sexual respectability reflects the politically inflammatory qualities of sex instruction in public schools, but it also reminds us of the belief that sexual self-restraint was essential to civilized whiteness. Indirection and euphemism modeled that restraint and so were integral parts of young people's education in sexual normality as it was offered via nature study.

In the unusually progressive school districts where teachers went beyond pious avian metaphors about family life to offer students some information about human beings, the discreet and reproductive nature of civilized white sexuality meant that almost all instructional materials were more articulate about the biology of conception and fetal development than about the behaviors, pleasures, and pains of sexual experience. However, it would be an error to interpret such reticence as evidence that evolutionary sex education was opposed to eroticism. It would be more accurate to say that the narrative of the evolutionary family attempted to harness sexual pleasure for civilized ends by containing it within loving white family life.

Nature study drew on a well-developed scientific tradition to make this claim. Since the turn of the century, a number of medico-sexological researchers had mobilized accounts of animal reproduction to suggest that desire became more refined with the progress of civilization. For instance, Havelock Ellis once argued that the "sexual system and sexual needs" of domesticated mammals were "more developed than in the wild species most closely related to them."[85] Even rodents, according to another investigator, displayed a

> stimulated power of reproduction . . . due to the advantages derived from their intimate relations with the luxuries of civilization. . . . It would seem highly probable . . . that the reproductive power of man has increased with civilization, precisely as it may be increased in the lower animals by domestication; that the effect of a regular supply of good food, together with all the other stimulating factors available and exercised in modern civilized communities, has resulted in such great activity of the generative organs . . . that conception in the healthy human female may be said to be possible almost at any time.[86]

Thus when Ellis wrote that the savage "sexual impulse is habitually weak, and only aroused to strength under the impetus of powerful stimuli, often acting periodically," he was asserting that savages were less erotically sensitive and sexually productive than lab rats, who, after all, were carefully bred and who lived under highly civilized conditions.[87] (The question of why such rats have been bred to be white is outside the bounds of the present discussion.) Even outside of the politically fraught context of public sex education, animal stories provided a politely indirect language in which moderns could communicate with one another about the erotic dimension of whiteness.

Modern sexologists generally agreed that, because "lower" species and races had not undergone the long evolutionary processes that refined the nervous system, and so the "nervous and psychic reflexes," they allegedly could not experience romance and sexual bliss with the sharp joy felt by normal Anglos.[88] This erotic insensitivity was widely represented as both a cause and an expression of their innate racial inferiority. In 1929 one scholar summarized the current professional literature on the subject by explaining that "in the struggle for existence a strong and well-developed sexual instinct has obviously an important survival value, and the higher races are undoubtedly to be credited with its possession."[89] This stance seems to reflect a widely shared assumption that "higher races," by definition, embodied evolutionary fitness.

To the extent that white superiority was rooted in nature, which required desire for the reproduction of the race, white people must possess powerful sexual feelings. Any appearance to the contrary was perforce either an illusion or a cultural pathology, to be addressed by the judicious application of sexual science. Therefore, when "savages" displayed more overt sexuality than was customary among civilized whites, enlightened moderns understood that this actually reflected the feebleness of erotic desire in primitive peoples:

> That the sexual impulse is relatively weak among savages, as compared with civilized peoples, is proved by the difficulty often shown in attaining sexual excitement—a difficulty which frequently has to be overcome by the indirect erethism of saturnalian proceedings . . . the sexual character of many [savage] festivals . . . demonstrates the need of artificial excitement.[90]

Such arguments implied that the sexual self-control and discretion characteristic of middle-class white moderns was not a sign of indifference to sex but rather meant that they had evolved beyond the need for "saturnalian" stimulation. Apparently this scholarly conclusion had a mass-cultural counterpart. Dozens of popular sexological works from this era include passages —even entire chapters—celebrating the rich satisfactions of modern, private love-unions by contrast to the "sensory and motor sluggishness," erotic inadequacy, and emotional poverty of sexual encounters among "primitive" peoples.[91]

Normal white moderns, then, combined passionate sexuality with an apparently instinctive preference for erotic privacy in the monogamous marital bedroom. Both passion and modesty were often represented as the natural result of long evolutionary processes.[92] In sex education as in sex research, the story of the evolutionary family taught that sexual desire was a precious social and racial resource, insofar as it was true to its essentially developmental and reproductive "nature." Margaret Sanger summed up the field with her usual directness when she explained to mothers that "the whole object of teaching the child about reproduction through evolution is to clear its mind of any shame or mystery concerning its birth and to impress it with the beauty and naturalness of procreation, in order to prepare it for the knowledge of puberty and marriage."[93] When sexual desire was conflated with legitimate procreation, there was no need for shame. There was also no thrill in deviant, public, or vulgarly explicit expressions of sex. According to the tale of the evolutionary family, sex was a profoundly pleasurable and satisfying experience *because* normal moderns restricted their sexuality to potentially reproductive activity within the private sphere of marriage. Sanger included in her list of things "every girl should know" the statement that an educated and restrained "sexual impulse . . . will make the purest, strongest and most sacred passion of adult life, compared to which all other passions pale into insignificance."[94] Intense private pleasure was the white reward for bearing the sexual responsibility for civilization in a disciplined, responsible fashion. In any case, erotic expression outside of loving marriage was biologically passé:

> Out of the original plan for double parentage of new individual bearers of the spark of living substance, there has developed through the ages of human life psychical or spiritual love with all its splendid possibilities as found in ideal family life. In other words, out of the material or physical aspects of reproduction have evolved or developed the possibilities of the conjugal affection of the parents for each other and parental affection for the offspring.[95]

In this self-consciously scientific point of view, the sexual urge was the ancient raw material out of which generations of white couples had gradually crafted love, civilized self-restraint, and modern family life. One sex education handbook described desire as the "germinating seed" that, when properly cultivated, gave rise to "the human qualities and associations most prized, namely, love, marriage, home, father, mother, love for the child, filial and paternal devotion, and from these a social system."[96] When Sanger and her contemporaries wrote about human mating in terms of love, marriage, and social responsibility, they were not simply evading discussions of desire. Rather, they were actively arguing that desire's most evolved nature was not only intimate and reproductive but also discreet. To distinguish modern white modesty from shame, they underscored that the normal, modern attitude to take toward sex was a scientifically enlightened one.

This highly white stance had the added virtue of allowing educators to implant heteronormative erotic values without mentioning perversion or describing actual human sexual behaviors in any detail. Instead, such arguments emphasized the rational and emotional dimensions of normal sexuality and the obligation of self-discipline that both reason and feeling imposed. All creatures reproduce, these educators reminded their young readers. The difference between humans and other animals is that "only people know how babies are born and they are the only creatures that plan to live together and have children" and that delay mating until they find "the one whom he or she can love."[97] Through nature study, in short, white children and adolescents were taught that evolution culminated in their rational ability to contain their sexuality inside emotionally and erotically charged monogamous marriage. They were also taught that the only really civilized way to talk about sex was indirectly, through an elaborate language of biological metaphors.

Conclusion

Indirection about desire, and reticence about its expression, were inseparable from the normalizing of whiteness. To the extent that sex education materials succeeded in defining modern marriage as normal, they taught that it was normal to cultivate erotic passion within carefully circumscribed boundaries. We have seen that some educators represented reproductive and social health as dependent on, even synonymous with, adherence to middle-class white ideals of gender. Others went a step further, claiming that those white ideals of normative gender, marriage, and family life were dictated not only by hygiene but also by evolution. Their sexological colleagues concurred that the discipline to contain and cultivate desire, the instinct for privacy, and the capacity for exquisite sensitivity were all evolved traits unique to civilized adults. As such, then, normality was racially and erotically specific to white, conventionally gendered heterosexuals. But being straight, white, and married wasn't quite enough: modern normality also required the performance of a sexual reticence once expected only of WASP elites. Whiteness and normality were sutured together even—better, especially—in the absence of explicit discussions of either race or what most people today would call sexuality. Sex education narratives about protecting the family, or about the birds and the bees, communicated a wealth of information about whiteness and normality not in spite but because of their apparent lack of address to either race or erotic longing.

An example will make the point clearer. When evolutionary sex educators told the story of the development of normal whiteness, they used a biological language that simultaneously universalized sexual growth (thus normalizing "adulthood," a.k.a. reproductive heterosexuality) and naturalized the hierarchy of races. According to this story, sexual growth toward reproductive heterosexuality began at conception, though the distinguishing marks of normal sexuality were not immediately apparent. Beginning life as tiny, rapidly dividing fertilized eggs, unborn potential humans passed through stages in which they had gills and tails; the embryos were indistinguishable from those of other creatures, whose ancient racial history humans had shared and were now recapitulating.[98] As one extremely successful manual explained:

> If you were to see the egg of a baby and the egg of an elephant and the egg of a mouse you would not know which was which. A rabbit that has been growing for a week seems so much like a baby that has been growing for three or four weeks that it would be hard for you to tell them apart. But the longer that animals and babies grow the more different from each other they become.[99]

In the context of evolutionary sex education, the difference in question was never neutral: humans were *better* than elephants, mice, or rabbits, in large part because human sexuality normally expressed itself in monogamous marriage and loving parenthood. This point was usually made in words, but sometimes an educator used drawings as well. Embryos were shown in vivid tables of comparative development that emphasized both the similarity of the process of growth across species and the difference of the product.[100] One particularly elaborate table, from a 1929 schoolbook on evolution by a prominent sex educator, shows "Parallelism in Development of Backboned Animals" through images of five species of embryos.[101] Read from top to bottom, the images in each column show the fetal development of increasingly species-specific traits (fins, beaks, and so forth). Read from left to right, the images in each row conform to the narrative of evolutionary development, with "lesser" races on the left and the "higher" ones on the right. This arrangement reflects the belief that evolution turns simple, primitive forms (fish) into complex, modern ones (humans), and so the table teaches hierarchy as well as parallelism in prenatal development. Such tables therefore imply not only that growth inevitably leads to heterosexual marriage and reproduction but also that some forms of beings are inherently better than others.

One final illustration will serve to remind us that modern mobilizations of evolutionary hierarchies usually had an important racial dimension in addition to their heterosexist one. A large-format picture book for small children, Marie Hall Ets's *The Story of a Baby* (1939), drew on what by that time were well-established visual and narrative conventions to tell the tale of the evolutionary family. As the human embryo in her narrative develops through the early stages of gestation, illustrations surrounding Ets's descriptive text contextualize the embryo's growth by references to "primitive" animals like fish and turtles, and later to the "lower" mammals (represented by seals). On other pages, however, the text is visually surrounded by pictures of comparatively "primitive" humans. From the "cave family," drawn with dark skin and dressed in crude bits of hide, the race progresses through ancient Egypt to the Vikings before it culminates in a white Victorian couple, who are shown courting in a surrey with a fringe on top. Each family grouping is drawn with paler skin (more precisely, with less cross-hatching) than the one before it, and the people wear more clothing and are surrounded with more sophisticated technologies in each successive image.

The story of "a" baby is clearly depicted as the story of the evolutionary development of a broadly inclusive modern American whiteness. But the racial specificity of the evolutionary family was not a subject for direct discussion with children. Rather, the evolution of white love was depicted as though it constituted an obvious parallel to the normal development of human fetuses. Just as well-bred indirection about eroticism was a subtle part of sex education's lessons in white normality, apparent indifference to race was a subtle but crucial element of sex education lessons about normal modern whiteness.

Whether they emphasized the venereal threat or focused on the biology of reproduction, modern sex education narratives taught young people that sexual desire was not normal unless it was the fertile expression of love between monogamous married spouses. Contemporary tales about the emotional and erotic impoverishment of "primitive" sexuality make it clear that many moderns understood such love as a racial achievement unique to whites. While sex instruction materials for children avoided direct discussion of homosexuality and race, popular and medical sex research for adults often drew an explicit connection between racial "primitivism" and sexual "perversion."

Instead of engaging in similarly direct discussions of racialized sexuality, narratives of venereal contagion used the language of military conquest and home protection to argue that white civilization depended on the restriction of eroticism to monogamous marriage. Similarly, lessons in the evolutionary development of the family used fables to support the claim that all other forms of sexual expression were primitive by comparison with modern marriage. In short, sex education was a social technology for the normalizing of ideal modern whiteness. Sex education taught hundreds of thousands, possibly millions, of young moderns that they ought to feel simultaneously afraid of, revolted by, and superior to sexual expression outside the normative boundaries of ideal white love. And these lessons, powerful though they were in communicating the racial and sexual superiority of heteronormativity, were effective precisely because they were reticent about race and sexuality. The sign of a successfully implanted norm is its silence.

Regarding Racial / Erotic Politics

I have argued in this book that "normality" has a long history as a covertly political phenomenon. Despite its superficial neutrality, the concept has worked to justify and further white racial dominance. That racial dominance, I have suggested, is not meaningfully separable from the political and cultural valorization of emotionally intimate monogamous marriage between gender-polarized opposite-sex adults as the only truly civilized, modern, and fully human site for sexual expression. One of the most powerful and long-lasting arguments for the legitimacy of white rule has taken the form of a claim to special racial access to self-control, and especially to private discipline expressing sensitivity to the good of the whole, which is regularly represented by and through "normal" marriage. I do not mean to suggest that racial and sexual norms have remained static since Joan Crawford was a jazz baby. Yet despite the massive cultural transformations of the past sixty or eighty years, the discursive connections that tie sexual and racial normality to legitimate membership in American culture have remained strong. Racial ideology continues to be implicated in the cultural and political dispossession of sexually non-normative people, who are still figured as the barbarians at the gates of culture. Sexual ideology continues to contribute to the burdens of racism that confront people of color, who still struggle against the dominant cultural expectation that their morality is inherently deficient.

Further, I have shown that the consolidation of "normal" sexuality helped to justify white dominance by depicting whiteness not only as superior but also as benign and innocent, in relation to racial "inferiors." Because "normality" took shape in and through sexual discourses focused on the meaning and ideal practice of "civilized" marriage and family life, its most overt content centered on intimate relationships characterized by mutual tenderness. A major goal of this project has been to shed light on the question of how whiteness has come to be so race-evasive and power-evasive, which is to say, so strikingly blind to its own racial existence and the power relations it instantiates, enforces, and profits from. The answer I have offered is that discourses of normal sexuality constructed the essence of white racial meaning as love: that is, as sensitivity to suffering and injustice, concern for equality across the gulf of difference, and affectionate responsibility for the young, the weak, and the vulnerable.

At the heart of ideal modern whiteness was a special, principled tenderness designed to bridge otherwise divisive differences between men and women, parents and children, old-stock WASPs and new immigrants, teachers and slum dwellers. All these people could, in theory, be "normal," so long as they willingly subjected themselves and their children to the bourgeois erotic and relational disciplines that certified their allegiance to the social and civic order on which white American civilization rested. In the texts I have explored here, the virtues of whiteness were represented simultaneously as personal and political, essential both to private happiness and to the common good. At the same time, because "normality" was a disciplinary ideal toward which individuals were urged to strive rather than a description of an actually existing state, it was easy to interpret the gap between racial ideology and racial reality as incidental, a matter of individual failures to live up to the essentially benevolent meaning of whiteness.

The chief questions of this book, then, are how whiteness came to be the race that seems to lack a racial position; why marital heterosexuality also became "normal" at approximately the same historical moment; and what specific racial and erotic meanings attached to this shared transparency. I have sketched out a handful of cultural and discursive strategies through which heteronormative whiteness was constructed as politically and morally innocent, and by means of which that racial/erotic construction was disseminated to early-twentieth-century Americans en masse. Each chapter of this discussion has highlighted a different aspect of the construction of normal whiteness as benign. " 'Barbarians Are Not Nervous' " used neurasthenia discourse to reconstruct the class-specific racial belief that well-bred white people were the natural owners of "civilization." Their capacity for refined sensation, and their tendency to translate that sensitivity both into cultural creativity and into sexual incapacity, was inseparable from the legitimacy of their dominance. In turn, their belief in their own weakness helped to excuse them from accountability for the suffering that made their privileged positions possible. "The Marriage Crisis" showed that, by the early twentieth century, white suffering in response to modernity had lost its earlier elite associations. Divorce could happen to anyone, given the impact of the machine age on marital partnership and sexual difference—but the democratization of potential sexual weakness also meant the extension of the disciplinary mandate to overcome it for the sake of the nation and the race.

The expansion of the normalizing requirements of racial/erotic self-discipline went hand in hand with their intimate intensification. While more different kinds of white people were called upon to be "normal," each white couple was solicited at an increasingly minute level.[1] Marital advice literature reflects and participated in this double movement of democratization and privatization of the political ideals of the republic in its representation of sexual difference between husbands and wives as a small-scale metaphor for the diversity of the United States. Marriage manuals, especially, suggest that mutually orgasmic sex mirrored and rehearsed the triumph of democratic justice in the nation as a whole. The literature of marital breakdown defined erotically charged, gender-polarized marriage, and the normative American whiteness to which it was essential, as self-governance in the service of love. This construction implied that those who could not or would not cultivate monogamous marital eroticism rejected discipline and thought only of themselves; thus they were bad citizens who deserved their social exclusion.[2] Through this construction of normality as a synonym for legitimate citizenship, whiteness excused itself from any political accountability for the pains of those who did not qualify as "normal."

Finally, "Birds, Bees, and the Future of the Race" delineated the indirect mode of expression characteristic of the pedagogy through which this democratized, self-congratulatory vision of whiteness was disseminated to millions of children and adolescents under the sign of the normal. The young people who grew up with their sexuality informed by modern sex education were simultaneously taught that whiteness was inseparable from normal love and family life, and that normal sexuality was inseparable from the performance of disciplined whiteness. On the level of content, modern sex education trained at least one generation to see normative whiteness as not only natural but as the pinnacle of evolutionary development. Through its rhetorical example, it also taught them that civilized normality required a very specific performance of mastery over one's language. The terms and tones in which one spoke about sex testified to one's status in relation to the normal. Endorsing alternative sexual cultures as legitimate, even if only by acknowledging their modes of address and points of view, could undermine the normality of the speaker as well as of his or her auditors. Thus normality was constructed in terms that implicitly proscribed political engagement with the hierarchical structures of difference that governed racial, gendered, and erotic politics. To object to white racial dominance, and to register protest against sexism and the pathologization of queer people, was to risk one's status as normal.

A book with such an argument can never be only academic or purely historical. To describe these features and strategies of normality necessarily involves engaging the politically charged paradoxes of modern white racial meaning. In what sense is whiteness both invisible and the dominant representation? How has it come to stand for the nation as a whole and also for its "best," most threatened part? How can whiteness represent a political system founded on the principle that the free expression of diverse opinion guarantees justice, while it demands that no one else speak or be heard without using its language and bowing to its political and moral superiority? How can it be both a powerfully, violently oppressive force and the standard of freedom to which others aspire? How can it be both empty, inherently devoid of culture, and yet notoriously defensive of its cultural purity?

One commonsense response to these questions is to dismiss whiteness's self-construction as simple ideology. Another is to try to adjudicate between their opposing claims by marshaling facts for and against their accuracy. A third approach is to draw attention to the terms of the historically specific definitions of normal race and sexuality that gave rise to these contradictory claims. I have chosen the latter course. This strategy reflects my political, as much as intellectual, convictions. I am persuaded that seeking to decide what whiteness is, or what value it has, on empirical grounds is a dubious use of progressive intellectual energy. It's not that such questions might not turn out to have answers, but rather that the (gendered and classed) structures of race and sexuality work together in such a way that factual responses to such questions are unlikely to enable significant forward movement.

My skepticism about the usefulness of strictly empirical approaches to the meaning of race stems, in part, from my observation that the dynamic interrelationship of sexual and racial normality has lasted much longer than the contents of the norms that governed daily life in the years when they were first sutured together. If we attend only to the content of norms and the immediate consequences of breaking them, cultural change appears so overwhelming that continuity in regulatory structures is hard to see. Yet it is undeniable that the above set of questions about the meaning of whiteness is just as pertinent in the first decade of the twenty-first century as it was in the third or fourth decade of the twentieth. On a more abstract level, my skepticism about too pure a reliance on empiricism reflects queer theoretical and political insights that are highly relevant to the linked racial and erotic politics of normality. One can substitute "heterosexuality" for "whiteness" in the above questions with no loss of clarity or cogency or political force, a fact that highlights the riskiness of an anti-racist strategy which seeks to mobilize facts alone against the force of white hegemony. David Halperin has developed an especially strong analysis of the political futility of empiricism as a means of contesting homophobia. As he points out, "homophobia cannot be refuted by means of rational argument" because it is "not reducible to a set of statements with a specifiable truth-content that can be rationally tested." Rather, he argues,

> Homophobic discourses contain no fixed propositional content. They are composed of a potentially infinite number of different but functionally interchangeable assertions, such that whenever any one assertion is falsified or disqualified another one—even one with a content exactly contrary to the original one—can be neatly and effectively substituted for it.[3]

Halperin goes on to argue that the logical incompatibility of homophobic claims about homosexuality—for example, that homosexuals are "both *sick* and *blameworthy* in respect of the same defect"—enhances their political efficacy. The same potent incoherence informs heterosexuality, which is

> (1) a social norm, (2) a perfectly natural condition into which everyone is born and into which everyone grows up, if no catastrophic accident interferes with normal, healthy, development, (3) a highly laudable accomplishment that one is entitled to take pride in and for which one deserves no small amount of personal and social credit, and (4) a

frighteningly unstable and precarious state that can easily be over-
thrown . . . and therefore needs to be militantly protected, defended,
and safeguarded by a constant mobilization of social forces.[4]

In this discursive situation it seems clear that responding to normalizing
judgments about non-normative people by directing critical energies toward
refuting or supporting any particular truth-claim about them may not be
particularly wise.

This is not because one claim about reality is as good as another. There
are often fairly clear grounds for assessing some claims as better (that is,
more nuanced or sensitive or accountable) in relation to facts, and there are
specific situations in which mobilizing such facts may be helpful. But there
are also some in which they are not. As Halperin says, "To refuse to allow
questions of truth to distract us from questions of politics is . . . a purely
strategic move, a way of shifting the ground of the argument. The point is
not that the truth of the matter has or should have no bearing on politics.
The point is rather that granting matters of truth precedence over politics is
itself a political strategy that may need to be resisted."[5] The paradoxical,
internally contradictory nature of the contemporary truth-claims about normative whiteness that I listed above suggests that the incoherence of the
category is one of the sources of its power. As a result, it seems likely that
academic refutations of one or another of those claims on factual grounds
will do little to undermine the discursive structures that render white racial
dominance simultaneously durable and deniable. The search for the "truth"
about white racial meaning absorbs critical energies that might be better
spent attending to the way that the paradoxical structures of whiteness are
constructed, so that we can address the ways in which they actually work.
Not only what "whiteness" means, but what it does; not what its truth is, but
what its construction in these paradoxical terms makes possible, and what it
makes difficult, impossible, or unlikely.

I want to emphasize that my use of queer theory to elucidate normative
meanings of whiteness does not constitute a mobilization of the troubling
analogy by which race is "like" sexuality, or a racialized position "like" a
gendered and erotically marked one. A number of scholars and activists have
pointed to the problematic nature of such analogies. Judith Butler's formulation is particularly apropos:

> It seems crucial to resist the model of power that would set up racism
> and homophobia and misogyny as parallel or analogical relations. The

assertion of their abstract or structural equivalence not only misses the specific histories of their construction and elaboration, but also delays the important work of thinking through the ways in which these vectors of power require and deploy each other for the purpose of their own articulation.[6]

One of my major goals in this book has been to highlight the extent to which racial and sexual meanings directly produce one another: their relationship is not analogical but mutually constitutive. So, what does this mutual construction of whiteness and heterosexuality do?

I have argued that the mutual construction of "normal" sexuality and modern white racial meaning has provided white racial dominance with an extraordinarily strong alibi. The historical construction of "normal" whiteness as love, vulnerability, and hard work actively facilitates white ignorance and confusion about racial power. Whiteness, in general, insists its privileges stem from its willing submission to disciplined self-control. White people — perhaps especially bourgeois ones, but also members of all classes who attend public elementary schools and stay awake during "social studies" — have long been taught to identify themselves with the nation's highest, most idealized sociopolitical virtues in a way that makes it extremely difficult for them to perceive that identification as complicitous in the failure of those same ideals.

Precisely the same constructions facilitate straight married people's ignorance of their privileged status and the extent to which it depends on and perpetuates the marginalization, exploitation, and oppression of sexually nonnormative people. The emergence and normalization of marital heterosexuality in terms of self-discipline for the common good meant, and continues to mean, that many Americans misinterpret the political, economic, and social disabilities that attend visible deviation from that norm as self-inflicted. From the power-evasive perspective of the normal, the vulnerability attendant on sexual and gender deviance often seems willfully, even self-destructively, chosen. This misinterpretation encourages people who conform to normative sexual expectations to believe that they have earned their relative safety and security, that they deserve it for their meritorious commitment to civilized marital self-discipline. The coercive force and state enforcement of heteronormativity thus disappear, such that the unequal distribution of social, civil, and human rights along lines of erotic and relational conformity seem to reflect objectively different qualifications for membership in the nation.

The belief that disciplined conformity to dominant culture's sexual norms will be rewarded by economic success, personal satisfaction, and invulnerability to bigots with baseball bats (or badges) provides a strong incentive for at least appearing to accept those norms. That belief simultaneously encourages indifference to—even self-righteous pleasure in—the vulnerability of those whose sexual non-normativity makes them second-class citizens. Thus the definition of normality in terms of the disciplined pursuit of monogamous, reproductive heterosexual love in marriage not only obscures its continuing racial, ethnic, and class specificity; it works against the very values of compassion and connection it claims to foster. In this way "normality" helps to perpetuate racist thinking as well as other justifications for an unjust social order.

NOTES

Introduction

1. Shapiro, "Portrait," 252.
2. Shapiro, "Portrait," 251. Though the discussions I cite here were published in 1945, Norma and Normman represent the "normal American" from the era *before* the Second World War. They incorporate statistics from 1910 through 1930s. Robert Latou Dickinson designed the statues (in collaboration with the sculptor Abram Belskie), and they are best understood in the context of his other graphic and sculptural works. Dickinson made drawings of his patients throughout his years of active practice (1882–1924), often including measurements of their pelvic anatomy in his case records. By the end of the 1920s he had condensed this information into standardized images of "the" sexual body, "drawn to scale [and] based upon an exhaustive study of actual measurements." See Exner, *The Sexual Side of Marriage*, 18. Dickinson turned to sculpture during his retirement in the 1930s, his efforts at three-dimensional representations culminating in the great popularity of his terra-cotta display at the 1939 World's Fair (letter from RLD to A. L. Rose, June 18, 1942, box 3, folder 45, Robert Latou Dickinson Papers, Countway Library of Medicine, Boston, Massachusetts). Norma and Normman thus grew out of an interest that spanned the years 1890–1940, the period of the current study.

    The photograph of Normman published in Shapiro's article wears a clay fig leaf; the surviving statue, in the Cleveland Health Museum, does not.
3. Shapiro, "Portrait," 255.
4. Frankenberg coined the terms "race-evasive" and "power-evasive" in *White Women, Race Matters*, 14.
5. MacKenzie, *Statistics in Britain 1865–1930*, 11. The quotation is from Karl Pearson's laudatory biography of Galton, *The Life, Letters, and Labors of Francis Galton*. For a

broader overview of the history of statistics, see Porter, *The Rise of Statistical Thinking 1820–1900*.

6. Bederman, *Manliness and Civilization*.

7. Omi and Winant discuss late-twentieth-century neoconservative avoidance of direct racial language, and the substitution of "code words" (e.g., "law and order") for race, in *Racial Formation in the United States*. They imply that such coding reflects a more or less conscious political strategy, perhaps originated by George Wallace, but developed in the 1970s and triumphant in the Reagan years. While they may well be correct in their assessment of conservative political maneuvering in the 1970s and 1980s, my analysis suggests that the avoidance of direct racial speech has much earlier roots in white U.S. culture. The reasons that such avoidance became so extraordinarily politically effective in the last decades of the twentieth century remain to be examined.

8. It is also not accidental that this same period is the period in which the United States most aggressively and consistently pursued first imperial conquest and, later, ideological dominance on the world stage; evolutionist thought was, if anything, even more convenient as a justification for empire abroad than for segregation at home. The civilized white contest for dominance was a global one.

9. Somerville is one of very few scholars who have interrogated the directly sexual component of evolutionary thinking about race and civilization; this work is indebted to her *Queering the Color Line*. See also Gilman, *Difference and Pathology*; Leys-Stepan, "Race and Gender"; Newman, *White Women's Rights*, especially 29–30.

10. This does not mean that love is genuinely outside the bounds of the political. Martin Luther King's mid-century vision of the "beloved community" as the opposite of racial segregation suggests that discourses of love, like civilization discourse for an earlier era of anti-racist activists, can be mobilized from many perspectives and for many ends. That suggestion is confirmed by Chela Sandoval's theorization of love as a political technology essential to resisting the neocolonial cultural imperatives of postmodern globalization. Even so, love did have and continues to have a gloss of purely personal sentiment and an overtone of selfless commitment to the beloved's well-being that make it a particularly valuable concept for political projects seeking to conceal their political nature.

11. Shapiro, "Portrait," 255, 254.

12. Ibid., 252.

13. "The average young man and woman of the Gay Nineties as portrayed in two figures scientifically constructed by Professor Dudley A. Sargent" appear in Shapiro, "Portrait," 253.

14. Shapiro, "Portrait," 252–53.

15. Ibid., 253.

16. Ibid., 252.

17. For additional examples of direct comparisons between the ancient Greek and modern American civilizations, see Beard, *American Nervousness*, 135–38; Abbott, "What Is Civilization?" 483.

18. Josephine Robertson, "Norma's Gym Suit in '90s Covered All," Cleveland *Plain Dealer*, September 12, 1945, 1, 8. The column is accompanied by a photograph of the local women's college basketball team of 1901, smothered in yards of black wool serge.

19. Robertson, "Gym Suit." Robertson attributed the story about the mountaineer to Miss Emily R. Andrews, director of physical education at Flora Stone Mather [women's] College, part of Western Reserve University.

20. Josephine Robertson, "Norma's Husband Better Be Good," Cleveland *Plain Dealer*, September 16, 1945.

21. Ibid.

22. Cf. Foucault's famous dictum that "the sodomite had been a temporary aberration; the homosexual was now a species." *The History of Sexuality*, vol. 1, 43. The historical literature examining this reorganization of sexuality is immense. See especially Simmons, "Companionate Marriage and the Lesbian Threat," 54–59; Chauncey, "Christian Brotherhood or Sexual Perversion?"; D'Emilio and Freedman, *Intimate Matters*, part 3.

23. Freedman, "The Prison Lesbian"; Carter, "Evolutionary Sexology and the Primitive Pervert," in "White Love," 307–370; Somerville, "Race and the Invention of the Homosexual Body," in *Queering the Color Line*, 15–38.

24. On the literal exclusion of sexual deviants from the United States, see Luibhéid, *Entry Denied*. On sexual citizenship, see Alexander, "Not Just (Any) Body Can Be a Citizen"; Berlant, *The Queen of America Goes to Washington City*; Brandzel, "Queering Citizenship?"; Canaday, "Building a Straight State"; Duggan, "Queering the State"; Phelan, *Sexual Strangers*; Somerville, "Queer *Loving*."

25. On scientific racism, see Gould, *The Mismeasure of Man*, and Kevles, *In the Name of Eugenics*. See also Kline, *Building a Better Race*. The thumbnail description of scientific racism I have given here is derived from Smedley, *Race in North America*, 27.

26. On glandular therapy in the 1950s, see Ordover, *American Eugenics*, 111–12.

27. Terry, *An American Obsession*, 188.

28. Kinsey, "Homosexuality: Criteria for a Hormonal Explanation of the Homosexual," *Journal of Clinical Endocrinology* 1.5 (May 1941): 425. Quoted in Terry, *An American Obsession*, 298.

29. It is less significant, but nonetheless true, that I was and am more curious about the development and rise of "normality" than about the manifestations of its dominance, which depress me.

30. Hale, *Making Whiteness*, 5–6, 144.

31. Pascoe, "Miscegenation Law, Court Cases, and Ideologies of 'Race' in Twentieth-Century America," 44–69.

32. See, among many possible examples, Ordover, *American Eugenics*, and the essays in Hodes, ed., *Sex, Love, Race*.

33. Ewald, "Norms, Discipline, and the Law," 154. My thanks to Paul Kelleher for loaning me this essay.

34. Burnham set this tone in his highly influential 1973 "The Progressive Era Revolution in American Attitudes about Sex." Another school of historical thought, focusing on the nineteenth century, has long argued that "Victorian" culture was not really characterized by sexual repression. See Degler, "What Ought to Be and What Was," and Foucault, *The History of Sexuality*, vol. 1. Despite such contributions, historians' tendency to reflect early-twentieth-century sources' rhetorical assertions of Victorian prudery continued well into the 1980s. For instance, see Trimberger, "Feminism, Men and Modern Love."

Though few professional historians of sexuality continue to use this framework of a modern revolution against Victorian repression, it has remained remarkably durable in popular culture. For an excellent characterization of this position and the process of its modification by historians, see D'Emilio and Freedman, *Intimate Matters*, xi–xix.

35. Robinson, *The Modernization of Sex*, 2.

36. Simmons first made this argument in the 1979 "Companionate Marriage and the Lesbian Threat." Similar arguments are advanced in Haag, "In Search of 'The Real Thing,'" and Neuhaus, "The Importance of Being Orgasmic."

37. Saxton, *The Rise and Fall of the White Republic*, 14.

38. Freud is a significant exception to this generalization; his unique contribution to the development of modern sexual normality was to incorporate a certain amount of perversion and neurosis into it. See, for instance, the essays collected under the title *Sexuality and the Psychology of Love*, especially " 'Civilized' Sexual Morality and Modern Nervousness" (1908), "The Most Prevalent Form of Degradation in Erotic Life" (1912); and "Some Psychological Consequences of the Anatomical Distinction between the Sexes" (1925). This insistence that there was no unproblematically natural, pure sexuality was one of the aspects of Freudian theory that made it unpalatable to many Americans, who tended to modify psychoanalysis in the direction of downplaying the nasty parts. The magisterial work on the subject is Nathan Hale's two-volume study *Freud and the Americans*.

39. Foucault, *Abnormal*, 50.

40. For an early instance (1882) of such African American criticism that focuses on the intersection of race and sexuality, see Wells-Barnett, *Southern Horrors*. Giddings offers a helpful overview of the events that led to Wells's analysis in *When and Where I Enter*, 17–31. Duggan contextualizes these events in an extraordinarily original and interesting way in *Sapphic Slashers*, chapter 1.

Gitlin draws the connection between Civil Rights and the New Left in *The Sixties*. The connection between political liberation movements and the rise of ethnic studies is described in the essays collected in Butler, *Color-Line to Border-lands*, especially those in section 2: "Institutional Structure and Knowledge Production." See also Doane "Rethinking Whiteness Studies," 6. Chafe provides a basic and widely available, if rather slender, overview of the political sequence by which working in the Civil Rights movement contributed to the emergence of a vocal feminism at the end of the 1960s in *The Unfinished Journey*, 328–36. See also Hayden and King, "Sex and Caste,"and other documents reprinted in Alpert and Alpert, eds., *The Sixties Papers*. For a later expression of explicitly anti-racist feminism, see Lorde, "The Master's Tools Will Never Dismantle the Master's House," among other pieces reprinted in Moraga and Anzaldúa, eds., *This Bridge Called My Back*. E. Frances White contextualizes the emergence of such theorizing in the "Black Feminist Interventions" chapter of *Dark Continent of Our Bodies*.

Garber points out that radical feminist theorizing, centrally including the work of poets of color such as Audre Lorde and Pat Parker, has been ignored in most recent genealogies of queer theory but that this reflects the heightened status of "critical theory" in the U.S. academy since the early 1990s more than it reflects the actual historical development of the field. See Garber, *Identity Poetics*. See also Turner, *A Genealogy of Queer Theory* for a Foucault-centered account that nonetheless acknowledges queer theory's debts both to feminism (white and otherwise) and to anti-racist critique.

41. Garber, *Identity Poetics*. For more on the long-standing significance of gender difference and gender relations in U.S. constructions of racial meaning, see Newman, *White Women's Rights,* and Wiegman, *American Anatomies*.

42. DuCille, *The Coupling Convention*, 145.

43. McDowell has written insightful and relevant introductions to several major works of twentieth-century African American women's literature, including Jessie Fauset's *Plum Bun: A Novel without a Moral* (Boston: Beacon Press, 1990); Ann Petry's *The Street* (Boston: Beacon Press, 1985); and Nella Larsen's *Quicksand* and *Passing* (New Brunswick, N.J.: Rutgers University Press, 1986). A different version of McDowell's introduction to this last is also available as " 'It's Not Safe. Not Safe at All,' " 616–25. Butler draws on and extends McDowell's reading of Larsen in *Bodies That Matter*, chapter 6, "Passing, Queering: Nella Larsen's Psychoanalytic Challenge," where she argues that homophobia does the work of white supremacy. Several essays in Abel et al., eds., *Female Subjects in Black and White,* engage relevant questions of the politics embedded in scholarly work on the race / sex / gender nexus.

For a more historically oriented approach to the problems of representing race and desire in a racist context, see Hine, "Rape and the Inner Lives of Black Women in the Middle West." On the general occlusion of such scholarship in white-defined sexuality studies, see Hammonds, "Black (W)holes and the Geometry of Black Female Sexuality."

44. Hall, *Queer Theories*, 149. For a more complete discussion of the common agendas of "queer" cultural, political, and intellectual projects around the turn of the millennium, as well as some suggestions about how historians of sexuality can use queer theory, see Carter, "On Mother-Love," especially 112–17.

Normative striving is not, of course, limited to straight people; gay neoconservatives (I like to call them "homocons") sometimes make careers out of summoning more flamboyant queers to sober up and settle down in "civilized commitment" (Eskridge, *The Case for Same-Sex Marriage*). The language of civilization suggests that racism is subtly in play when homocons try to use sexual shame to discipline perverse subjects. Warner analyzes the arguments of Eskridge and others like him in *The Trouble with Normal*, especially chapter 3, "Beyond Gay Marriage."

Because Warner has offered the only previous book-length work on the sexual politics of normality, and because he is usually credited with coining the term "heteronormativity," it seems appropriate to explain how I see the relationship between his scholarship and mine. Several people have asked whether my research provides the historical context for the political situation Warner describes. I would say, instead, that his work delineates one contemporary development or consequence of the earlier politics of the normal that I engage, but his work is severely limited by his lack of attention to race.

Warner's argument proceeds as though sexuality alone—or in tandem with its derivative, gender—determines access to normality and its privileges. In contrast, I hold in this book that normality sutures race to sexual object–choice, erotic activity, and gender expression, such that they cannot be fully understood when isolated from one another. Racism in the United States very often works through the sexual abjection of people of color, whose alleged inferiority, bestiality, irrationality, or what-have-you is routinely signified through depictions of their erotic conduct and affective expression as deviant, pathological, abnormal. One consequence is that attempts to claim "normality" have historically also been attempts to claim at least some of the privileges of whiteness. Warner's assumption that normality is racially neutral leads to a serious flaw in his political analysis: he forgets that normative strivings do not imply political quiescence or complicity with dominant power structures in quite the same way in all contexts. When race is brought back into the analytic frame, movements toward normativity can be reinterpreted as potentially revolutionary along racial lines, even as they are immensely risky along the lines of sexuality and gender.

45. My specification of the U.S. American context is not meant to imply that critical work in these areas always or necessarily focuses on this country but only to acknowledge that queer theory, feminism, and antiracism have different political histories in different places. It seems that globalization may be pushing the different threads of radical social and political critique closer together than they have

been since the 1960s; I am thinking of the recent emphasis on race in queer theory as well as of the emergence of "borderland studies" as a newly organized field which concentrates on the zones where nation-states, identities, sexualities, ethnicities, and bodies collide. See, for instance, the "What's Queer about Queer Studies Now?" special issue of *Social Text* in Fall–Winter 2005, edited by David Eng with Judith Halberstam and José Esteban Muñoz.

46. Katz, *The Invention of Heterosexuality*, sketches the major developments in modern heterosexual identity from its sexological inception in the late-nineteenth and early-twentieth centuries to the present and notes that the identity category seems to have been influenced by the fact that its most influential early articulators were all white men (18). In "The Prison Lesbian," Freedman has written about the way in which lesbian bodies and desires were constructed as inherently primitive within the disciplinary context of early-twentieth-century prisons, while Terry has investigated similar themes in medical discourses (*An American Obsession*). In *Queering the Color Line*, Somerville has expanded this subject to address the mutually constitutive pathologizing of blackness and homosexuality in early-twentieth-century culture, and the ways in which African American authors worked within and against this discourse in their own representations of race and sex. Somerville shows that the hardening of the color line also involved a hardening of gender and erotic boundaries. Ferguson develops a similar theme in *Aberrations in Black* but focuses on the constitution of blackness as "nonheteronormative" in canonical sociology and African American fiction. In *The Color of Sex* Stokes points to the conventional romantic narrative structure of many popular white-supremacist novels of this period, suggesting that the resolution of plot tension in heterosexual union is a necessary element of the narrative of triumphant whiteness that these stories rehearse. White (*Dark Continent of Our Bodies*) and Reid-Pharr (*Black Gay Man*) analyze the impact of the conflation of whiteness with normality on African American gender and sexual politics, especially as these shape fiction and literary criticism.

The present study has been influenced by all these authors and also by the diverse group of literary and cultural critics collectively known as "queer theorists." A full list of acknowledgments would run for many pages; among those whose published work has profoundly shaped my thinking about what it means to study sexuality are Dorothy Allison, Judith Butler, Pat Califia, Samuel Delaney, Michel Foucault, David Halperin, Isaac Julien, Cherríe Moraga, Carol Queen, Robert Reid-Pharr, Gayle Rubin, Eve Kosofsky Sedgwick, and Michael Warner. The queer theorists whose nonprint cultural productions have most influenced my work are Edward Goehring and Catherine Opie.

47. The most significant exception to this generalization is Stoler, *Race and the Education of Desire*. I suspect that it is no accident that the work on the intersection of race and sexuality most tightly focused on Foucault is also the most attentive to

the making of good bourgeois subjects and citizens. For all his fame in gay, lesbian, and queer circles, Foucault actually wrote much more about the processes of normalization and discipline that are central to modern whiteness as the foundation of the nation-state. See especially *Discipline and Punish*, 177–84.

48. Again, there are exceptions. Segrest, *Memoir of a Race Traitor*, speaks of the intersection of whiteness and heterosexuality in the late twentieth century. Newman, *White Women's Rights*, focuses on late-nineteenth- and early-twentieth-century feminism's origins in white racialist thinking but makes occasional references to sexuality; see especially her discussion of Margaret Mead (163). Kline, *Building a Better Race*, is among the most sustained discussions of the intersection of "normal" sexuality and "normal" whiteness in the twentieth-century United States.

49. For instance, Delgado's and Stefancic's widely used anthology *Critical White Studies* opens with the observation that "whites have found their whiteness both opaque and transparent," a theme that informs many of the contributions to the volume. For an example of the assertion that whiteness is invisible, see Bonnie Kae Grover, "Growing Up White in America," 34; for analysis of what Barbara Flagg calls "the transparency phenomenon," see Flagg, "Transparently White Subjective Decisionmaking," 87; for the sociological claim that transparency may be on the wane, see Charles Gallagher, "White Racial Formation: Into the Twenty-First Century," 7. See also the essays collected in Doane and Bonilla-Silva, eds., *White Out*, and especially Doane, "Rethinking Whiteness Studies," 6–8.

50. Warner, *Fear of a Queer Planet*, xxiii.

51. Think, for instance, of George W. Bush's eyes.

52. Hale, *Making Whiteness*, xi; Frankenberg, *White Women, Race Matters*, 6.

53. This perspective informs much of Terry's work, such as "Lesbians under the Medical Gaze," where the urge to investigate appears synonymous with the attempt to master deviance. It is also a major theme of Minton, *Departing from Deviance*. Foucault, though more explicitly skeptical about the extent to which "normality" actually allows freedom from the operations of power, also saw the production of expert knowledge as a crucial technique of power. See, for instance, "Scientia Sexualis," part 3 of *The History of Sexuality*, vol. 1.

There is a large and relevant body of literature on the persistent tendency to figure lesbian sexuality as an invisibility or absence. The best-known work on the subject is Castle, *The Apparational Lesbian*; for a distinctly different approach to the problem of lesbian invisibility, see Garber, "Where in the World Are the Lesbians?" Against the widespread assumption that antihomophobic scholarship will necessarily seek to render lesbianism more clearly visible, see Jagose, *Inconsequence*. My thanks to Julia Shaw for alerting me to this last.

54. Though I thought I learned this from feminism, I am informed that this argument for the well-rounded perception of social structures by the oppressed is really

drawn from Hegel: the master / slave dialectic, to be precise; see *Phenomenology of Spirit*, 114. My thanks to Amy Ninetto for this citation.

55. See Hale, *Making Whiteness*. Outlaw makes a similar point when he argues that "experiences of whiteness as transparent and invisible are likely to be much more characteristic in postapartheid conditions in this country than in earlier conditions: that is, after substantial dismantling of the formal institutions and explicitly racialized and regulated practices of segregated race relations governed by agendas of White Supremacy. . . . For during the long period of postslavery formal apartheid, white folks marshaled and invoked their whiteness in myriad ways as the powerful identification card that it was. Visibility and recognition as white, consciousness of the ability—the power—to marshal and invoke whiteness, and to require that it be recognized and deferred to as supreme, were normal routines and assumptions structuring daily life. Invisibility and transparency are conditions of significantly different historical, social, political conditions." "Rehabilitate Racial Whiteness?" 168–69.

56. Roediger, *The Wages of Whiteness*, 13.

57. Marable, "The Problematics of Ethnic Studies," in Marable, ed., *Dispatches from the Ebony Tower*, 244.

58. See Ignatiev and Garvey, eds., *Race Traitor*, and Roediger, *Toward the Abolition of Whiteness*. For a helpful, if hostile, summary and assessment of the "new abolitionism," see Winant, "White Racial Projects."

59. Kolchin argues for the importance of such historical methods in "Whiteness Studies." Kolchin argues that the failure to attend adequately to real social relations—"inattention to context" and overemphasis on "image, representation, and literary depiction" (161)—bedevils whiteness studies and produces a characteristic analytical weakness in the field. In Kolchin's view, both causality and really existing differences in social power and political conviction disappear when scholars pay too much attention to representation. Kolchin's implicit definition of "real" history in terms of empiricism and issues of "interest and politics" (162) leads him to evaluate other approaches as presentist, more assertive than argumentative, more subjective than objective, and tainted by what he calls a "postmodern accentuation of self" (166). It is this kind of response I have in mind when I suggest that some readers will not find the present work to be "history."

60. Kolchin again provides a useful example: "The 1790 law that limited naturalization to 'free white persons' allowed Irish immigrants entrance as 'white persons'; in what sense, then, should one speak of their subsequently 'becoming' white? This can make sense if whiteness is to be understood metaphorically, meaning 'acceptable,' but . . . whiteness studies authors clearly intend the term to serve as more than a metaphor" (163). The comparative construction suggests that for Kolchin, metaphors are inherently less substantive, revealing, or consequential than legal classifications. Further, the contradictory character of nineteenth-

century Irish immigrants' relation to the category of whiteness is presented as though it were the consequence of an analytical failure among whiteness studies scholars, rather than an insight into the real complexity of racial meaning, its conceptual mobility, and its incommensurability with the material real.

61. Sedgwick, *Epistemology of the Closet*, 22.

62. The implication that discursive analysis is good for progressive political thinking as well as historical analysis will seem utterly bizarre to many (straight?) survivors of the academic theory wars of the late 1980s and early 1990s. Among the many works by historians that denounced poststructuralist theory as tending to political paralysis, see Palmer, *Descent into Discourse*. A more thoughtful piece, also directed at the "linguistic turn," is Christian, "The Race for Theory," which asks important questions about the race of the "subject" whose death was routinely announced at this time.

Women's historians and other feminist scholars were also often wary of the way that the "linguistic turn" seemed to threaten the conceptual space for paying attention to women and to gender. Foucault's discursive analyses came under especially heavy fire, primarily because his histories of sexuality neither spoke much about female subjects nor mobilized gender as an interpretative tool, despite the fact that those studies addressed a field of study long and well studied by feminists. For a representative feminist-historical argument against taking discourse analysis seriously because Foucault doesn't discuss women enough and feminists had already said it anyway, see Richlin, "Foucault's *History of Sexuality*." Such arguments' fear lest discourse analysis undermine the political agency of oppressed people is explored and addressed by McWhorter in *Bodies and Pleasures*; see especially chapter 3, "Why I Shouldn't Like Foucault (So They Say)." For further engagements of Foucault from a politicized, explicitly queer perspective, see Halperin, "Forgetting Foucault," and *Saint Foucault*.

I hesitate to date my argument by situating this work in relation to "theory wars" that are now fifteen years old, but feel it necessary because it appears that my side lost. Few Ph.D. candidates in history are currently being trained to use the kinds of theoretical and interpretative tools that scholars in interdisciplinary sexuality studies often find most useful. That means that fewer people are being trained to do specifically historical studies of sexuality. Worse, those who try will find relatively few mentors who can introduce them to the theory and methods of the field. The professional practice of the history of sexuality is more often sponsored by English, Women's Studies, and American Studies than by history departments, which is a shame because doctoral training in history has yielded some brilliant work on sexuality—and also because there's no good reason that language and literature students should have all the fun. Nobody has yet collected and analyzed the data on the disciplinary homes of sexuality studies scholars in general, but since a significant amount of work on the history of sexuality addresses lesbian and gay subjects, Marc Stein's analysis of hiring patterns among practitioners of lesbian and gay history is suggestive. See American Historical Association, "Committee on Lesbian and Gay History Survey on LGBTQ History Careers," June 2001, available online at http://www.usc.edu/isd/archives/clgh/reports.html. A shorter version of this material can be also be found in "Committee on Lesbian and Gay History Survey on LGBTQ History Careers."

63. Foucault discusses the link between taxonomic classification and the disciplined modern subject in *Discipline and Punish*, 148–49.

64. My formulation in this paragraph is so profoundly indebted to Gail Bederman's representation of her approach to gender that it hovers between paraphrase and plagiarism; I have omitted quotation marks primarily because I couldn't find a syntactically accurate way to indicate the divergence between her comments about manhood and my larger claims about identity in general. See Bederman, *Manliness and Civilization*, 7.

65. See Newitz, "White Savagery and Humiliation," 145–46, for a brilliant exploration of whiteness by analogy to the Lacanian Phallus.

66. See Maclean, *Behind the Mask of Chivalry*; Wade, *The Fiery Cross*; and Blee, *Women of the Klan*.

67. The classic essay on prescriptive literature is Degler, "What Ought to Be and What Was."

68. See, for instance, Higham, *Strangers in the Land*, esp. chapter 6; Allen, *The Invention of the White Race*; Ignatiev, *How the Irish Became White*; Conzen, "German-Americans and the Invention of Ethnicity"; Orsi, "The Religious Boundaries of an Inbetween People;" Barrett and Roediger, "Inbetween Peoples." For an important reconsideration of the relationship between "race" (Irish, Italian, etc.) and "color" (white, tawny, yellow, etc.) in this era, see Guglielmo, "Rethinking Whiteness Historiography." Guglielmo argues that, while the Southern Italians he studied were consistently identified and discriminated against on racial grounds, they were simultaneously colored "white on arrival" in a way that makes it misleading to represent them as "becoming" white or as "in-between people" (51–52). My understanding of the role of sexuality and its class-specific management is in alignment with Guglielmo's work in that it emphasizes the hierarchies within the racial category "white," the varying degrees of access different kinds of people could have to the racial ideal.

69. Jacobson, *Whiteness of a Different Color*.

70. Ibid., 4.

71. The comparisons between the "modern" normals and their "Victorian" grandparents were possible because late-nineteenth-century investigators had recorded the dimensions of students at the most elite and prestigious Eastern colleges and universities. Norma and Normman "lived" in the heartland, but their "grandparents" had gone to Harvard and Radcliffe. See Shapiro, "Portrait," 251, 254.

72. This definition of the "normal" or "average" American by reference to people who were admittedly not "average" in any statistical sense appears also in Lynd and Lynd, *Middletown* (1929). "Middletown" was selected as the focus for the Lynds' study not because it was genuinely "normal" ("A typical city, strictly speaking, does not exist"—3) but because it represented an ideologically defined "normality" better than any more statistically average city could. "Middletown," a.k.a. Muncie, Indiana, had a very small black population and virtually no recent immigrants. Thus, the Lynds explained, "instead of being forced to handle two major variables, racial change and cultural change, the field staff was enabled to concentrate upon cultural change. The study thus became one of the interplay of a relatively constant native American stock and its native environment" (8). Muncie was "Middletown" *because it was white.*

73. Shapiro, "Portrait," 252.

74. Caption on "Search-For-Norma Entry" form. Cleveland *Plain Dealer*, September 9, 1945, 8.

75. Josephine Robertson, "Theater Cashier, 23, Wins Title of 'Norma,' Besting 3,863 Entries." Cleveland *Plain Dealer*, September 23, 1945, 1. Interestingly, this young woman seems to have been "average" in its more everyday and depressing sense. Martha Skidmore was twenty-three, married, and quite plain. When interviewed by the *Plain Dealer*, Mrs. Skidmore "indicated that she was an average individual in her tastes and that nothing out of the ordinary had ever happened to her until the Normal Search came along" R(1).

76. See Haney-Lopez, *White by Law.*

77. Jacobson, *Whiteness of a Different Color*, 26. This discussion is derived from Takaki, *Iron Cages*, 3–15.

78. Daniel Ullman, "The Constitution of the United States," Daniel Ullman Papers, New York Historical Society, Reel #5, frame 231; quoted in Jacobson, *Whiteness of a Different Color*, 71.

79. Though John Hartigan Jr.'s ethnographic researches do not speak directly to the racial formations of the early twentieth century, his argument about the ways in which some white people are racially marked as "rednecks," "hillbillies," and "white trash" does seem to confirm the ongoing centrality of self-control to "normal" whiteness. That normative self-control has two dimensions that resonate with the current work—first is the requirement of a particular kind of sexual respectability, preferably limited to intraracial marriage, and second is the requirement of reticence about race. See Hartigan, "Who Are These White People?"

80. I do not want to make an argument for the exact moment of mass culture's emergence. I have some sympathy with arguments that place that occurrence in the late nineteenth century, with the rise of the dime novel and the expansion of the periodical press, while I also concur with those who argue that our own mass culture, defined by audiences in the millions, is a phenomenon that coincided

with the advent of television. For my purposes, the important thing is that the racial and sexual discourses I analyze increasingly addressed themselves to an immense and undifferentiated white audience which was solicited as normal precisely through the absence of class, ethnic, religious, and regional cultural markers. The fact that that audience was fictional is beside the point. I suspect, though I have not argued, that the rise of the concept of the "normal" in the 1920s and 1930s provided the cultural foundation for the emergence of a genuinely standardized cultural product after the Second World War. For a helpful summary of the professional debate about the difference between popular and mass culture, see Kammen, *American Culture, American Tastes*.

81. Dell, *Love in the Machine Age*, 6.

82. Ibid., 15.

83. Ibid., 6, 14–16, 29.

84. Ibid., 6.; emphasis in original.

85. Ibid., 237.

86. *Our Dancing Daughters* (Harry Beaumont, 1928).

87. *The Birth of a Nation* (D. W. Griffith, 1915) played for fifteen years in the South, according to Richard Delgado and Jean Stefancic, "Images of the Outsider in American Law and Culture," *Cornell Law Review* 77 (1992); reprinted in Delgado and Stefancic, *Critical White Studies*, 172. See Lears, *No Place of Grace*, chapter 3, for a fascinating discussion of the antimodernist reclamation of "knightly" violence and its connection with white supremacy. Floyd Dell offers us another view of the stock character represented by the Southern gentleman in *Our Dancing Daughters*. Dell describes such a man as "both shocked and bewildered" by flappers, because he "is accustomed to divide girls into two categories, the 'chaste' and the 'unchaste.' He has his . . . uses for both." Modern "petters" like Crawford fit neither camp, and therefore the old-fashioned man feels "that there is something unnatural about . . . this betwixt-and-between behavior" (*Love in the Machine Age*, 169).

88. Interestingly, Page's character's erotic insensitivity is suggested through her practice of rewarding herself for each month of marriage by buying a diamond bracelet. She refers to these as her "service stripes," a term commonly used at this time for the presents with which men compensated their mistresses for their unmarriagability. The suggestion is that she is providing a service for her husband rather than that they are lovers; the "Victorianism" of this view is underscored by her confusion of marriage with a legal form of prostitution.

89. *Our Modern Maidens* (Jack Conway, 1929) also starred Crawford, as did *Our Blushing Brides* (Harry Beaumont, 1930).

1. "Barbarians Are Not Nervous"

1. Beard, *A Practical Treatise on Nervous Exhaustion (Neurasthenia)* (1880), *American Nervousness* (1881), and *Sexual Neurasthenia* (1884). These works are highly repetitive. In the interests of brevity and simplicity in my notes, I have cited this material as it appears in *American Nervousness*. The other volumes are cited where they are more relevant or concise.

2. Beard, *Sexual Neurasthenia*, 73.

3. Haller and Haller, *The Physician and Sexuality in Victorian America*, 5–43.

4. Wood, " 'The Fashionable Diseases' "; Lears, *No Place of Grace*, 50.

5. Mumford, " 'Lost Manhood' Found," 87.

6. The newest explorations of the social relationships embedded in the diagnosis, and therefore its variable meanings in different cultural settings, are in *Cultures of Neurasthenia*, ed. Gijswift-Hofstra and Porter. These essays focus on the mobilization and uses of the diagnosis outside the United States.

7. The importance of claims to weakness or victim status in contemporary constructions of whiteness have drawn the attention of several scholars. See Newitz, "White Savagery and Humiliation"; Gressing, *The Recovery of Race in America*; Sklar, "Dying American Dream," and others. To my knowledge none of this literature has explored the possibility that claims of weakness might be a relatively durable element of American whiteness. The sole exception is Linda Williams's *Playing the Race Card*, which examines the way that representations of suffering have informed and been informed by racial politics since the mid-nineteenth century.

8. Gosling, *Before Freud*, 13. Tom Lutz nuances this claim with the observation that both sanatoria and VA hospitals continued to use both the diagnosis and some of its classic therapies until late in the 1920s; see "Varieties of Medical Experience," in *Cultures of Neurasthenia*, ed. Gijswift-Hofstra and Porter, 65–66. Lutz further notes that the diagnosis retains its usefulness and explanatory power in China to this day (67).

9. Rosenberg, *No Other Gods*, 98.

10. Some of these cases are straightforward, usually brief, accounts published in American medical journals. Others were collected, packaged into appealing narratives, and published by Silas Weir Mitchell, one of the most prominent American doctors of the nineteenth century and the chief proponent of nervousness after Beard's untimely demise in 1883. Mitchell was also a popular middlebrow novelist. Because these histories were written by a man who knew both the medical literature on nervousness and the respectable public's standards for a satisfying story, they illustrate the interpretations of nervousness most likely to appeal to a broad late-nineteenth-century audience. The Mitchell case histories I have used here are from *Fat and Blood, and How to Make Them*, originally published in 1877 and

reprinted in 1902 and 1907. These reprintings suggest that *Fat and Blood* retained a certain relevance into the new century. See also S. Weir Mitchell, *Wear and Tear, or Hints for the overworked* (1871), a popular volume on overworked nerves that went through at least five editions. For a full biographical (not to say hagiographical) treatment, see Burr, *Weir Mitchell, His Life and Letters*. Mitchell's novels were historical romances for men, most of them set during the Revolutionary War.

11. Beard, *American Nervousness*, vi.

12. For the unique competitiveness of modern civilization, see Beard, *Practical Treatise*, 255; for commentary on the rapid pace of modern life, Beard, *American Nervousness*, 103–05, 113–15.

13. Beard, *American Nervousness*, 25. The example of hemophilia as an aristocratic hereditary disease is mine, not Beard's, and is intended simply as an illustration likely to be familiar to readers. Research into the transmission of hemophilia and its linkage with other hereditary traits was, however, among the original projects of the prestigious Galton Laboratory in London at the turn of the century. In 1936, Julia Bell and J. B. S. Haldane published "the first certain pedigree demonstration of linkage in human beings," which addressed the connection between hemophilia and color-blindness. See Kevles, *In the Name of Eugenics,* 202. On the "symbolics of blood" and its relation to sexuality in the making of modern racism, see Foucault, *The History of Sexuality,* vol. 1, 146–50; see also Stoler's gloss on and extension of this passage in *Race and the Education of Desire*, 37–53.

14. Beard emphasized that "the nervous diathesis can only exist in civilization" (*American Nervousness*, 177), and that neurasthenia was the result of civilization acting on that predisposed body (176). No amount of strain or self-indulgence could make a barbarian nervous.

15. Beard, *American Nervousness*, 26.

16. Ibid.

17. Ibid.

18. See Kasson, "Table Manners and the Control of Appetite," in *Rudeness and Civility*.

19. Edward P. Thwing, untitled review in the *Quarterly Journal of Inebriety* 10 (January 1888): 44.

20. Beard, *American Nervousness*, 2.

21. Ibid., 2–3.

22. Ibid., 4.

23. Ibid., 26.

24. Richard White, personal communication.

25. Gosling, *Before Freud*, 55, 92, 96.

26. On the consolidation of distinct and relatively permanent classes in this era, and hence the loss of faith in the American dream of independent self-sufficiency for most workers, see Beckert, *The Monied Metropolis*, especially chapters 7 and 8. Newman also notes the connection between the late-nineteenth-century refor-

mulation of race and gender relations, the fear felt by "Anglo-Saxon elites" lest the social changes they witnessed should undermine their dominance, and the "continuing pressure on urban wages." *White Women's Rights*, 28, 15.

27. Roediger, *The Wages of Whiteness*.

28. See Gosling, *Before Freud*; on the work ethic, see also Lutz, *American Nervousness, 1903*.

29. Beard, *American Nervousness*, 103–14. My list of the causes of American nervousness is partial—Beard's discussion of the topic covers an entire chapter of *American Nervousness*.

30. Beard, *American Nervousness*, 114–15.

31. Theodore Dreiser's (unfinished) novel *An Amateur Laborer*, though written in the first decade of the twentieth century, is revealing as a description of exactly this bind. The protagonist, a journalist suffering from nervousness, cannot write and must eventually find wage labor or starve; but the very nervous sensitivity that blocks his creative use of the pen makes it impossible for him to tolerate other work. See Lutz, *American Nervousness, 1903*, 44. See also Adams, *The Education of Henry Adams*, for the most famous expression of this position.

32. Sicherman details the ways in which the neurasthenia diagnosis could be a source of prestige for both doctors and patients in "The Uses of a Diagnosis."

33. Beard, *American Nervousness*, 9–10.

34. Of course, some neurasthenes were both rich and powerful, and in the Gilded Age the cautious Yankee thrift Beard seemed to be advocating was not an especially good way to amass a fortune. I have already noted that Leland Stanford, Henry Villard, and Collis Huntington all had nervous collapses; and as Richard White has pointed out, these men and their peers lived and got rich off other people's money. Had they relied on their own resources they would never have become fabulously wealthy. Yet the Beardian emotional economy of nervousness applies to them too. People like Stanford and Huntington were especially vulnerable to nervousness because their fortunes depended on resources they did not own and could not control. Their social standing, and their ability to make yet more money, depended on that unstable and appropriated wealth; their place in the ongoing development of civilization was far from secure. Such insecurity, combined with the strain of constant attention to the tickertape, made attacks of nervous weakness completely predictable.

35. Barker-Benfield, *The Horrors of the Half-Known Life*.

36. Beard, *Sexual Neurasthenia*, 156–57. See also Mumford, " 'Lost Manhood' Found."

37. The language of the "narrow margin" and of "nervous bankruptcy" appears in Beard, *American Nervousness*, 10, 13; the description of "true spermatorrhea" comes from Beard, *Sexual Neurasthenia*, 157. Gosling, *Before Freud*, table 2 (63) indicates that a fairly large number of cases in his sample—24 percent of men, 14 percent of women—were reported without their conclusions.

38. Gosling, *Before Freud*, 96–97; Willard, *A White Life for Two* (1890). Willard's definition of a white life centered on abstention from alcohol and pre- and extramarital sex; the exercise of self-control and restraint seemed to her to be the essence of civilization. She appears to have been incapable of recognizing any other definition of whiteness and has become well-known for refusing to accept Ida B. Wells's claim that white women sometimes chose to have sex with black men. See Bederman, *Manliness and Civilization*, 66–67; Ware, *Beyond the Pale,* 200–205; and, more generally, Tyrell, *Woman's World, Woman's Empire.*

39. Wood, " 'The Fashionable Diseases.' "

40. Mitchell, *Fat and Blood*, 144–45.

41. Clarke, *Sex in Education* (1878).

42. Mitchell borrowed this case from his esteemed British colleague William Playfair, who described it in *The Systematic Treatment of Nerve Prostration and Hysteria* (published in the United States in 1883). Mitchell seems to have assumed that this patient, though English, illustrated the nervous "type" as he and his readers saw it in the United States.

43. Mitchell, *Fat and Blood*, 161; the statement that the patient was "naturally fine and highly cultivated" appears on 164.

44. Ibid., 161–63.

45. Ibid.

46. Ibid., 163.

47. Ibid., 165.

48. Beard, *Sexual Neurasthenia*, 154.

49. Beard, *American Nervousness*, 97.

50. Pick has made a similar argument in relation to European discourses of degeneracy; he holds that degeneracy expressed "danger from internal transgressions rather than inter-racial 'pollution.' " *The Faces of Degeneration*, 39.

51. See Brumberg, *Fasting Girls*; O'Connor, "Pictures of Health."

52. The secondary literature on hysteria is immense. I have relied especially on Gilman et al., *Hysteria beyond Freud*, and Micale, *Approaching Hysteria*.

53. Dixon, *Woman and her Diseases from the Cradle to the Grave*, 134, 140. A similar example can be found in Charcot, "Isolation in the Treatment of Hysteria," in *Clinical Lectures*, 368.

54. Carter, *On the Pathology and Treatment of Hysteria*, 46.

55. This account of the Fancher case is drawn from Brumburg, *Fasting Girls*, 78–89. Brumberg, too, notes the important role of deception in the diagnosis of hysteria (85).

56. Ibid., 83.

57. Ibid., 80; Beard, *Sexual Neurasthenia*, 190.

58. Beard, *Practical Treatise*, 137.

59. Ibid.

60. Beard, *American Nervousness*, 114–15.

61. See Carter, "White Love," 114–52, for an (over)extended discussion of these issues and the problem of differential diagnosis.

62. Though I can't develop this argument here, it is likely that the neurasthenia diagnosis simultaneously reflects the ambiguous status of the United States in relation to its "parent," i.e., British, civilization. Stoler and other postcolonial scholars have shown that very similar issues of cultural ownership, purity, duplicity, and legitimacy structured the political, economic, racial, and social relations of colonies and metropoles to one another. (See, e.g., Stoler's discussion of "fraudulent recognitions" in "Sexual Affronts and Racial Frontiers.") America's position in the Gilded Age was unique in that it was an ex-colony seeking to become an imperial nation in its own right, but there are enough commonalities between the anxieties of "native whites" in the United States and those of "European" ancestry in the Dutch colonies Stoler studies to suggest that further study of the consolidation of white racial identity in the United States should engage with the contradictory imperial status of the nation.

63. For the Beecher-Tilton affair, see Fox, *Trials of Intimacy*. For more on Victoria Woodhull, see Goldsmith, *Other Powers*; Frisken, "Sex in Politics"; and McGarry, "Spectral Sexualities."

64. Godkin, "Chromo-Civilization," 201. My thanks to Colin Fisher for directing my attention to this editorial.

65. This is, for instance, pretty much what Ida B. Wells did in the aftermath of the lynching of her friends in Memphis in 1892. See Bederman, *Manliness and Civilization*, chapter 2, "The White Man's Civilization on Trial."

66. Godkin, "Chromo-Civilization," 202.

67. Marzio, *The Democratic Art*, offers a thorough account of the development of chromolithography both as a craft and as a business. Oddly, we see here the editor of a mass-distributed weekly suggesting that the mass distribution of culture would undermine civilization; the strangeness is compounded when we recall that Godkin himself was an Irishman made good, who took up the cudgels to defend WASP civilization from one of its native sons. It seems likely that Godkin's attack on chromolithography derived from two sources. First, he probably knew that Beecher's sisters Catharine and Harriet (author of *Uncle Tom's Cabin*) had bestowed lavish praise on the chromo as a vector for middle-class morality in their famous and influential 1869 work *The American Woman's Home: or Principles of Domestic Science*. Second, *The Nation* was founded to provide the masses with access to "real" culture in the hope that eventually refinement would permeate all classes of the American democracy. To a certain extent, then, the sticky sentimentality and commercialism of most chromos constituted direct competition for Godkin's project of using mass-production printing technology to uplift and refine popular taste and morals.

68. Godkin, "Chromo-Civilization," 202.

69. McGarry, "Spectral Sexualities," 21.

70. Beard, *American Nervousness*, 98–99.

71. That Beard believed machines could evolve, and that adaptation involved humans and machines evolving together, is clearest in this passage about the Third Avenue elevated train in New York City: "When first organized . . . the noise of the trains was a source of distress to all or nearly all, who lived on or very near the avenue and streets through which it passed. . . . Those who were so unfortunate as to be confined to the house by any form of sickness in some cases suffered so severely that it was feared their lives would be sacrificed; and some were obliged to dispose of their property and move away. The majority of residents, however, in the course of a few months became so used to the din that . . . it ceased to be painfully annoying; they had adapted themselves to their environment; the nervous system had become to a degree benumbed, so that the vibrations striking on the ear gave rise to no conscious or memorable sensation. This process of [adaptation] was made much easier and shorter by . . . the fact that the structure of the road had been so affected by use that its vibrations were less rasping to the nerves. It would appear that the vibrations were both changed in quality and diminished in loudness" (*American Nervousness*, 110–11).

72. Ibid., 12.

73. Unsigned editorial from the London *Times*, reprinted as a long footnote in Beard, *American Nervousness*, 100–102.

74. Ibid.

75. Roediger, *The Wages of Whiteness*, 13.

76. See also Harris, "Whiteness as Property"; Lipsitz, *The Possessive Investment in Whiteness*.

77. On race relations between the Civil War and the Second World War, see Williamson, *The Crucible of Race*. On the rise of the myth of the "black beast rapist" in the 1890s, see Hodes, "The Sexualization of Reconstruction Politics." On the Ku Klux Klan, see Wade, *The Fiery Cross*, and Blee, *Women of the Klan*.

78. See Chauncey's discussion of the "pansy craze" in *Gay New York*, chapter 11; Simmons explores contempt for "mannish" women in "Companionate Marriage and the Lesbian Threat"; Carter describes the "primitive pervert" in "White Love," chapter 5, as does Somerville in *Queering the Color Line*.

2. The Marriage Crisis

1. *A Doll's House* was originally performed in 1879, and while the simple portrayal of marriage as constraining to women had lost its novelty by the 1920s, Ibsen's heroine continued to resonate as a symbol of the modern woman who preferred the risks of independence to the suffocation of secure but infantilized, femininity.

For examples, see Messer, *The Family in the Making*, xvii; Wile and Winn, *Marriage in the Modern Manner*, 29.

2. Macfadden, *Sweethearts for Life*, 71.

3. See, for instance, Carpenter, *Love's Coming of Age*, 78–96; Emerick, "College Women and Race Suicide"; Howard, *Facts for the Married*, x–xii. Observers across the political spectrum commonly ascribed the "revolution in manners and morals" to the effects of the Great War. For a left-radical articulation of this view, see Calverton, *The Bankruptcy of Marriage*, 14–20; on the far nativist right, see Stoddard, *Clashing Tides of Color*. See also Hirschfeld, *The Sexual History of the World War*.

4. Katherine B. Davis published part of the research for her 1929 scholarly monograph, *Factors in the Sex Life of 2200 Women*, as an article called "Why They Failed to Marry" in *Harper's Monthly*. Similarly, G. V. Hamilton's 1929 *A Research in Marriage* was condensed and revised for readability and republished in 1930 as *What Is Wrong with Marriage*.

5. "Danger Rocks in Married Life" appeared in the *Ladies' Home Journal*, September 1912, 11–12; "Twenty Rules for a Happy Marriage" in the *American Magazine*, November 1920, 51; "Is Marriage Breaking Down?" in the *Literary Digest*, February 17, 1923, 36; "Modernization of Marriage" in *Current Literature*, October 1912, 436–37.

6. Quoted in Wile and Winn, *Marriage in the Modern Manner*, x.

7. Fliegelman, *Prodigals and Pilgrims*, and Demos, *A Little Commonwealth*. For an account of the dramatic changes in the religious and political context of marriage, family life, and the structure of the household over the course of the nineteenth century, see Ryan, *Cradle of the Middle Class*; see also Bushman, *The Refinement of America*, for an exploration of the shifts in the physical space and aesthetic ideal of the household during this period.

8. Simmons remains the outstanding feminist interpreter of the gendered dimensions of the literature of modern marriage; see "Companionate Marriage and the Lesbian Threat" and "Modern Sexuality and the Myth of Victorian Repression." Haag offers a similar interpretation in "In Search of 'The Real Thing.' " Other scholars have begun revising Simmons's position, acknowledging its power but nuancing its feminism to allow for greater ambiguity in gender politics: see Neuhaus, "The Importance of Being Orgasmic," and Laipson, " 'Kiss Without Shame, for She Desires It.' "

9. Brandzel says, with admirable succinctness, "As a site of citizenship production, the institution of marriage is critical to the formation of a properly gendered, properly racialized, properly heterosexual America" ("Queering Citizenship?" 172).

10. This formulation is indebted to Berlant's articulation of the Reaganite configuration of citizenship in crisis in *The Queen of America Goes to Washington City*.

11. Anderson's "imagined community" of the nation originates with print culture's creation of a community of readers; see *Imagined Communities*, 47.

12. Hinkle, "The Chaos of Modern Marriage," 1.

13. Ibid., 2–3.

14. Ibid., 3–4.

15. This representation is about the same age as the United States, appearing in England almost synchronously with the first hints of industrialization. It draws on a much older tradition of representing agrarian life as a source of the calm self-presence that leads to virtue, in contrast to the distracting urban turmoil that leads to vice. In the nineteenth-century United States, the social alienation associated with urban life led some doctors to think that cities contributed to mental alienation, or insanity. See Rothman, *The Discovery of the Asylum*, 115.

16. The classic text on the rich history of the intimate American opposition between nature and the machine is Marx, *The Machine in the Garden*.

17. Horsman, *Race and Manifest Destiny*, 5.

18. Ibid., 6.

19. Though I do not know of scholarship examining the significance of marriage to the formation and meaning of whiteness, I have developed the ideas in this discussion in relation to an excellent body of scholarship on the political significance of marriage for American black people. See, for instance, Tate, *Domestic Allegories of Political Desire*; Jones, *Labor of Love, Labor of Sorrow*; and, for a more literary investigation, DuCille, *The Coupling Convention*.

20. Franke, "Becoming a Citizen"; see also Stanley, *From Bondage to Contract*.

21. As G. Stanley Hall put it, "differentiation and civilization are practically synonymous." "The Question of Co-education," 589. On the racial significance of sexual differentiation, see Carter, "Normality, Whiteness, Authorship," especially 161–64, and Terry, *An American Obsession*, 46.

22. Repellier, "The Decay of Sentiment," 68.

23. Groves and Ogburn, *American Marriage and Family Relationships*, 17–18. In addition to founding the professional specialty of marriage counseling, Ernest Groves was active and influential in the development of college curricula aimed at training undergraduates to make strong marriages.

24. Ibid., 20.

25. Sumner, "Modern Marriage," *Yale Review* 13 (January 1924): 275.

26. Lynd and Lynd, *Middletown*, 119–20, 134–35.

27. Adams, *The Tempo of Modern Life*, 56.

28. Ibid., 94.

29. Violent images of modernity's impact can be found in diverse sources. See Calverton and Schmalhausen, *New Generation*, 10, where "old values have been shattered." Groves and Ogburn wrote that "the old [attitudes] are disintegrating more rapidly than the new are being satisfactorily formed" (*American Marriage and Family Relationships*, 13). Floyd Dell wrote simply (and approvingly) that "the mechanization of the modern world is destroying . . . the last remnants of the patriarchal family" (*Love in the Machine Age*, 6).

30. Knight, "The Companionate and the Family," 260.

31. Lindsey and Evans, *Companionate Marriage*, 9.

32. *Modern Times* (Charles Chaplin, 1936).

33. The image of the married couple as representative of the nation significantly predates Hinkle's essay. For a thoughtful exploration of the political uses of this image in the early nineteenth century, see Norma Basch, "Marriage, Morals, and Politics in the Election of 1828."

34. Alexander Geppert tells us that upon its initial publication in England, *Married Love* "sold over two thousand hardback copies in the first two weeks, went through six editions, and sold more than seventeen thousand copies in the first year alone. . . . By 1925, after thirty-nine reprints, sales . . . had passed the half-million mark [and by] 1955, 1,032,250 copies had been printed in twenty-eight editions" ("Divine Sex, Happy Marriage, Regenerated Nation," 396–97). The volume was banned from the United States as an obscene publication until 1931, but references to it in other manuals indicate both that it was getting into this country and that many Americans accepted Stopes's descriptions and suggestions as relevant to their experiences.

35. Stopes, *Married Love*, 17.

36. Fosdick, "Our Machine Civilization—A Frankenstein Monster?" 366.

37. Ibid., 367.

38. Stoddard, *Clashing Tides of Color*, 3.

39. My political interpretation here is indebted to Christina Simmons's work on the modernization of marriage, though my emphasis on race and democracy is my own. Newman, *White Women's Rights*, 28, offers a useful overview of the demographic, economic, and cultural changes of the period from the 1880s through the 1920s that she sees as foundational to transformations in gender and racial meanings during this era.

40. Wile and Winn, *Marriage in the Modern Manner*, 29.

41. Van de Velde, *Ideal Marriage*, 172.

42. Exner, *The Sexual Side of Marriage*, 104.

43. Lindsey and Evans, *Companionate Marriage*, 109.

44. Ibid.

45. Dickinson and Beam, *A Thousand Marriages*, 59.

46. Van de Velde, *Ideal Marriage*, 199. See also Exner, *The Sexual Side of Marriage*: "An amazingly large number of men seem to have no better idea of technique than to take the shortest route between desire and satisfaction, that is, to finish as quickly as possible" (119). The description of such men as "running for the train" also suggests that their sex was embedded in the world of commerce and efficiency.

47. For instance, when Judge Lindsey was telling the story of the "Smiths" and their marital problems, he included the detail that "Mr. Smith" had been seeing a girl he met at a dance hall. This girl was, apparently, willing to accept Mr. Smith as

always in a hurry, since she had allowed him to move in with her (*Companionate Marriage*, 104).

48. See, e.g., Groves and Ogburn, *American Marriage and Family Relationships*, 23.

49. Lindsey and Evans, *Companionate Marriage*, 110–11.

50. Hendry and Podolsky, *Secrets of Love and Marriage*, 13.

51. Stone and Stone, *A Marriage Manual*, 158–59.

52. Chideckel, *The Single, the Engaged, and the Married*, 21.

53. Ibid.

54. Van de Velde, *Ideal Marriage*, 250. Emphasis in original.

55. Exner, *The Sexual Side of Marriage*, 106. See also Hendry, *Secrets of Love and Marriage*, 85; Van de Velde, *Ideal Marriage*, 189.

56. Macfadden, *Sweethearts for Life*, 71.

57. Stopes, *Married Love*, 1–2. See also Exner, *The Sexual Side of Marriage*, 30, for a less breathless exposition of the same perspective.

58. This position was (and in many instances remains) a basic tenet of psychoanalysis, but it found frequent expression outside of psychoanalytic contexts; rather than seeing that fact as evidence of the reach of Freudianism, I see it as evidence of the larger discursive context that Freud's work crystallized, expressed, and developed in particular directions. American intellectuals of the early twentieth century had their own, not always especially Freudian commitments that led them to collapse heterosexuality into adulthood and thence into the progressive development of civilization. Overall, Americans were relatively uninterested in the Freudian claim—or insight, if you prefer—that "normal" development takes place in a matrix of trauma and perverse desire. They usually preferred a much more optimistic vision of a kind of manifest destiny of the mind, in which "growing up" meant being "normal" unless some negative influence disrupted natural growth. For an instance of this American position, see Dell, *Love in the Machine Age*, 14–15, 324. For American reactions to classical psychoanalytic theory, see Hale, *Freud and the Americans*.

59. Exner, *The Sexual Side of Marriage*, 37–39.

60. Groves and Groves, *Sex in Marriage*, 39.

61. Exner, *The Sexual Side of Marriage*, 178.

62. Sanger, *Happiness in Marriage*, 157.

63. The apparently neutral scientificity of the language of "adjustment" should not be taken at face value. The term had disciplinary implications that are clear in much contemporary usage. For instance, a 1941 symposium of Philadelphia-area schoolteachers titled "Our Schools and the American Way of Life" described their district's response to "flagrantly anti-social behavior" in students as characterized by "speed, concentration, dynamic action, economy of effort, prevention of overlapping or duplication," and other virtues of the assembly line. The teachers reported that when wayward girls were treated as industrial problems, "sensible adjustment" was possible in a "truly amazing" number of cases. A "steady decline

in arrests" supported their contention that "adjustment" was synonymous with good citizenship, and indeed with "the American way of life." See the Fulton School, "Building Better Citizens," 15.

The note of self-satisfied coercion embedded and denied in the language of "adjustment" is more immediately obvious in the case of the Philadelphia school-teachers than in the literature of marital breakdown. Nonetheless, in marriage manuals as in public schools, "adjustment" was something transmitted by experts to people who were discursively positioned as in need of training about how to be properly normal. For instance, M. J. Exner's popular manual *The Sexual Side of Marriage* explained that most "maladjustment" arose "out of ignorance," and that "the work of the psychologist in adjusting these families is largely the teaching of simple facts in regard to the . . . sex life" (77–78). The psychologist, like the schoolteacher, transfers disciplinary skills which will help married couples avoid "maladjustment," the intimate spousal version of "anti-social behavior."

Given the discursive definition of the real, legitimate American as one deeply concerned about the state and future of marriage, the normalizing of sexual expression through the internalization of discipline was not optional but rather an essential element of "the American way of life." In this sense it was coercive even in situations where the transfer of disciplinary skill was voluntary and unsupervised, as in the relationship between the writers and readers of marriage manuals. But that coercion is disavowed by the ostentatiously neutral scientificity of the language of "adjustment" and, indeed, of the larger discursive structure of the literature of marital advice. Exner's usage reinforces the sense that "adjustment" was simply a matter of educated rationality, applied to marriage as though it were a machine which could be tweaked to its maximum level of performance and productivity. The mechanical resonances of the term emphasize the neutrality of the expert in relation to the married couple, just as the list of industrial techniques ("speed, concentration, dynamic action, economy of effort, prevention of overlapping or duplication") underscores the objectivity of the Philadelphia teachers in relation to their students.

64. Stopes, *Married Love*, chapter 2, "The Fundamental Pulse."
65. Some authors held that passion was closest to the surface just before the menses; others, during or just after; still others argued for a peak of desire halfway between periods. See, for instance, Fielding, *Sex and the Love-Life*, 113, 145; Sanger, *Happiness in Marriage*, 154, 158; Groves and Brooks, *Readings in the Family*, 77; Groves and Groves, *Sex in Marriage* 161, 176; Hendry, *Secrets of Love and Marriage*, 55–59; Van de Velde, *Ideal Marriage*, 283–86. Since there was, as yet, no consensus about when women were most fertile, it is impossible to demonstrate a correlation between claims about the monthly peak of desire and beliefs about the monthly peak of fertility.
66. Chideckel, *The Single, the Engaged, and the Married*, 30. Some manuals went out of

their way to assure readers that men's desire did not fluctuate. For instance, Stopes, *Married Love*, 54: "In the average man of our race desire knows no season. . . . Some men have observed in themselves a faintly marked monthly . . . rhythm; but in the majority of men desire, even if held in firm check, is merely slumbering." At the opposite end of the tonal spectrum, Hayden's *The Art of Marriage* explained civilized women's capacity for desire at any season thus: "In the course of evolution, when the early human race developed hands for holding, no doubt the males raped the females as often as they chose. During long ages the women gradually took advantage of their plight by learning how to enjoy the sex act at all times; and they now should be thankful that those prehistoric ancestors were incessant rapists" (61). The implication is, of course, that constant sexual arousal is the normal state for males. In a related discussion about the pattern of pleasure experienced in copulation, Van de Velde acknowledges that men's desires and sensations do vary; nevertheless, his charts show variation in women's response, unvaried repetition in men's. See *Ideal Marriage*, graphs A–D (181–88) and the footnote on 188.

67. The common sense of both eugenics and heteronormativity is still in action today in multiple cultural sites. For instance, fetal imaging and amniocentesis are simultaneously technologies of eugenicism and heterosexuality in that their two chief justifications are (a) establishing the presence of "birth defects" in order to give parents the option to abort "defective" offspring, and (b) establishing the sex of the fetus in order to give parents and everyone else the opportunity to guarantee that, months before birth, the child is inserted into the system of heteronormative gender that is supposed to produce manly men and womanly women—that is, "normally" sexed and gendered adults.

68. Some sources assume moderns will try to set a schedule and keep to it. For instance, Exner, *The Sexual Side of Marriage*, 129, says that routine is "common," and Stone and Stone warn their readers that a set routine is inappropriate (*A Marriage Manual*, 170).

69. Hendry, *Secrets of Love and Marriage*, 44–45.

70. Groves and Groves, *Sex in Marriage*, 174–75. See also Hendry, *Secrets of Love and Marriage*, 24, and Durant, "The Breakdown of Marriage," 157.

71. Chideckel, *The Single, the Engaged, and the Married*, 136.

72. Groves and Groves, *Sex in Marriage*, 159. See also Exner, *The Sexual Side of Marriage*, 224, and Hendry, *Secrets of Love and Marriage*, 30: "He should know . . . that following a set routine grows boresome, and that variety is the spice of life. Nothing will so deaden marital love as to fall into the habit of coming together on set days, along the same unvarying lines, year in and year out."

73. Groves, *Marriage*, 239.

74. This argument is advanced by Laipson in " 'Kiss without Shame, for She Desires It.' "

75. Van de Velde, *Ideal Marriage*, graphs A–D, 181–88.

76. Hendry, *Secrets of Love and Marriage*, 85. Emphasis in original.

77. Exner, *The Sexual Side of Marriage*, 218.

78. Sanger, *Happiness in Marriage*, 137–39.

79. Perhaps the most extreme example of this tendency appears in a manual written for use as a textbook in college marital-education courses. Bowman's *Marriage for Moderns* opens with a chapter titled "Some Differences between Men and Women."

80. Fear of censorship certainly played a role at a purely practical level, but censored works such as *Married Love* and the novels *The Well of Loneliness* and *Ulysses* circulated freely enough in the early-twentieth-century United States that authors' unambivalent commitment to erotic education could have produced relatively unambiguous representations of erotic technique; there was, after all, a thriving trade in pornography at this time. In addition, the fact that a few widely available manuals did include some information on technical matters (Van de Velde, for instance, describes the importance of clitoral stimulation and lubrication) suggests that marriage manuals' general, generic avoidance of sexual detail had a source beyond Comstockery or reluctance to be perceived as pornographic.

81. Hendry, *Secrets of Love and Marriage*, 86.

82. Exner, *The Sexual Side of Marriage*, 119–20.

83. Stopes, *Married Love*, 109–10.

84. Fielding, *Sex and the Love-Life*, 125.

85. Robie, *Sex and Life*, 375. Emphasis implied, but not made typographically, in original.

86. Aline Brouthier Morris Fund, *American Citizenship*, 15.

87. Horowitz, *Rereading Sex*.

88. Van de Velde, *Ideal Marriage*, 54. Moore and Clark report somewhat different conclusions in "Clitoral Conventions and Transgressions." The early-twentieth-century anatomy texts they examined were less interested in the homologies between clitoris and penis than late-Victorian ones had been, though more so than midcentury works that rarely discuss the clitoris in detail. This may reflect a divergence of internal medical culture from the medicosocial treatments that dominated mass-market marriage manuals. Moore and Clarke do note that Robert L. Dickinson's *Human Sex Anatomy* is a marked exception to their rule of midcentury silence about clitoral structure, function, and sensation. This may be significant, since Dickinson was the only author of a major anatomy text who was also an influential sexologist, sex educator, and marriage counselor. *Human Sex Anatomy* had its most recent reprinting in 1972 and is still in use as a teaching tool in some universities.

89. In fact, this vision of heterosexuality could and did flourish outside of the context of marital advice. Some anarchists and other radicals, from V. F. Calverton to Emma Goldman, viewed the breakdown of marriage as a desired end to a struc-

ture of economic and sexual exploitation and alienation, and many of them hoped to replace that structure with freely chosen individual unions. Simmons's work on "sex radicals" of this era draws a connection between this individualism and that of several contemporary white women's defenses of lesbianism as a personal choice that freed women from dependence on men (see "Women's Power in Sex Radical Challenges to Marriage in the Early-Twentieth-Century United States"). On her own evidence, however, it seems clear that most of the radical analyses with which moderns contested the normalization of monogamous marriage assumed that freeing sex would tend to heighten women's desire for men and their willingness to pursue it outside of wedlock.

90. Jacobson, *Whiteness of a Different Color*, 111.

91. Ibid., 111, 113.

92. Bederman, *Manliness and Civilization*, chapter 3.

93. Aline Brouthier Morris Fund, *American Citizenship*, 13–14.

94. Trixie's "probationary" status is clearer than her exact ethnic position. Her name and some of her mannerisms resonate with contemporary film versions of tough Irishness, while the actress who played her (Lillian Roth, née Rutstein) was Jewish. The difficulty of securing an ethnic reading for her character probably reflects the decreased relevance of the specific differences between "probationary" whites of comparable class status—whether Irish or Jewish, Trixie is not a "normal" white woman because she has no sexual or emotional self-control and is much more sensitive to the lure of diamond bracelets than she is to the sanctity of marriage.

95. Dell, *Love in the Machine Age*, 237.

96. Ibid., 6.

97. Ibid., 6, 98.

98. Ibid., 236–37.

99. Brady, "Night Message," 38. I have inferred the immigrant character of Brady's audience from the fact that the evening high school of which she was principal was on the Lower East Side of New York City. This inference is supported by the re-publication of her remarks in Griscom, *Americanization*, a handbook designed simultaneously to teach American thoughts and correct pronunciation to adult immigrants.

100. Jacobson, *Whiteness of a Different Color*, 57–68. See also Maclean, "The Leo Frank Case Reconsidered."

101. Lindsey and Evans, *Companionate Marriage*, 272.

102. Stone and Stone, *A Marriage Manual*, 4.

3. Birds, Bees, and the Future of the Race

1. Davenport did not report the exact date of this meeting in her 1924 description of it, but internal evidence locates it between 1916 and 1922. See *Salvaging of American*

Girlhood, 19–22. Miss Davenport was a sister of the eugenicist Charles Davenport of the Eugenics Record Office at Cold Spring Harbor, New York. She began teaching at the New York Training School for Teachers in 1905, served as its principal for some time, and earned her doctorate in psychology from Columbia University in 1923. By the time she wrote *Salvaging of American Girlhood* she had approximately nineteen years of experience as a sex educator. Unfortunately, her single-minded focus on her research into "adolescent interests" regarding sex led her to omit her answers to the questions they asked.

2. Davenport, *Salvaging of American Girlhood*, 22–23.

3. Ibid., 2, 10, 12–13, 22, 36, and passim. The quoted words appear on 22.

4. Ibid., 23–25.

5. Ibid., 27.

6. Davenport emphasized her students' normality in part by specifying their class location in the larger American culture: all were "high school graduates and members of middle or more fortunate working class families," and thus "somewhat above the average for the total population" in cultural and educational status. Again we can see that the "normal" was not exactly the "average" in any statistical sense (*Salvaging of American Girlhood*, 27). Similar accounts of normal modern youth seeking sex information can be found in Bigelow, "The Educational Attack on the Problems of Social Hygiene," 173; California State Board of Health, *The Problem of Sex Education in Schools*, Pamphlet No. 15, 3; Peabody, "Sex Education in the Home and High School," 373–74; and many others.

7. Davenport, *Salvaging of American Girlhood*, 34, 88–89.

8. Ibid., 132.

9. Ibid., 158.

10. Ibid., 188.

11. Ibid., 16. Davenport's thoughts on the scientific point of view are detailed on 183.

12. Ibid., 16.

13. Ibid., 284–87.

14. Indeed, the critic Allan Bloom has argued that one ought to read books 4 and 5 of *Emile* as treatises on sex education, the theme which holds together Rousseau's discussions of the nature of God and the responsibilities of citizens. In any case, it is clear that Emile makes the transition from childhood to manhood, from dependent pupil to independent citizen, through the process of acquiring knowledge of the passions and their place in his universe. Rousseau emphasizes that this is the crux of his whole system of education: if Emile is corrupted by vice or false knowledge derived only from experience of the senses, the care with which he has been guided up to puberty has all been for nothing. See Rousseau, *Emile*, especially the introduction by Bloom, 15–17, 212, 320.

15. Davenport, *Salvaging of American Girlhood*, 212.

16. Bigelow, "The Educational Attack on the Problems of Social Hygiene," 166–67.

17. This is true despite the fact that European historians, and careful readers of Foucault's *History of Sexuality,* volume 1, will recognize this erotically evasive modern style of sexual discourse from the eighteenth century on. What is new about twentieth-century sex education is not its insistence on its own modernity, nor its devotion to reticence, nor its usefulness as a site for the implantation of racial and gender norms. Rather, it is its commitment to making modern, reticent normality available to the entire population through a publicly funded educational technology. Foucault gives an example of "cherub-faced boys who, in front of adults, had skillfully woven the garlands of discourse and sex" (29). The fact of the exhibition of their skill suggests that in 1776 it was noteworthy, exceptional, to be celebrated: they won applause for the enlightened calm with which they discussed procreation. By the 1930s in the United States, what was noteworthy was that most people could not sustain such a performance. The shift toward a universal prescription and a normalized educational practice is clear.

18. Hine, "Rape and the Inner Lives of Black Women in the Middle West."

19. Ibid., 915.

20. Higginbotham, "African-American Women's History and the Metalanguage of Race," 262.

21. Simmons, "African Americans, Marriage Education, and Women's Sexuality in the 1940s."

22. Peiss, *Cheap Amusements*; Chauncey, "Christian Brotherhood or Sexual Perversion?"

23. See especially Terry, *An American Obsession*; Chauncey, *Gay New York.*

24. For more on the sexological construction of erotic normality through the textual performance of distance from perversion, see Carter, "White Love," 307–18, 338–50.

25. Sanger, *What Every Girl Should Know,* 60; Smith, "Medical Phases," 33; Rice, *In Training,* 32; Moore, *Keeping in Condition,* 64.

26. For more on the differences between these schools of thought in the interwar years, see Carter, "Birds, Bees, and Venereal Disease." For an excellent discussion of the early years of social-hygiene activism, see Brandt, *No Magic Bullet.*

27. For instance, developmental knowledges form the core of influential early texts like Bigelow, *Sex Education* (1916), while in *Teaching Sex* Moran shows that during the Depression, venereal-disease education had more funding than any other branch of sex education (113–16). Since that funding was distributed through state boards of health, who were primary distributors of sex-information pamphlets, it seems plain that the knowledge of contagion continued to be widely disseminated even before the Second World War encouraged renewed emphasis on disease control among the troops. Therefore, though the knowledge of contagion dominated the teens and the knowledge of development gained visibility during the twenties, the two approaches to sex education coexisted and were in conversation with one another throughout the period under study here.

28. One aspect of the culture against which sex educators wrote is beautifully delineated in Chauncey, *Gay New York*; see also Ullman, " 'The Twentieth-Century Way.' " For a brief but enticing genealogical description of the multiple popular sexual cultures of the late nineteenth century, see Horowitz, "Victoria Woodhull, Anthony Comstock, and Conflict over Sex in the United States in the 1870s."

29. Eliot, "The American Social Hygiene Association," 1–2. Charles Eliot, who had restructured university education during his presidency at Harvard, was the grand old man of Progressive Era reforms. His name on the ASHA's letterhead signaled that social hygiene had arrived at the status of a fully legitimate, worthy cause. See the long entry on Eliot in the *National Cyclopedia of American Biography*. Jones, *Bad Blood*, suggests that Eliot was not alone in seeing venereal disease as a problem primary for the "white race."

30. Brandt, *No Magic Bullet*, 59 et seq.

31. Ibid., 62.

32. Brandt, *No Magic Bullet*, observes this in a caption on the first unpaginated section of illustrations.

33. Brandt, *No Magic Bullet*, 66.

34. Rice, "Venereal Disease," 19.

35. Sisson, "Educational Phases," 100.

36. This is, of course, a restatement of Kipling's theme in the "The White Man's Burden" (1899), which exhorts the civilized nations to "send forth the best ye breed" to "serve" by improving the physical and moral environments of the primitive and weak.

37. Sisson, "Educational Phases," 101–02, and Moore, "Teaching Phases," 152. Patricia Campbell has named this kind of sex-education literature the "bully boys" school of thought, a phrase which nicely captures the Rooseveltian flavor of the books' exhortations to live cleanly and strenuously. See Campbell, *Sex Guides*, chapter 3, for a description of the major works in the genre.

38. Steinhardt, *Ten Sex Talks to Boys*. The arrangement of the text into a tombstone-appropriate format is my addition.

39. Moore, *Keeping in Condition*, 102.

40. Hodge, "Instruction in Social Hygiene in the Public Schools," 307–08.

41. Sanger, *What Every Girl Should Know*, 65.

42. Ibid., 3; Cabot, "Education versus Punishment as a Remedy for Social Evils," 39.

43. California State Board of Health, *The Problem of Sex Education in Schools*, 3. This pamphlet is a reprint of one originally published by the USPHS. See also the chapter "Training and National Progress," in Moore's *Keeping in Condition*, which concludes with the reminder that "as in the past national immorality has meant national decadence, so will it in the future; and as in the past national purity has meant national power, so will it to our nation" (125). Girls, too, were warned that their physical "fitness" was consequential. For instance, the Illinois Department

of Public Health published a pamphlet titled *Healthy Happy Womanhood* that included this warning: "In some of the war-ravaged countries of Europe more than half of the babies who are born die during the first year of life. . . . Why? Largely because the strength of the mothers has been sapped by food shortage and over-work so that they cannot give their babies proper nourishment" (4). A nation whose children were subject to the horrors of war drew "hope for the future" from "healthy, happy womanhood." Extending its military message further, this pamphlet compared girls who took good care of their bodies to Joan of Arc, who, it said, "symbolizes the woman of the twentieth century, eager to take a part in the work of the world" (3).

44. California State Board of Health, *The Problem of Sex Education in Schools*, 4; California State Board of Health, *When They Come Home*, Pamphlet No. 11. For an especially explicit connection between venereal disease and the Hun, see Massachusetts State Department of Health, "To Girls: About the Enemy at Home."

45. "How Shall We Teach?" was the name of a regular column in *Social Hygiene* (and later the *Journal of Social Hygiene*) in the era under discussion.

46. Eliot, "American Social Hygiene Association," 2.

47. American Federation for Sex Hygiene, *Report of the Special Committee on the Matter and Methods of Sex Education*, 3.

48. Ibid. (the quotation, though not the conclusion that sex education was undesirable).

49. Quoted in Burnham, "The Progressive Era Revolution in American Attitudes toward Sex," 904.

50. See Moran, " 'Modernism Gone Mad,' " 502–5.

51. Gruenberg, *Parents and Sex Education*, 4.

52. Exner, "The Sex Factor in Character Training," 389.

53. Ibid.

54. Foster, "The Social Emergency," 51. On this era's intensifying fear of the city as a moral contaminant and source of perversion, see Terry, *An American Obsession*, 88–96.

55. Foster, "Social Emergency," 51.

56. Ibid.

57. Exner, "Sex Factor in Character Training," 394.

58. Funk and Beatty, "Relating Sex to Life," 235.

59. Descriptions of babies born with syphilis or gonorrhea ranged from the hideously over-detailed to the truncated and incidental, but in one form or another such descriptions appear in quite a few manuals for adolescents of both sexes. See Corner, *Attaining Womanhood*, 88; Smith, "Medical Phases," 35; Wood-Allen, *What a Young Girl Ought to Know*, 237; Rice, *In Training*, 32; Rice, *How Life Goes On and On*, 27.

60. Steinhardt's manual *Ten Sex Talks to Girls* devotes several pages (95–98) to spelling out the contrasts between healthy babies and syphilitic babies.

61. Sisson, "Educational Phases," 102. See also Coleman, "Moral and Religious Phases," 176: "Motives of cautious fear are always weak with full-blooded and generous youth."

62. Winfield Scott Hall, a renowned sex educator, explained in another context that appeals to the desire to protect the weak were effective with teenagers because they were recapitulating the Middle Ages: "Young people at this age are living over again the impulses and the instincts of chivalry. . . . So, the youth of today can be very easily inspired to adopt this code of honor and to be ready to fight for it" ("The Relation of Education in Sex to Race Betterment," 76–77). See also Coleman, "Moral and Religious Phases," 170, for an argument that the sexual awakening of adolescence is inseparable from the "rapid development of social sympathy" at that age.

63. Steinhardt, *Ten Sex Talks to Girls*, 96.

64. Ibid., 96, 98.

65. Halttunen, "Humanitarianism and the Pornography of Pain in Anglo-American Culture."

66. I would add that white sympathetic suffering with slaves also constituted a kind of white training in the evasion of really existing racial power relations. If, for well-bred whites, looking at a picture of a whipping scene could arouse outrage at the gross violation of black personhood, it could also seem to transfer the site of suffering from the black body to the refined white one in a way that elides the difference between the two experiences of pain and that seems to render the white viewer imaginatively vulnerable and abject in a faintly pleasurable way. The real suffering of the enslaved is thus rendered both distant and titillating, and the real racial power of the white viewer is denied.

67. Bigelow, "The Established Points in Social Hygiene Education," 9. See also Kassoy, "A History of the Work of the American Social Hygiene Association in Sex Education," 95.

68. Davenport, *Salvaging of American Girlhood*, 237–38.

69. On the history of recapitulation theory both within biological science and in culture, see Gould, *Ontogeny and Phylogeny*.

70. Though recapitulation theory lost favor among biologists between 1900 and 1930, it remained influential in sexological literature at least through 1940. Rasmussen, "The Decline of Recapitulationism in Early Twentieth-Century Biology."

71. Lydston, *The Diseases of Society and Degeneration*, 377.

72. Carter, "Normality, Whiteness, Authorship," 161–63.

73. Hodge, "Instruction in Social Hygiene in the Public Schools," 307–8.

74. In fact, since the lessons offered small children were usually repeated in more advanced grades, sex education for all ages began with flowers more often than not. See Wood-Allen, *What a Young Girl Ought to Know*, "Twilight Talks" II and III; Howard, *Confidential Chats with Girls*, 3; American Federation for Sex Hygiene,

Report of the Sex Education Sessions, 6; Garrett, "Sex Education for Children before the Age of Fifteen," 258; California State Board of Health, *The Problem of Sex Education in Schools*, 14–15; Bigelow, "The Established Points in Social Hygiene Education," 8; United States Public Health Service, *Sex Education in the Home*, Pamphlet No. 61, 2; Cady and Cady, *The Way Life Begins*, 23; De Schweinitz, *Growing Up*, 23–24.

75. See, e.g., Gaffney, "A Father's Plan for Sex Instruction," 270.

76. See, e.g., Rice, *The Story of Life*, 8–14; Mason, " 'Fathers Aren't Any Blood Relation to the Children,' " 429–30.

77. De Schweinitz, *Growing Up*, 41.

78. Ibid., 98.

79. Rice, *The Story of Life*, 14–15.

80. Ibid., 20.

81. For instance, Rice, *How Life Goes On and On*, 8, includes the story of an oriole "mother" who died protecting her nest.

82. Garrett, "Some Methods of Teaching Sex Hygiene," 59.

83. American Federation for Sex Hygiene, *Report of the Special Committee on the Matter and Methods of Sex Education*, 6.

84. Peabody, "Sex Education in the Home and High School," 365.

85. Ellis, "Analysis of the Sexual Impulse," in *Studies in the Psychology of Sex*, vol. 3, 207–9.

86. G. Adlerz, "Periodische Massenvermehrung als Evolutionsfaktor," *Biologisches Centralblatt* 22 (1902): 108. Quoted in Crawley, *Studies of Savages and Sex*, 9.

87. Ellis, "The Sexual Instinct in Savages," in *Studies in the Psychology of Sex*, vol. 1, part 2, 265.

88. Lydston, *The Diseases of Society and Degeneration*, 47.

89. Crawley, *Studies of Savages and Sex*, 5.

90. Ibid., 3–4.

91. Lydston, *The Diseases of Society and Degeneration*, 47. See also Butterfield, *Sex Life in Marriage*, 27–32; Hayden, *The Art of Marriage*, 46.

92. For instance, Ellis's *Studies in the Psychology of Sex* opens with a section titled "The Evolution of Modesty."

93. Sanger, *What Every Girl Should Know*, 2.

94. Ibid., 41.

95. Bigelow, "Established Points in Social Hygiene Education," 5.

96. Cady and Cady, *The Way Life Begins,* 17.

97. De Schweinitz, *Growing Up*, 104.

98. On common embryological forms, see Cady and Cady, *The Way Life Begins*, 68–69; Rice, *In Training*, 25. On recapitulation of eras before the division of sex, see Cady and Cady, *The Way Life Begins*, 60–61.

99. De Schweinitz, *Growing Up*, 75.

100. Verbal descriptions of the similarity of form and development among embryos of different species are widespread and include Corner, *Attaining Womanhood*, 30–31, 33, and Rice, *In Training*, 25. Drawings of embryos appear in Cady and Cady, *The Way Life Begins*, 68.

101. Gruenberg, *The Story of Evolution,* 130. One of the most beautiful sex education books is Ets's large-format picture book *The Story of a Baby*, which, though clearly intended for very small children, included a good deal of similar information by explaining the developing fetus as having gills at one point, and at another, "flippers and flappers" like those of "a sea turtle or a whale." Ets made the connection between such animals and the human embryo by the simple device of drawing pictures of them on the same pages.

Epilogue

1. This simultaneous capacity to bring far more people under surveillance, while attending more minutely to each subject, is one of the hallmarks of modern disciplinary regimes of power as Foucault described them in *Discipline and Punish,* part 3: Discipline.

2. Stoler makes a similar point: "Discourses of sexuality . . . have mapped the moral parameters of European nations. These deeply sedimented discourses on sexual morality could redraw the 'interior frontiers' of national communities. . . . These nationalist discourses . . . marked out those whose claims to property rights, citizenship, and public relief were worthy of recognition and whose were not." *Race and the Education of Desire*, 8–9.

3. Halperin, *Saint Foucault*, 32–33.

4. Ibid., 46.

5. Ibid., 198–99, note 37.

6. Butler, *Bodies That Matter,* 18.

BIBLIOGRAPHY

Abbott, Wilbur Cortez. "What Is Civilization? The Answer of Modern America." *Forum* 74.4 (October 1925): 481–90.

Abel, Elizabeth, Barbara Christian, and Helene Moglen, eds. *Female Subjects in Black and White: Race, Psychoanalysis, Feminism*. Berkeley: University of California Press, 1997.

Abelove, Henry. *Deep Gossip*. Minneapolis: University of Minnesota Press, 2003.

Abelove, Henry, Michele Aina Barale, and David Halperin, eds. *The Lesbian and Gay Studies Reader*. New York: Routledge, 1993.

Adams, Henry. 1905. *The Education of Henry Adams*. New York: Penguin, 1995.

Adams, James Truslow. *The Tempo of Modern Life*. New York: Albert and Charles Boni, 1931.

Alexander, M. Jacqui. "Not Just (Any) Body Can Be a Citizen: The Politics of Law, Sexuality, and Postcoloniality in Trinidad and Tobago and the Bahamas." *Feminist Review* 48 (1994): 5–23.

Alexander, Ruth M. *The Girl Problem: Female Sexual Delinquency in New York, 1900–1930*. Ithaca, N.Y.: Cornell University Press, 1995.

Aline Brothier Morris Fund. *American Citizenship*. New Haven, Conn.: Yale University Press, 1933.

Allen, Theodore. *The Invention of the White Race*. London: Verso, 1994.

Alpert, Judith, and Stewart Alpert, eds. *The Sixties Papers: Documents of a Rebellious Decade*. New York: Praeger, 1984.

American Federation for Sex Hygiene. *Report of the Sex Education Sessions of the Fourth International Congress on School Hygiene, and of the Annual Meeting of the Federation*. New York: AFSH, 1913.

——. *Report of the Special Committee on the Matter and Methods of Sex Education*. New York: AFSH, 1912.

American Historical Association. "Committee on Lesbian and Gay History Survey on LGBTQ History Careers." Compiled by Marc Stein. *Perspectives* 39.5 (May 2001): 29–31.

Anderson, Benedict. *Imagined Communities: Reflections on the Origin and Spread of Nationalism.* London: Verso, 1983.

Barker-Benfield, J. G. *The Horrors of the Half-Known Life: Male Attitudes toward Women and Sexuality.* New York: Harper and Row, 1976.

Barrett, James, and David Roediger. "Inbetween Peoples: Race, Nationality, and the New Immigrant Working Class." *Journal of American Ethnic History* 16.3 (Spring 1997): 3–45.

Basch, Norma. "Marriage, Morals, and Politics in the Election of 1828." *Journal of American History* 80.3 (December 1993): 890–918.

Beard, George M. *American Nervousness.* New York: G. P. Putnam's Sons, 1881.

——. *A Practical Treatise on Nervous Exhaustion (Neurasthenia).* New York: G. P. Putnam's Sons, 1880.

——. *Sexual Neurasthenia.* New York: E. B. Treat, 1884.

Beckert, Sven. *The Monied Metropolis: New York City and the Consolidation of the American Bourgeoisie, 1850–1896.* Cambridge: Cambridge University Press, 2001.

Bederman, Gail. *Manliness and Civilization: A Cultural History of Gender and Race in the United States, 1880–1917.* Chicago: University of Chicago Press, 1995.

Berlant, Lauren. *The Queen of America Goes to Washington City: Essays on Sex and Citizenship.* Durham, N.C.: Duke University Press, 1997.

Berlet, Chip, ed. *Eyes Right! Challenging the Right Wing Backlash.* Boston: South End Press, 1995.

Bigelow, Maurice A. "The Educational Attack on the Problems of Social Hygiene." *Social Hygiene* 2.1 (January 1916): 165–77.

——. "The Established Points in Social Hygiene Education, 1905–1924." *Journal of Social Hygiene* 10.1 (January 1924): 2–11.

——. 1916. *Sex Education: A Series of Lectures concerning Knowledge of Sex in Its Relation to Human Life.* New York: Macmillan, 1918.

Bigelow, William F., ed. *The Good Housekeeping Marriage Book: Twelve Ways to a Happy Marriage.* New York: Prentice Hall, 1938.

Blanchard, Phyllis. 1920. *The Adolescent Girl: A Study from the Psychoanalytic Viewpoint.* New York: Dodd, Mead, 1924.

Blee, Kathleen. *Women of the Klan: Racism and Gender in the 1920s.* Berkeley: University of California Press, 1991.

Bowman, Henry. *Marriage for Moderns.* New York: McGraw-Hill, 1942.

Brady, Mary L. "Night Message." In Ellwood Griscom, ed., *Americanization: A School Reader and Speaker,* 37–39. New York: Macmillan, 1920.

Brandt, Allan. *No Magic Bullet: A Social History of Venereal Disease in the United States since 1880.* Oxford: Oxford University Press, 1985.

Brandzel, Amy. "Queering Citizenship? Same-Sex Marriage and the State." *GLQ* 11.2 (2005): 171–204.

Brumberg, Joan Jacobs. *Fasting Girls: The Emergence of Anorexia Nervosa as a Modern Disease*. Cambridge, Mass.: Harvard University Press, 1988.

Burnham, John C. "The Progressive Era Revolution in American Attitudes toward Sex." *Journal of American History* 59.4 (March 1973): 885–908.

Burr, Anna Robeson. *Weir Mitchell, His Life and Letters*. New York: Duffield, 1929.

Bushman, Richard. *The Refinement of America: Cities, Houses, Persons*. New York: Vintage, 1993.

Butler, Johnella, ed. *Color-Line to Borderlands: The Matrix of American Ethnic Studies*. Seattle: University of Washington Press, 2001.

Butler, Judith. *Bodies That Matter: On the Discursive Limits of "Sex."* New York: Routledge, 1993.

Butterfield, Oliver. 1937. *Sex Life in Marriage*. New York: Emerson Books, 1946.

Cabot, Hugh. "Education versus Punishment as a Remedy for Social Evils." In American Federation for Sex Hygiene, *Report of the Sex Education Sessions of the Fourth International Congress on School Hygiene*, 35–44. New York: AFSH, 1913.

Cady, Bertha Chapman, and Vernon Mosher Cady. 1917. *The Way Life Begins*. New York: AFSH, 1926.

California State Board of Health. *The Problem of Sex Education in Schools*. Pamphlet no. 15. San Francisco: n.d. [c. 1918?].

——. *When They Come Home*. Pamphlet no. 11. San Francisco: n.d. [c. 1918].

Calverton, V. F. *The Bankruptcy of Marriage*. New York: Macaulay Company, 1928.

Calverton, V. F., and Samuel D. Schmalhausen, eds. *The New Generation: The Intimate Problems of Modern Parents and their Children*. New York: Macaulay Company, 1931.

Campbell, Patricia. *Sex Guides: Books and Films about Sexuality for Young Adults*. New York: Garland Publishing, 1986.

Canaday, Margot. "Building a Straight State: Sexuality and Social Citizenship under the 1944 G.I. Bill." *Journal of American History* 90. 3 (December 2003): 935–57.

Carpenter, Edward. *Love's Coming of Age*. New York: Boni and Liveright, 1911.

Carter, Julian B. "Birds, Bees, and Venereal Disease: Toward an Intellectual History of Sex Education." *Journal of the History of Sexuality* 10.2 (April 2001): 213–49.

——."Normality, Whiteness, Authorship: Evolutionary Sexology and the Primitive Pervert." In Vernon Rosario, ed., *Science and Homosexualities*, 155–76. New York: Routledge, 1997.

——. "On Mother-Love: History, Queer Theory, and Non-Lesbian Identity." *Journal of the History of Sexuality* 14.1–2 (2005): 107–38.

——. "White Love: Sexual Normality and the Future of the Race, 1890–1940." Ph.D. dissertation, University of California, Irvine, 1998.

Carter, Robert B. *On the Pathology and Treatment of Hysteria*. London: J. Churchill, 1853.

Castle, Terry. *The Apparational Lesbian: Female Homosexuality and Modern Culture*. New York: Columbia University Press, 1995.

Chafe, William. *The Unfinished Journey: America since World War II*. New York: Oxford University Press, 1995.

Charcot, Jean-Martin. *Clinical Lectures on Diseases of the Nervous System.* Translated by Thomas Savill. London: New Sydenham Society, 1889.

Chauncey, George. "Christian Brotherhood or Sexual Perversion? Homosexual Identities and the Construction of Sexual Boundaries in the World War I Era." In M. Duberman, M. Vicinus, and G. Chauncey, eds., *Hidden from History: Reclaiming the Lesbian and Gay Past,* 294–317.

——. *Gay New York: Gender, Urban Culture, and the Making of the Gay Male World, 1890–1940.* New York: Basic Books, 1994.

Chideckel, Maurice. *The Single, the Engaged, and the Married.* New York: Eugenics Publishing Company, 1936.

Christian, Barbara. "The Race for Theory." *Cultural Critique* 6 (Spring 1987): 51–63.

Clarke, Edward H. *Sex in Education, or A Fair Chance for Girls.* Boston, 1878.

Coleman, Norman. "Moral and Religious Phases." In Foster, ed., *The Social Emergency,* 168–89.

Conzen, Kathleen. "German-Americans and the Invention of Ethnicity." In Frank Trommler and Joseph McVeigh, eds., *America and the Germans: An Assessment of a Three Hundred Year History,* vol. 1, 131–47. Philadelphia: University of Pennsylvania Press, 1985.

Corner, George W. *Attaining Womanhood: A Doctor Talks to Girls about Sex.* New York: Harper and Brothers, 1939.

Coward, Noel. 1930. *Private Lives: An Intimate Comedy in Three Acts.* New York: Signet, 1983.

Crawley, Ernest. *Studies of Savages and Sex.* Edited by Theodore Besterman. London: Methuen, 1929.

Davenport, F. Isabel. *Salvaging of American Girlhood: A Substitution of Normal Psychology for Superstition and Mysticism in the Education of Girls.* New York: E. P. Dutton, 1924.

Davis, Katherine Bement. *Factors in the Sex Life of 2200 Women.* New York: Harper and Brothers, 1929.

——. "Why They Failed to Marry," *Harper's Monthly Magazine,* March 1928, 460–69.

Degler, Carl. "What Ought to Be and What Was: Women's Sexuality in the Nineteenth Century." *American Historical Review* 79 (December 1974): 1467–90.

Delgado, Richard, and Jean Stefancic, eds. *Critical White Studies: Looking behind the Mirror.* Philadelphia: Temple University Press, 1997.

Dell, Floyd. *Love in the Machine Age: A Psychological Study of the Transition from Patriarchal Society.* New York: Farrar and Rinehart, 1930.

D'Emilio, John. "Capitalism and Gay Identity." In M. Abelove, M. A. Barale, and D. Halperin, eds., *The Lesbian and Gay Studies Reader,* 467–76.

D'Emilio, John, and Estelle Freedman. *Intimate Matters: A History of Sexuality in America.* New York: Harper and Row, 1988.

Demos, John. 1970. *A Little Commonwealth: Family Life in Plymouth Colony.* New York: Oxford University Press, 2000.

De Schweinitz, Karl. *Growing Up: The Story of How We Become Alive, are Born, and Grow Up*. New York: Macmillan, 1928.

Diamond, Irene, and Lee Quinby, eds. *Feminism and Foucault: Reflections on Resistance*. Boston: Northeastern University Press, 1988.

Dickinson, Robert Latou. "Bicycling for Women from the Standpoint of the Gynecologist." *American Journal of Obstetrics and Diseases of Women and Children* 31 (January 1895): 24–37.

——. *Human Sex Anatomy: A Topographical Hand Atlas*. Baltimore: Williams and Wilkins, 1933.

Dickinson, Robert Latou, and Lura Beam. *A Thousand Marriages: A Medical Study of Sex Adjustment*. Baltimore: Williams and Wilkins, 1931.

——. *The Single Woman*. Baltimore: Williams and Wilkins, 1934.

Dixon, Edward H. *Woman and her Diseases from the Cradle to the Grave: Adapted Exclusively to her Instruction in the Physiology of her System, and all the Diseases of her Critical Periods*. New York: A. Ranney, 1857.

Doane, Ashley. "Rethinking Whiteness Studies." In A. Doane and E. Bonilla-Silva, eds., *White Out*, 3–20.

Doane, Ashley, and Eduardo Bonilla-Silva, eds. *White Out: The Continuing Significance of Racism*. New York: Routledge, 2003.

Duberman, Martin, Martha Vicinus, and George Chauncey Jr., eds. *Hidden From History: Reclaiming the Lesbian and Gay Past*. New York: Penguin, 1989.

DuCille, Ann. *The Coupling Convention: Sex, Text, and Tradition in Black Women's Thinking*. New York: Oxford University Press, 1997.

Duggan, Lisa. "Queering the State." *Social Text* 39 (Summer 1994): 1–14.

——. *Sapphic Slashers: Sex, Violence, and American Modernity*. Durham, N.C.: Duke University Press, 2000.

Durant, Will. "The Breakdown of Marriage." In J. F. McDermott, ed., *The Sex Problem in Modern Society*, 147–69.

Eliot, Charles W. "The American Social Hygiene Association." *Social Hygiene* 1.1 (December 1914): 1–2.

Ellis, Havelock. *Studies in the Psychology of Sex*. New York: Random House, 1936.

Emerick, Charles. "College Women and Race Suicide." *Political Science Quarterly* 24.2 (1909): 269–83.

Engelhardt, H. Tristram. "The Disease of Masturbation: Values and the Concept of Disease." In J. W. Leavitt and R. Numbers, eds., *Sickness and Health in America*, 13–21.

Eskridge, William. *The Case for Same-Sex Marriage: From Sexual Liberty to Civilized Commitment*. New York: Free Press, 1996.

Ets, Marie Hall. *The Story of a Baby*. New York: Viking, 1939.

Everett, Millard S. *The Hygiene of Marriage*. New York: Vanguard Press, 1932.

Ewald, Francois. "Norms, Discipline, and the Law." *Representations* 30 (Spring 1990): 138–61.

Exner, Max J. "The Sex Factor in Character Training." *Journal of Social Hygiene* 10.7 (October 1924): 385–96.

———. *The Sexual Side of Marriage*. New York: W. W. Norton, 1932.

Ferguson, Roderick. *Aberrations in Black: Toward a Queer of Color Critique*. Minneapolis: University of Minnesota Press, 2004.

Fielding, William J. *Sex and the Love-Life*. New York: Blue Ribbon Books, 1927.

Fitzgerald, F. Scott. *The Great Gatsby*. New York: Scribner, 1995.

Fliegelman, Jay. *Prodigals and Pilgrims: The American Revolution against Patriarchal Authority, 1750–1800*. Cambridge: Cambridge University Press, 1982.

Fosdick, Harry Emerson. *The Challenge of the Present Crisis*. New York: Association Press, 1918.

Fosdick, Raymond B. "Our Machine Civilization—A Frankenstein Monster?" *Current Opinion*, September 1922, 365–67.

Foster, William T. "The Social Emergency." In American Federation for Sex Hygiene, *Report of the Sex Education Sessions of the Fourth International Congress on School Hygiene*, 45–54.

Foster, William T., ed. *The Social Emergency: Studies in Sex Hygiene and Morals*. Boston: Houghton Mifflin, 1914.

Foucault, Michel. *Abnormal: Lectures at the Collège de France, 1974–1975*. New York: Picador, 1999.

———. *Discipline and Punish: The Birth of the Prison*. Translated by Alan Sheridan. New York: Vintage, 1995.

———. *The History of Sexuality*. Vol. 1: *An Introduction*. Translated by Robert Hurley. New York: Pantheon, 1978.

Fout, John C., and Maura Shaw Tantillo, eds. *American Sexual Politics: Sex, Gender, and Race since the Civil War*. Chicago: University of Chicago Press, 1993.

Fox, Richard Wightman. *Trials of Intimacy: Love and Loss in the Beecher-Tilton Scandal*. Chicago: University of Chicago Press, 1999.

Franke, Katherine M. "Becoming a Citizen: Reconstruction Era Regulation of African-American Marriages." *Yale Journal of Law and the Humanities* 11 (1999): 251–309.

Frankenberg, Ruth. *White Women, Race Matters: The Social Construction of Whiteness*. Minneapolis: University of Minnesota Press, 1993.

Freedman, Estelle. "The Prison Lesbian: Race, Class, and the Construction of the Aggressive Female Homosexual." *Feminist Studies* 22.2 (Summer 1996): 397–423.

Freud, Sigmund. *Sexuality and the Psychology of Love*. Edited by Philip Rieff. New York: Simon and Schuster, 1963.

Frisken, Amanda. "Sex in Politics: Victoria Woodhull as an American Public Woman." *Journal of Women's History* 12.1 (2000): 89–110.

Fulton School. "Building Better Citizens." In *Our Schools and the American Way of Life*, by Philadelphia Public Schools, 14–17. Philadelphia: n.p., 1941.

Funk, Margaret, and Willard Beatty. "Relating Sex to Life." *High School Clearing House* 8.4 (December 1933): 235–38.

Gaffney, Charles E. "A Father's Plan for Sex Instruction." *Social Hygiene* 1.2 (March 1915): 270–71.

Garber, Linda. *Identity Poetics: Race, Class, and the Lesbian-Feminist Roots of Queer Theory.* New York: Columbia University Press, 2001.

——. "Where in the World Are the Lesbians?" *Journal of the History of Sexuality* 14.1–2 (2005): 28–50.

Garrett, Laura B. "Sex Education for Children before the Age of Fifteen." *Social Hygiene* 1.2 (March 1915): 257–66.

——. "Some Methods of Teaching Sex Hygiene." In American Federation for Sex Hygiene, *Report of the Sex Education Sessions of the Fourth International Congress on School Hygiene,* 55–63.

Geppert, Alexander C. T. "Divine Sex, Happy Marriage, Regenerated Nation: Marie Stopes' Marital Manual *Married Love* and the Making of a Best-Seller, 1918–1955." *Journal of the History of Sexuality* 8.3 (1998): 389–433.

Giddings, Paula. *When and Where I Enter: The Impact of Black Women on Race and Sex in America.* New York: William Morrow, 1984.

Gijswift-Hofstra, Marijke, and Roy Porter, eds. *Cultures of Neurasthenia: From Beard to the First World War.* Amsterdam: Rodopi, 2001.

Gilman, Sander. *Difference and Pathology: Stereotypes of Sexuality, Race, and Madness.* Ithaca, N.Y.: Cornell University Press, 1985.

Gilman, Sander, Helen King, Roy Porter, G. S. Rousseau, and Elaine Showalter. *Hysteria beyond Freud.* Berkeley: University of California Press, 1993.

Gitlin, Todd. *The Sixties: Years of Hope, Days of Rage.* New York: Bantam, 1987.

Godkin, E. L. "Chromo-Civilization." *The Nation,* September 24, 1874, 201–2.

Goldberg, David Theo, ed. *The Anatomy of Racism.* Minneapolis: University of Minnesota Press, 1990.

Goldsmith, Barbara. *Other Powers: The Age of Suffrage, Spiritualism, and the Scandalous Victoria Woodhull.* New York: Alfred A. Knopf, 1998.

Gordon, Linda. *The Moral Property of Women: A History of Birth Control Politics in America.* Urbana: University of Illinois Press, 2002.

Gosling, F. G. *Before Freud: Neurasthenia and the American Medical Community, 1870–1910.* Urbana: University of Illinois Press, 1987.

Gould, Stephen Jay. *The Mismeasure of Man.* New York: W. W. Norton, 1993.

——. *Ontogeny and Phylogeny.* Cambridge, Mass.: Harvard University Press, 1977.

Gressing, Aaron. *The Recovery of Race in America.* Minneapolis: University of Minnesota Press, 1995.

Griscom, Ellwood, ed. *Americanization: A School Reader and Speaker.* New York: Macmillan, 1920.

Groves, Ernest R. *Marriage.* New York: Henry Holt, 1933.

Groves, Ernest R., and Lee M. Brooks. *Readings in the Family.* Philadelphia: J. B. Lippincott, 1934.

Groves, Ernest R., and Gladys Hoagland Groves. *Sex in Marriage.* New York: Macauley Company, 1932.

Groves, Ernest R., and William Ogburn. *American Marriage and Family Relationships*. New York: Henry Holt, 1928.

Gruenberg, Benjamin C. 1928. *Parents and Sex Education, for Parents of Young Children*. New York: Viking, 1932.

——. *The Story of Evolution: Facts and Theories on the Development of Life*. New York: D. Van Nostrand, 1929.

Guglielmo, Thomas. "Rethinking Whiteness Historiography: The Case of Italians in Chicago, 1890–1945." In A. Doane and E. Bonilla-Silva, eds., *White Out*, 49–61.

Haag, Pamela. "In Search of 'The Real Thing': Ideologies of Love, Modern Romance, and Women's Sexual Subjectivity in the U.S., 1920–1940." *Journal of the History of Sexuality* 2.4 (1992): 547–57.

Hale, Grace Elizabeth. *Making Whiteness: The Culture of Segregation in the South, 1890–1940*. New York: Pantheon Books, 1998.

Hale, Nathan. *Freud and the Americans: The Beginnings of Psychoanalysis in the United States, 1876–1917*. New York: Oxford University Press, 1971.

Hall, Donald. *Queer Theories*. New York: Palgrave Macmillan, 2003.

Hall, G. Stanley. "The Question of Co-education." *Munsey's Magazine* 34.5 (February 1906): 588–92.

Hall, Winfield Scott. "The Relation of Education in Sex to Race Betterment." *Social Hygiene* 1.1 (December 1914): 67–80.

Haller, John, and Robin Haller. *The Physician and Sexuality in Victorian America*. Urbana: University of Illinois Press, 1974.

Halperin, David. "Forgetting Foucault: Acts, Identities, and the History of Sexuality." *Representations* 63 (Summer 1998): 93–120.

——. *Saint Foucault: Toward a Gay Hagiography*. New York: Oxford University Press, 1995.

Halttunen, Karen. "Humanitarianism and the Pornography of Pain in Anglo-American Culture." *American Historical Review* 100.2 (April 1995): 303–35.

Hamilton, G. V. 1929. *A Research in Marriage*. New York: Garland, 1986.

——. *What Is Wrong with Marriage*. New York: Albert and Charles Boni, 1930.

Hammonds, Evelyn. "Black (W)holes and the Geometry of Black Female Sexuality." In Elizabeth Weed and Naomi Schor, eds., *Feminism Meets Queer Theory*, 136–56. Bloomington: Indiana University Press, 1997.

Haney-Lopez, Ian. *White by Law: The Legal Construction of Race*. New York: New York University Press, 1996.

Harris, Cheryl. "Whiteness as Property." *Harvard Law Review* 106.8 (1993): 1707–91.

Hartigan, John Jr. "Who Are These White People? 'Rednecks,' 'Hillbillies,' and 'White Trash' as Marked Racial Subjects." In A. Doane and E. Bonilla-Silva, eds., *White Out*, 95–112.

Hayden, Jesse. 1926. *The Art of Marriage: A Scientific Treatise*. High Point, N.C.: Book Sales Agency, 1936.

Hegel, G. W. F. *Phenomenology of Spirit*. Translated by A. V. Miller. New York: Oxford University Press, 1979.

Hendry, James Parker, and Edward Podolsky. 1933. *Secrets of Love and Marriage*. New York: Herald, 1939.

Higginbotham, Evelyn Brooks. "African-American Women's History and the Metalanguage of Race." *Signs* 17.2 (1992): 251–74.

Higham, John. *Strangers in the Land: Patterns of American Nativism, 1865–1925*. New Brunswick, N.J.: Rutgers University Press, 1955.

Hine, Darlene Clark. "Rape and the Inner Lives of Black Women in the Middle West: Preliminary Thoughts on the Culture of Dissemblance." In Roger Lancaster and Micaela DiLeonardo, eds., *The Gender/Sexuality Reader*, 434–39. New York: Routledge, 1997.

Hinkle, Beatrice M. "The Chaos of Modern Marriage." *Harper's Monthly Magazine*, December 1925, 1–13.

Hirschfeld, Magnus. *The Sexual History of the World War*. New York: Panurge Press, 1934.

Hodes, Martha. "The Sexualization of Reconstruction Politics: White Women and Black Men in the South after the Civil War." *Journal of the History of Sexuality* 3 (1992): 402–17.

——. *Sex, Love, Race: Crossing Boundaries in North American History*. New York: New York University Press, 1999.

Hodge, C. F. "Instruction in Social Hygiene in the Public Schools." *School Science and Mathematics* 11 (1911): 304–14.

hooks, bell. "Feminism: A Transformational Politic." In Deborah L. Rhode, ed., *Theoretical Perspectives on Sexual Difference*, 185–93. New Haven, Conn.: Yale University Press, 1990.

Horowitz, Helen Lefkowitz. *Rereading Sex: Battles over Sexual Knowledge and Suppression in Nineteenth-Century America*. New York: Alfred A. Knopf, 2002.

——. "Victoria Woodhull, Anthony Comstock, and Conflict over Sex in the United States in the 1870s." *Journal of American History* 87.2 (September 2000): 403–34.

Horsman, Reginald. *Race and Manifest Destiny: The Origins of American Racial Anglo-Saxonism*. Cambridge, Mass.: Harvard University Press, 1981.

Howard, William Lee. *Confidential Chats with Girls*. New York: E. J. Clode, 1911.

——. *Facts for the Married*. New York: E. J. Clode, 1912.

Ignatiev, Noel. *How the Irish Became White*. New York: Routledge, 1995.

Ignatiev, Noel, and John Garvey, eds. *Race Traitor*. New York: Routledge, 1996.

Illinois Department of Public Health. *Healthy Happy Womanhood*. Springfield, Ill., n.d. [c. 1942?].

Jacobson, Matthew Frye. *Whiteness of a Different Color: European Immigrants and the Alchemy of Race*. Cambridge, Mass.: Harvard University Press, 1998.

Jagose, Annamarie. *Inconsequence: Lesbian Representation and the Logic of Sexual Sequence*. Ithaca, N.Y.: Cornell University Press, 2002.

Jones, Jacqueline. *Labor of Love, Labor of Sorrow: Black Women, Work, and Family from Slavery to the Present*. New York: Vintage, 1985.

Jones, James. *Bad Blood: The Tuskegee Syphilis Experiment*. New York: Free Press, 1981.

Jung, C. G. "The Sex Problem of the Student." In J. F. McDermott, ed., *The Sex Problem in Modern Society*, 327–50.

Katz, Jonathan Ned. *The Invention of Heterosexuality*. New York: Plume Books / Penguin, 1996.

Kammen, Michael. *American Culture, American Tastes: Social Change and the Twentieth Century*. New York: Alfred A. Knopf, 1999.

Kasson, John. *Rudeness and Civility: Manners in Nineteenth-Century Urban America*. New York: Hill and Wang, 1990.

Kassoy, Irving. "A History of the Work of the American Social Hygiene Association in Sex Education, 1876–1930." Master's thesis, College of the City of New York, 1931.

Kevles, Daniel. *In the Name of Eugenics: Genetics and the Uses of Human Heredity*. Cambridge, Mass.: Harvard University Press, 1998.

Kipling, Rudyard. "The White Man's Burden." *The Complete Verse*. London: Kyle Cathie, 1990.

Kline, Wendy. *Building a Better Race: Gender, Sexuality, and Eugenics from the Turn of the Century to the Baby Boom*. Berkeley: University of California Press, 2001.

Knight, M. M. "The Companionate and the Family." *Journal of Social Hygiene* 10.5 (May 1924): 257–67.

Kolchin, Peter. "Whiteness Studies: The New History of Race in America." *Journal of American History* 89.1 (June 2002): 154–73.

Laipson, Peter. " 'Kiss without Shame, for She Desires It': Sexual Foreplay in American Marital Advice Literature, 1900–1925." *Journal of Social History* 29.3 (1996): 507–22.

Larmour, David, Paul Miller, and Charles Platter, eds. *Rethinking Sexuality: Foucault and Classical Antiquity*. Princeton, N.J.: Princeton University Press, 1998.

Lears, T. J. Jackson. *No Place of Grace: Antimodernism and the Transformation of American Culture, 1880–1920*. New York: Pantheon, 1981.

Leavitt, Judith Walzer, ed., *Women and Health in America*. Madison: University of Wisconsin Press, 1984.

Leavitt, Judith Walzer, and Ronald Numbers, eds. *Sickness and Health in America*. Madison: University of Wisconsin Press, 1985.

Leys-Stepan, Nancy. "Race and Gender: The Role of Analogy in Science." In D. T. Goldberg, ed., *The Anatomy of Racism*, 38–57.

Lindsey, Judge Ben B., and Wainwright Evans. *Companionate Marriage*. New York: Boni and Liveright, 1927.

Lipsitz, George. *The Possessive Investment in Whiteness: How White People Profit from Identity Politics*. Philadelphia: Temple University Press, 1998.

Luibhéid, Eithne. *Entry Denied: Controlling Sexuality at the Border*. Minneapolis: University of Minnesota Press, 2002.

Lutz, Tom. *American Nervousness, 1903: An Anecdotal History*. Ithaca, N.Y.: Cornell University Press, 1991.

Lydston, G. F. *The Diseases of Society and Degeneration: The Vice and Crime Problem*. Philadelphia: J. B. Lippincott, 1904.

Lynd, Robert, and Helen Merrell Lynd. *Middletown: A Study in American Culture*. New York: Harcourt, Brace, 1929.

Macfadden, Bernarr. *Sweethearts for Life: Or, Marriage Idealized*. New York: Physical Culture Publishing, 1903.

MacKenzie, Donald. *Statistics in Britain 1865–1930: The Social Construction of Scientific Knowledge*. Edinburgh: Edinburgh University Press, 1981.

Maclean, Nancy. *Behind the Mask of Chivalry: The Making of the Second Ku Klux Klan*. New York: Oxford University Press, 1994.

——. "The Leo Frank Case Reconsidered: Gender and Sexual Politics in the Making of Reactionary Populism." *Journal of American History* 78.3 (December 1991): 917–48.

Marable, Manning, ed. *Dispatches from the Ebony Tower: Intellectuals Confront the African American Experience*. New York: Columbia University Press, 2000.

Marx, Leo. *The Machine in the Garden: Technology and the Pastoral ideal in America*. New York: Oxford University Press, 1964.

Marzio, Peter. *The Democratic Art: Pictures for a Nineteenth-Century America*. Fort Worth, Tex.: Amon Carter Museum of Western Art, 1979.

Mason, Mary A. " 'Fathers Aren't Any Blood Relation to the Children.' " *Social Hygiene* 1.3 (June 1915): 429–30.

Massachusetts State Department of Health. "To Girls: About the Enemy At Home." Boston: n.d. [c. 1917].

McDermott, John Francis, ed. *The Sex Problem in Modern Society*. New York: Modern Library, 1931.

McDougall, William. "Marriage and the Home." *Forum* 80 (July 1928): 11–14.

McDowell, Deborah. " 'It's Not Safe. Not Safe at All': Sexuality in Nella Larsen's *Passing*." In Ablove et al., eds., *The Lesbian and Gay Studies Reader*, 616–25.

McGarry, Molly. "Spectral Sexualities: Nineteenth-Century Spiritualism, Moral Panics, and the Making of U.S. Obscenity Law." *Journal of Women's History* 12.2 (2000): 8–29.

McWhorter, Ladelle. *Bodies and Pleasures: Foucault and the Politics of Sexual Normalization*. Bloomington: Indiana University Press, 1999.

Messer, Mary Burt. *The Family in the Making*. New York: G. P. Putnam's Sons, 1928.

Micale, Mark. *Approaching Hysteria: Disease and its Interpretations*. Princeton, N.J.: Princeton University Press, 1995.

Minton, Henry. *Departing from Deviance: A History of Homosexual Rights and Emancipatory Science in America*. Chicago: University of Chicago Press, 2002.

Mitchell, Silas Weir. 1877. *Fat and Blood, and How to Make Them*. Philadelphia: J. B. Lippincott, 1907.

——. *Wear and Tear, or Hints for the overworked*. Philadelphia: J. B. Lippincott, 1871.

Moore, Harry H. *Keeping in Condition: A Handbook on Training for Older Boys*. New York: Macmillan, 1915.

———. "Teaching Phases: For Boys." In W. T. Foster, ed., *The Social Emergency*, 127–53.

Moore, Lisa Jean, and Adele E. Clark. "Clitoral Conventions and Transgressions: Graphic Representations in Anatomy Texts, c. 1900–1991." *Feminist Studies* 21.2 (Summer 1995): 255–301.

Moraga, Cherríe, and Gloria Anzaldúa, eds. *This Bridge Called My Back: Writings by Radical Women of Color*. New York: Kitchen Table Press, 1981.

Moran, Jeffrey P. "'Modernism Gone Mad': Sex Education Comes to Chicago, 1913." *Journal of American History* 83.2 (September 1996): 481–513.

———. *Teaching Sex: The Shaping of Adolescence in the Twentieth Century*. Cambridge, Mass.: Harvard University Press, 2000.

Morgan, Lewis Henry. *Ancient Society: Researches in the Lines of Human Progress from Savagery, through Barbarism, to Civilization*. New York: Holt, 1877.

Mumford, Kevin. "'Lost Manhood' Found: Male Sexual Impotence and Victorian Culture in the United States." In J. C. Fout and M. S. Tantillo, eds., *American Sexual Politics*, 75–99.

Neuhaus, Jessamyn. "The Importance of Being Orgasmic: Sexuality, Gender, and Marital Sex Manuals in the U.S., 1920–1963." *Journal of the History of Sexuality* 9.4 (2000): 447–73.

Newitz, Annalee. "White Savagery and Humiliation: or A New Racial Consciousness in the Media." In Annalee Newitz and Matt Wray, eds., *White Trash: Race and Class in America*, 131–54. New York: Routledge, 1997.

Newman, Louise Michele. *White Women's Rights: The Racial Origins of Feminism in the United States*. New York: Oxford University Press, 1999.

O'Connor, Erin. "Pictures of Health: Medical Photography and the Emergence of Anorexia Nervosa." *Journal of the History of Sexuality* 5.4 (1995): 535–72.

Omi, Michael, and Howard Winant. *Racial Formation in the United States: From the 1960s to the 1990s*. 2d ed. New York: Routledge, 1994.

Ordover, Nancy. *American Eugenics: Race, Queer Anatomy, and the Science of Nationalism*. Minneapolis: University of Minnesota Press, 2003.

Orsi, Robert. "The Religious Boundaries of an Inbetween People: Street *Feste* and the Problem of the Dark-Skinned Other in Italian Harlem, 1920–1990." *American Quarterly* 44.3 (September 1992): 313–47.

Outlaw, Lucius. "Rehabilitate Racial Whiteness?" In George Yancy, ed., *What White Looks Like*, 159–72. New York: Routledge, 2004.

Palmer, Bryan. *Descent into Discourse: The Reification of Language and the Writing of Social History*. Philadelphia: Temple University Press, 1990.

Pascoe, Peggy. "Miscegenation Law, Court Cases, and Ideologies of 'Race'." *Journal of American History* 83.1 (1996): 44–69.

Peabody, James E. "Sex Education in the Home and High School." *Social Hygiene* 2.5 (July 1916): 363–74.

Pearson, Karl. *The Life, Letters, and Labours of Francis Galton.* 3 vols. Cambridge: Cambridge University Press, 1914–30.

Peiss, Kathy. *Cheap Amusements: Working Women and Leisure in Turn-of-the-Century New York.* Philadelphia: Temple University Press, 1986.

Phelan, Shane. *Sexual Strangers: Gays, Lesbians, and Dilemmas of Citizenship.* Philadelphia: Temple University Press, 2001.

Pick, Daniel. *The Faces of Degeneration: A European Disorder, c. 1848–1918.* New York: Cambridge University Press, 1989.

Playfair, William. *The Systematic Treatment of Nerve Prostration and Hysteria.* Philadelphia: Lea, 1883.

Porter, Theodore M. *The Rise of Statistical Thinking 1820–1900.* Princeton, N.J.: Princeton University Press, 1986.

Rasmussen, Birgit, Eric Klinenberg, Irene Nexica, and Matt Wray, eds. *The Making and Unmaking of Whiteness.* Durham, N.C.: Duke University Press, 2001.

Rasmussen, Nicolas. "The Decline of Recapitulationism in Early Twentieth-Century Biology." *Journal of the History of Biology* 24.1 (1991): 51–89.

Reed, James. 1978. *The Birth Control Movement and American Society: From Private Vice to Public Virtue.* Princeton, N.J.: Princeton University Press, 1984.

Reid-Pharr, Robert. *Black Gay Man: Essays.* New York: New York University Press, 2001.

Repellier, Agnes. "The Decay of Sentiment." *Atlantic Monthly* 60 (1897): 67–76.

Rice, Thurman B. *How Life Goes On and On.* Chicago: American Medical Association, 1933.

———. *In Training: For Boys of High School Age.* Chicago: American Medical Association, 1933.

———. *The Story of Life: For Boys and Girls of Ten Years.* Chicago: American Medical Association, 1933.

———. *Venereal Disease.* Chicago: American Medical Association, 1933.

Richlin, Amy. "Foucault's *History of Sexuality*: A Useful Theory for Women?" In Larmour et al., *Rethinking Sexuality,* 138–70.

Robie, William F. 1916. *Rational Sex Ethics: A Physiological and Psychological Study of the Sex Lives of Normal Men and Women, with Suggestions for a Rational Sex Hygiene with Reference to Actual Case Histories.* Boston: Richard G. Badger, 1918.

———. *Sex in Life: What the Experienced Should Teach and the Inexperienced Should Learn.* Boston: Richard G. Badger, 1920.

Robinson, Paul. *The Modernization of Sex.* New York: Harper and Row, 1976.

Roediger, David. *Toward the Abolition of Whiteness: Essays on Race, Politics, and Working-Class History.* New York: Verso, 1994.

———. *The Wages of Whiteness: Race and the Making of the American Working Class.* New York: Verso, 1991.

Rosenberg, Charles S. 1961. *No Other Gods: On Science and American Social Thought.* Baltimore: Johns Hopkins University Press, 1976.

Rothman, David. *The Discovery of the Asylum: Social Order and Disorder in the New Republic.* Boston: Little, Brown, 1971.

Rousseau, Jean-Jacques. 1762. *Emile: or, On Education.* Edited by Allan Bloom. New York: Basic Books, 1979.

Ryan, Mary P. *Cradle of the Middle Class: The Family in Oneida County, New York, 1790–1865.* Cambridge: Cambridge University Press, 1981.

Sanger, Margaret. 1926. *Happiness in Marriage.* Elmsford, N.Y.: Maxwell Reprint Company, 1969.

———. 1920. *What Every Girl Should Know.* New York: Belvedere Publishing, 1980.

Saxton, Alexander. *The Rise and Fall of the White Republic: Class Politics and Mass Culture in Nineteenth Century America.* London: Verso, 1990.

Sedgwick, Eve Kosofsky. *Epistemology of the Closet.* Berkeley: University of California Press, 1990.

Segrest, Mab. *Memoir of a Race Traitor.* Boston: South End Press, 1994.

Shapiro, Harry L. "A Portrait of the American People." *Natural History,* June 1945, 248–55.

Sicherman, Barbara. "The Uses of a Diagnosis: Doctors, Patients, and Neurasthenia." In J. W. Leavitt and R. Numbers, eds., *Sickness and Health in America,* 22–39.

Simmons, Christina. "African Americans, Marriage Education, and Women's Sexuality in the 1940s." Paper presented at "Women's Sexualities: Historical, Interdisciplinary, and International Perspectives," Indiana University, November 15, 2003.

———. "Companionate Marriage and the Lesbian Threat." *Frontiers* 4.3 (1979): 54–59.

———. "Modern Sexuality and the Myth of Victorian Repression." In Kathy Peiss and Christina Simmons, *Passion and Power: Sexuality in History,* 157–77. Philadelphia: Temple University Press, 1989.

———. "Women's Power in Sex Radical Challenges to Marriage in the Early-Twentieth-Century United States." *Feminist Studies* 29.1 (Spring 2003): 169–98.

Sisson, Edward Octavius. "Educational Phases." In W. T. Foster, ed., *The Social Emergency,* 84–103.

Sklar, Holly. "The Dying American Dream and the Snake Oil of Scapegoating." In C. Berlet, ed., *Eyes Right!,* 113–34.

Smedley, Audrey. *Race in North America: Origin and Evolution of a Worldview.* Boulder, Colo.: Westview, 1993.

Smith, Andrew C. "Medical Phases." In W. T. Foster, ed., *The Social Emergency,* 32–44.

Snitow, Ann, Christine Stansell, and Sharon Thompson, eds. *Powers of Desire: The Politics of Sexuality.* New York: Monthly Review Press, 1983.

Somerville, Siobhan. *Queering the Color Line: Race and the Invention of Homosexuality in American Culture.* Durham, N.C.: Duke University Press, 2000.

———. "Queer Loving." *GLQ* 11.3 (2005): 335–70.

Soto, Sandra K. "Cherríe Moraga's Going Brown: 'Reading Like a Queer.'" *GLQ* 11.2 (2005): 237–63.

Stanley, Amy Dru. *From Bondage to Contract: Wage Labor, Marriage, and the Market in the Age of Slave Emancipation.* New York: Cambridge University Press, 1999.

Steinhardt, Irving. *Ten Sex Talks to Boys.* Philadelphia: Lippincott, 1914.

——. *Ten Sex Talks to Girls.* Philadelphia: Lippincott, 1913.

Stoddard, Lothrop T. *Clashing Tides of Color.* New York: Charles Scribner's Sons, 1935.

Stoler, Ann Laura. *Race and the Education of Desire: Foucault's "History of Sexuality" and the Colonial Order of Things.* Durham, N.C.: Duke University Press, 1995.

——. "Sexual Affronts and Racial Frontiers: European Identities and the Cultural Politics of Exclusion in Colonial Southeast Asia." *Comparative Studies in Society and History* 34.2 (July 1992): 514–51.

Stokes, Mason. *The Color of Sex: Whiteness, Heterosexuality, and the Fictions of White Supremacy.* Durham, N.C.: Duke University Press, 2001.

Stone, Abraham, and Hannah Stone. *A Marriage Manual: A Practical Guide-Book to Sex and Marriage.* Rev. ed. New York: Simon and Schuster, 1935.

Stopes, Marie C. 1918. *Married Love.* New York: Eugenics Publishing, 1931.

Sumner, William Graham. "Modern Marriage." *Yale Review* 13 (January 1924): 249–75.

Takaki, Ronald. *Iron Cages: Race and Culture in Nineteenth Century America.* Seattle: University of Washington Press, 1982.

Tate, Claudia. *Domestic Allegories of Political Desire.* New York: Oxford University Press, 1992.

Terry, Jennifer. *An American Obsession: Science, Medicine, and Homosexuality in Modern Society.* Chicago: University of Chicago Press, 1999.

——. "Lesbians under the Medical Gaze: Scientists Search for Remarkable Differences." *Journal of Sex Research* 27.3 (1990): 317–39.

Thomas, William I. *Sex and Society: Studies in the Social Psychology of Sex.* Chicago: University of Chicago Press, 1907.

Thornton, Henry, and Freda Thornton. *How to Achieve Sex Happiness in Marriage.* New York: Citadel Press, 1934.

Tichi, Cecelia. *Shifting Gears: Technology, Literature, Culture in Modernist America.* Chapel Hill: University of North Carolina Press, 1987.

Trimberger, Ellen Kay. "Feminism, Men and Modern Love: Greenwich Village, 1900–1925." In A. Snitow, C. Stansell, and S. Thompson, eds., *Powers of Desire*, 131–52.

Turner, William B. *A Genealogy of Queer Theory.* Philadelphia: Temple University Press, 2000.

Tyrell, Ian. *Woman's World, Woman's Empire: The Woman's Christian Temperance Union in International Perspective, 1880–1930.* Chapel Hill: University of North Carolina Press, 1999.

Ullman, Sharon. "'The Twentieth-Century Way': Female Impersonation and Sexual Practice in Turn-of-the-Century America." *Journal of the History of Sexuality* 5.4 (1995): 573–600.

United States Public Health Service. *Sex Education in the Home.* Pamphlet no. 61. Washington: Government Printing Office, 1930.

Van de Velde, Theodore H. 1926. *Ideal Marriage: Its Physiology and Technique*. New York: Random House, 1930.

Wade, Wyn Craig. *The Fiery Cross: The Ku Klux Klan in America*. New York: Oxford University Press, 1998.

Ware, Vron. *Beyond the Pale: White Women, Racism, and History*. London: Verso, 1992.

Warner, Michael, ed. *Fear of a Queer Planet: Queer Politics and Social Theory*. Minneapolis: University of Minnesota Press, 1993.

——. *The Trouble with Normal: Sex Politics, and the Ethics of Queer Life*. Cambridge, Mass.: Harvard University Press, 1999.

Welke, Barbara Young. *Recasting American Liberty: Gender, Race, Law, and the Railroad Revolution, 1865–1920*. Cambridge: Cambridge University Press, 2001.

Wells-Barnett, Ida B. *Southern Horrors: Lynch Law in All Its Phases*. New York: New York Age, 1892.

White, E. Frances. *Dark Continent of Our Bodies: Black Feminism and the Politics of Respectability*. Philadelphia: Temple University Press, 2001.

Wiegman, Robyn. *American Anatomies: Theorizing Race and Gender*. Durham, N.C.: Duke University Press, 1995.

Wile, Ira S., and Mary Day Winn. *Marriage in the Modern Manner*. New York: Century, 1929.

Willard, Frances E. *A White Life for Two*. Chicago: Women's Temperance Publishing Association, 1890.

Williams, Linda. *Playing the Race Card: Melodramas of Black and White from Uncle Tom to O. J. Simpson*. Princeton, N.J.: Princeton University Press, 2001.

Williams, Patricia J. *The Alchemy of Race and Rights*. Cambridge, Mass.: Harvard University Press, 1991.

Williamson, Joel. *The Crucible of Race: Black-White Relations in the American South since Emancipation*. New York: Oxford University Press, 1984.

Winant, Howard. "White Racial Projects." In B. Rasmussen, E. Klinenberg, I. Nexica, and M. Wray, eds., *The Making and Unmaking of Whiteness*, 106–8.

Wood, Ann Douglas. "'The Fashionable Diseases': Women's Complaints and Their Treatment in Nineteenth Century America." In J. W. Leavitt, ed., *Women and Health in America*, 222–38.

Wood-Allen, Mary. *What A Young Girl Ought to Know*. Philadephia: Vir Publishing, 1897.

INDEX

Gender (*continued*)
  expression of, 13; in sex education
  materials, 134, 139–140, 142–144. *See
  also* Sexes, difference of
Gender politics, 11, 21, 43, 60, 77, 92–93,
  107–108. *See also* Depoliticization;
  Disavowal
Gender relations, instability of, 21, 85, 92,
  107–108
Gentility. *See* Refinement
Globalization, economic, 50. *See also*
  Imperialism
Godkin, E. L., 64–67, 73
Gonorrhea, 127, 129–131, 137
Great War. *See* World War I

Health, 2, 7, 10, 16, 24, 48, 56, 98, 101, 122,
  126
Heterosexuality: as adulthood, 36–37, 40,
  97, 113, 141, 149–150, 183 n.58; civilization, vector for transmission of, 9, 36,
  40–41, 58, 88, 119; democracy and, 14,
  33–38, 76–77, 81, 90, 98, 107–108, 113,
  115, 138; eroticization of sex and gender
  difference, 21, 77, 79, 97, 100–101; as
  fundamental to human beings, 27, 97;
  as modern, 24, 36–41, 113; and political
  innocence, appearance of, 19, 24, 27,
  78, 87–88, 101, 114; as reproductivity,
  21, 97, 116–117, 141–150; social order
  and, 78, 88, 98, 159. *See also* Marriage
Heterosexual pleasure, 24, 77, 89–90, 98–
  99, 105–108, 155
History: American, as marital, 80–81, 87–
  88; of civilization, 7–10, 23–24, 58, 82,
  87
History, academic discipline of, 19–20, 24;
  methods, 30–32
Homosexuality, 13, 14, 16–17, 19, 26, 73,
  141, 152, 179 n.78
Hysteria, 60, 62, 119

Identity categories, 17, 30–31
Ideology. *See* Disavowal; Innocence,
  political
Illness. *See* Disease
Immigrants, 33, 35, 50, 62, 87–88, 171 n.68;
  Americanization of, 37, 96, 112–115, 120,
  187 n.99
Immigration, 19, 72; restriction of, 58, 109
Imperialism, 11, 43, 82, 86
Impotence, 13, 43, 67
Industrialization, 19, 46, 50, 71, 80–81, 91
Inheritance: biological, 5, 117, 119; cul-
  tural, 9, 12, 14, 24, 46, 52, 66, 70, 117, 119
Innocence, political, 7, 9, 19, 22–23, 27, 32,
  44, 68, 71–72, 101, 114, 154
Insensitivity, 81, 84, 89, 95–96, 110
Interpretation, politics of, 17, 19, 22–23,
  25–29, 31–32
Invisibility. *See* Disavowal; Visibility

Justice, 9, 11, 51, 77–78, 92, 114, 139, 155–156

Literature, marital advice. *See* Marital
  advice literature
Literature of marital breakdown. *See*
  Marital breakdown, literature of
Love: apolitical, 6, 14, 162 n.10; citizens
  connected by, 77, 88, 108; civilization
  and, 98, 148; marital, 79, 97–98, 108,
  140, 142; parental, 97–98, 142–144, 148;
  whiteness and, 2, 74, 88, 95, 98, 105,
  115–116, 127, 154

Machine age, 36–37, 50, 68, 76, 80–81, 86,
  102, 116
Machines, 50–51, 61, 65–69, 74, 77, 84;
  nature vs., 80–83, 89–90, 99, 106;
  undermining intimacy, 75, 81, 85–87,
  89, 102, 116. *See also* Technology
Male dominance, 21. *See also* Gender
  politics

Manifest destiny, 82

Manliness. *See* Gender

Marital advice literature, 14–15, 17, 90, 116, 155

Marital breakdown, literature of, 83, 87, 90, 98; major themes in, 76–77, 79

Marriage: breakdown of, 80–81, 83–86, 90; civilization dependent on, 40, 98; civilization transmitted through, 7–9, 18, 20, 36; as cradle of democracy, 35, 76, 81, 90 (*see also* Heterosexuality); as discipline, 78, 98, 115, 119, 121; egalitarian, 13, 77; maturation and, 98, 113, 119; metaphor for relations of citizens, 76–77, 81, 88, 90, 92, 105, 107, 114–115, 155; modern, 38, 76, 79, 87, 99, 110, 113; modernization as threat to, 75–76, 79–81, 90, 93–94, 116; normal, affection as foundation of, 3, 13, 77, 121, 140, 142–145, 149, 151; normality and, 2–3, 7, 17, 20, 78, 99, 121; privilege linked to race, 82–83; sexual self-cultivation and, 98–107, 147–148; women's suffering in, 74–75, 99

Marriage Charts, 100–101, 103

Marriage manuals. *See* Marital advice literature

Mass culture, 12, 14–15, 36, 64, 67, 172 n.80; heteronormativity emerging in, 78–79, 97, 111–113; sex instruction as, 14–15

Mass media, 64–66, 75–76, 86

Masturbation, 53–55, 96

Materialism: historical, 30, 71; scientific, 45, 51–52, 61–62

Mechanical reproduction, 65–67, 71; of art of love, 103

Mechanical violence, 86, 106

Medical profession, 45, 61–62

"Middletown," 85, 172 n.72

Miscegenation, 20

Modernism, sexual, 23–24

Modernity, 1–2, 37–38; inhumanity of, 85, 105; internalized, 89; intimacy vs., 14, 79–81, 99, 102; nervousness and, 42; re / productive capacity of, 44, 65–70; transition to, 68, 72, 81; triumphant, 14, 73, 99. *See also* Civilization, modern white; Divorce

Modern marriage. *See* Marriage: modern

Modern people: Americans as, 46, 80; cold and insensitive, 76, 84, 109; rational, 47, 51, 61, 73, 101–102; superiority of, 8–9, 37, 47–48, 62, 70

Modern whiteness, 8, 9, 15, 36–41, 44, 46–51, 61–62, 65–70, 72–73, 78–79, 113–115, 124

Monogamy, 15, 120–121, 140

Morality, sexual. *See* Self-discipline; Whiteness: self-control and

Nation: as consistent relational ideals, 36, 78, 87, 89; as democracy, 10, 105, 113–114; imagined as white, 5, 34, 83, 87, 107; marriage a synecdoche for, 76–77, 81, 88, 92, 105, 107, 114–115; possessive interest in, 82

Native Americans, 11, 47, 88

Nervous breakdown, 45, 49

Nervous diathesis, 47

Nervousness, 12, 42, 45, 52, 67–68; class and, 43, 47–49, 52; clinical treatment of, 45, 49, 54–55, 61, 71; etiology of, 46–50; hysteria vs. (*see* Differential diagnosis); in men, 43, 49, 54–55; normality, providing context for, 42–43; in women; 49–50, 55, 96; white sexual weakness and, 12, 43, 54–58

Neurasthenia discourse, 12, 18, 45, 58–59, 70

Newspapers, 10–11, 62–66

Non-normativity, critical insight and, 13, 22, 26

Racial backsliding, 62, 96, 125, 138. *See also* Degeneration

Racial body, 46–47, 59, 68–69

Racial boundaries and credentials, 20–21, 33, 47–51, 58–62, 65–66

Racial pedagogy, 123. *See also* Sex education

Racism, scientific, 16, 163 n.25

Recapitulation, 98, 141, 145

Refinement, 8, 12, 47–48, 56, 59, 65–66, 73, 78

Religion, 11, 51, 54, 62, 65

Representation, 169 n.59; of democracy in modern America, 9, 11; normal texts and, 18–19, 21; 32, 125, 132, 151, 156; race-evasive and power-evasive strategies of, 2, 76, 78, 87–88, 92–93, 114; restraint in, 125, 139, 146, 149; sex education and, 126, 140; of whiteness as normal, major themes in, 13

Reproduction: of images, 65–67, 136; of love, 102; mode of, 7; nonhuman biology of, 142–144, 146, 150–151; sex as, 141–149; of white bodies, 7–8, 11, 13, 43, 117, 119; of white civilization, 5–8, 13–14, 18, 20–21, 36, 44–45, 55, 58, 74, 117, 119, 126

Reproductive weakness, 12–13, 42–43, 54–58, 67–68, 74, 131–133

Reproductivity. *See* Heterosexuality

Reticence, 2, 6, 82, 122–123, 125–126, 129–130, 133, 140–141, 144–145, 148–149, 151

Science: evolutionary, 5, 11, 50–51, 126, 162 n.8; of sex, 16, 18, 41, 118, 141, 149

Scientific racism, 16, 163 n.25

Segregation, 16, 19–23, 58, 123, 169 n.55

Self-cultivation, 34, 65, 77–78, 98, 103, 111–112, 139

Self-discipline: citizenship and, 78–79, 114–115; civilization dependent on, 15, 59, 65–67, 94, 116; competing ideals of, 62, 73; modern marriage and, 40, 78, 94–95, 98, 103–105, 125–126; nervousness and, 50, 54, 56, 70; normal heterosexuality and, 13, 98, 147–148; ownership of civilization justified by, 31, 44–47, 59, 64–66, 70, 82–83, 98, 107–109, 155, 159; racial hierarchy and, 47, 112–113; reticence and, 122–123, 133, 145, 147–151; sexual and temporal difference and, 99–105, 108; strategy for preserving white dominance, 12, 44, 116, 133; white manhood and, 54, 94–96, 128–132, 144–145

Self-government. *See* Democracy; Self-discipline

Selfishness, sexual, 94–96, 109–110, 119, 129

Self-referentiality. *See* Solipsism

Self-starvation, 55, 57, 59–61

Sensitivity. *See* Whiteness: sensitivity and

Sex, interest in, 118–119

Sex advice. *See* Marital advice literature

Sex education, 118–119, 144, 151–152, 155–156; evolutionary family and, 126–127, 140–141, 146–149, 151; expressive etiquette of, 125, 135, 140, 145 (*see also* Reticence); generic features of, 15, 18–19, 120, 128; professional practice of, 125, 135; on venereal contagion, 127–133; whiteness universalized via, 121–122, 124, 126–127, 144–145

Sexes, difference of, 8, 141; deepened by modernity, 76, 80–81, 83, 86–87, 90; desire and, 77, 97, 107–108, 184–185 n.66; image for diversity in polity, 77, 81–82, 87; as temporal difference, 91, 95–96, 99–105, 110

Sexual failure, 12–13, 37, 54–55, 93–94, 104, 141, 155

Sexual fitness. *See* Eugenics; Fitness, sexual and racial

Julian B. Carter is an assistant professor of critical studies at the California College of the Arts in Oakland and San Francisco.

Library of Congress Cataloging-in-Publication Data

Carter, Julian B.

The heart of whiteness : normal sexuality and race in America, 1880–1940 / Julian B. Carter

p. cm.

Includes bibliographical references and index.

ISBN 978-0-8223-3937-3 (cloth : alk. paper)

ISBN 978-0-8223-3948-9 (pbk. : alk. paper)

1. Heterosexuality—United States—History. 2. Sexual ethics—United States—History. 3. Race awareness—United States—History. 4. Whites—Race identity—United States—History.

5. Social norms. 6. Marriage—United States—History.

7. United States—Social conditions—1918–1932.

8. United States—Social conditions—1933–1945.

9. United States—Social conditions—1865–1918.

I. Title.

HQ18.U5C36 2007

306.76'408900973—dc22   2006037279